THE WORLD'S GREATEST COMIC MAGAZINE!

DEADPOOL

DEADPOOL #13

GERRY DUGGAN, CHARLES SOULE & DAVID WALKER
writers

JACOPO CAMAGNI, GUILLERMO SANNA, ELMO BONDOC & PACO DIAZ
artists

VERONICA GANDINI, MAT LOPES, NOLAN WOODARD & ISRAEL SILVA
color artists

VC's JOE SABINO & CLAYTON COWLES
letterers

FRANCISCO HERRERA & FRANCESCA RIZO
cover art

HEATHER ANTOS, CHRIS ROBINSON & KATHLEEN WISNESKI
assistant editors

JORDAN D. WHITE, JAKE THOMAS & MARK PANICCIA
editors

DEADPOOL: LAST DAYS OF MAGIC #1

GERRY DUGGAN
writer

SCOTT KOBLISH
artist

GURU-eFX
color artist

VC's JOE SABINO
letterer

HUMBERTO RAMOS & EDGAR DELGADO
cover art

HEATHER ANTOS
assistant editor

JORDAN D. WHITE
editor

collection editor JENNIFER GRÜNWALD
associate managing editor KATERI WOODY
associate editor SARAH BRUNSTAD
editor, special projects MARK D. BEAZLEY
vp production & special projects JEFF YOUNGQUIST
svp print, sales & marketing DAVID GABRIEL
book designer ADAM DEL RE

editor in chief AXEL ALONSO
chief creative officer JOE QUESADA
publisher DAN BUCKLEY
executive producer ALAN FINE

DEADPOOL created by ROB LIEFELD & FABIAN NICIEZA

DEADPOOL: WORLD'S GREATEST VOL. 4 — TEMPORARY INSANITATION. Contains material originally published in magazine form as DEADPOOL #13 and DEADPOOL: LAST DAYS OF MAGIC #1. First printing 2016. ISBN# 978-1-302-90091-5. Published by MARVEL WORLDWIDE, INC., a subsidiary of MARVEL ENTERTAINMENT, LLC. OFFICE OF PUBLICATION: 135 West 50th Street, New York, NY 10020. Copyright © 2016 MARVEL No similarity between any of the names, characters, persons, and/or institutions in this magazine with those of any living or dead person or institution is intended, and any such similarity which may exist is purely coincidental. **Printed in Canada.** ALAN FINE, President, Marvel Entertainment; DAN BUCKLEY, President, TV, Publ ... ORT, SVP of Publishing; DAVID BOGART, SVP of Business Affairs & Operations, Publishing & Partnership; C.B. CEBULSKI, VP of Brand Management & Dev ... NGQUIST, VP of Production & Special Projects; DAN CARR, Executive Director of Publishing Technology; ALEX MORALES, Director of Publishing Operations; ... ation regarding advertising in Marvel Comics or on Marvel.com, please contact Vit DeBellis, Integrated Sales Manager, at vdebellis@marvel.com. For Ma ... 9/2/2016 and 10/10/2016 by SOLISCO PRINTERS, SCOTT, QC, CANADA.

10 9 8 7 6 5 4 3 2 1

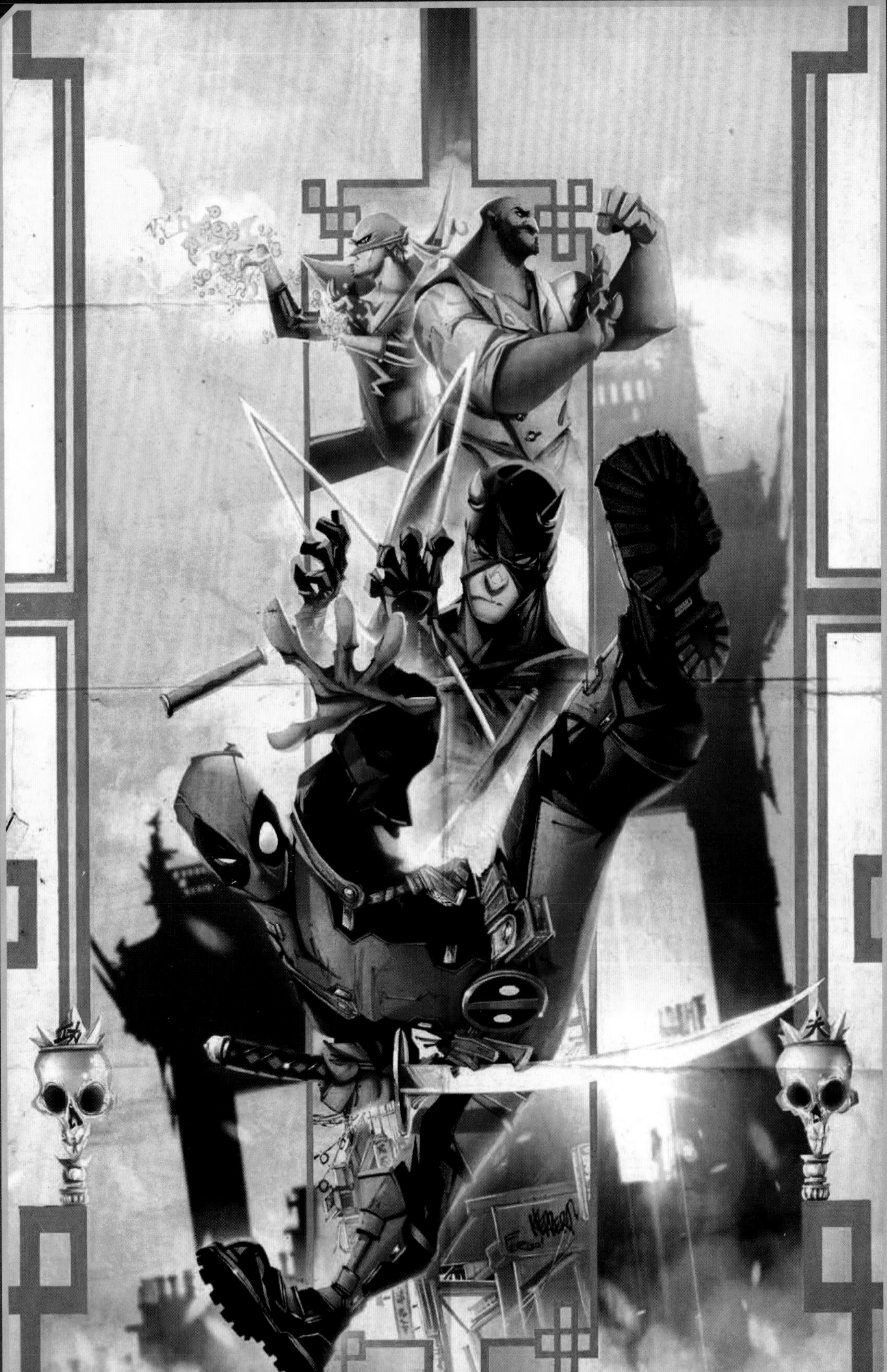

Avenger...Assassin...Superstar...Smelly person...Possibly the world's most skilled mercenary, definitely the world's most annoying, Wade Wilson was chosen for a top-secret government program that gave him a healing factor allowing him to heal from any wound. Somehow, despite making his money as a gun for hire, Wade has become one of the most beloved "heroes" in the world. Call him the Merc with the Mouth...call him the Regeneratin' Degenerate...call him...

DEADPOOL

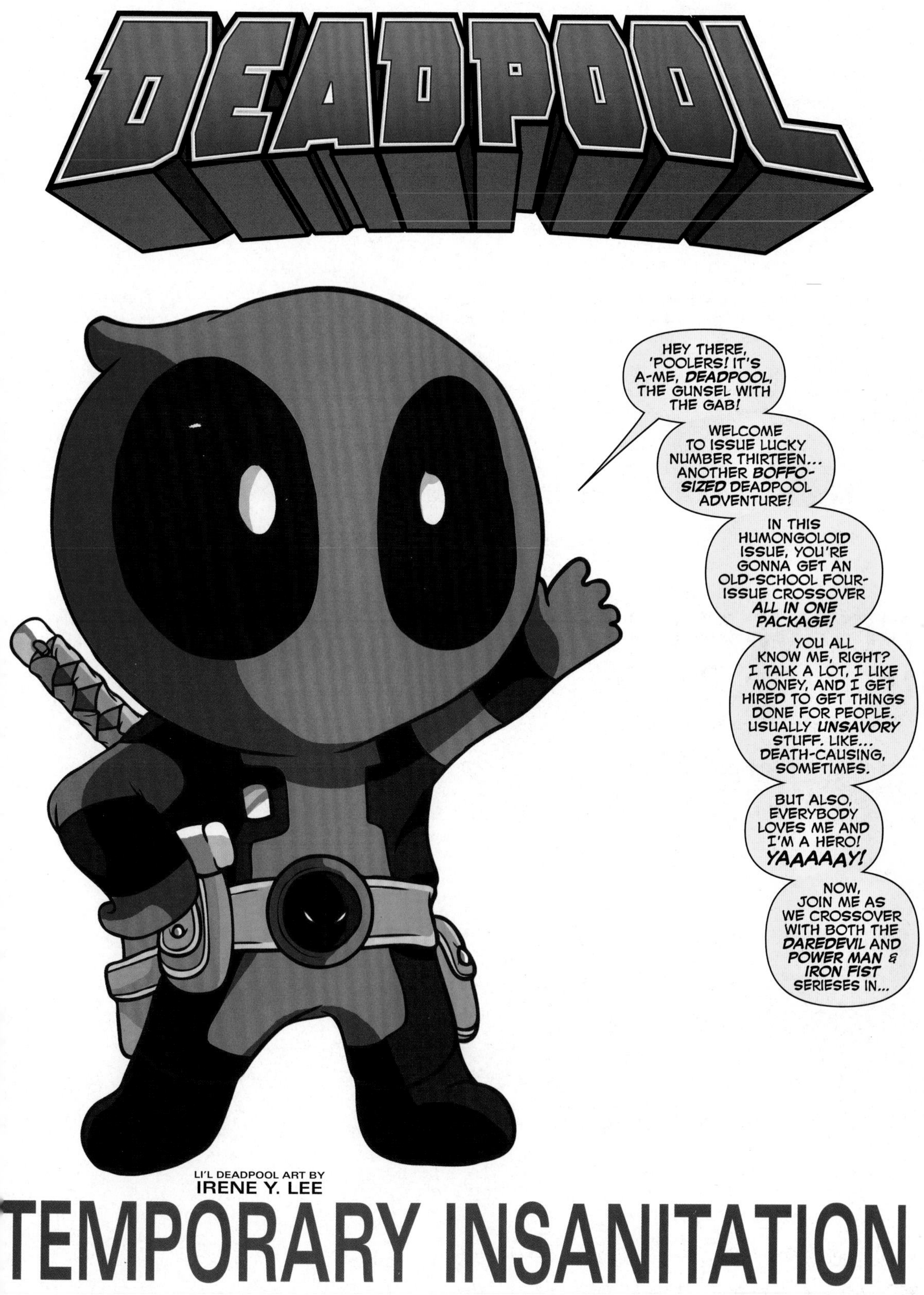
HEY THERE, 'POOLERS! IT'S A-ME, ***DEADPOOL***, THE GUNSEL WITH THE GAB!
WELCOME TO ISSUE LUCKY NUMBER THIRTEEN... ANOTHER ***BOFFO-SIZED*** DEADPOOL ADVENTURE!
IN THIS HUMONGOLOID ISSUE, YOU'RE GONNA GET AN OLD-SCHOOL FOUR-ISSUE CROSSOVER ***ALL IN ONE PACKAGE!***
YOU ALL KNOW ME, RIGHT? I TALK A LOT, I LIKE MONEY, AND I GET HIRED TO GET THINGS DONE FOR PEOPLE. USUALLY ***UNSAVORY*** STUFF. LIKE... DEATH-CAUSING, SOMETIMES.
BUT ALSO, EVERYBODY LOVES ME AND I'M A HERO! ***YAAAAAY!***
NOW, JOIN ME AS WE CROSSOVER WITH BOTH THE ***DAREDEVIL*** AND ***POWER MAN & IRON FIST*** SERIESES IN...

LI'L DEADPOOL ART BY
IRENE Y. LEE

TEMPORARY INSANITATION

DEADPOOL #13
TEMPORARY INSANITATION PART ONE

Gerry Duggan
writer

Jacopo Camagni
artist

Veronica Gandini
colorist

VC's Joe Sabino
letterer

Heather Antos
assistant editor

Jordan D. White
editor

DAREDEVIL #7.1
TEMPORARY INSANITATION PART TWO

Charles Soule
writer

Guillermo Sanna
artist

Mat Lopes
colorist

VC's Clayton Cowles
letterer

Chris Robinson
assistant editor

Mark Paniccia
editor

POWER MAN AND IRON FIST #4.1
TEMPORARY INSANITATION PART THREE

David Walker
writer

Elmo Bondoc
artist

Nolan Woodard
colorist

VC's Clayton Cowles
letterer

Kathleen Wisneski
assistant editor

Jake Thomas
editor

DEADPOOL #13.1
TEMPORARY INSANITATION PART FOUR

Gerry Duggan
writer

Paco Diaz
artist

Israel Silva
colorist

VC's Joe Sabino
letterer

Heather Antos
assistant editor

Jordan D. White
editor

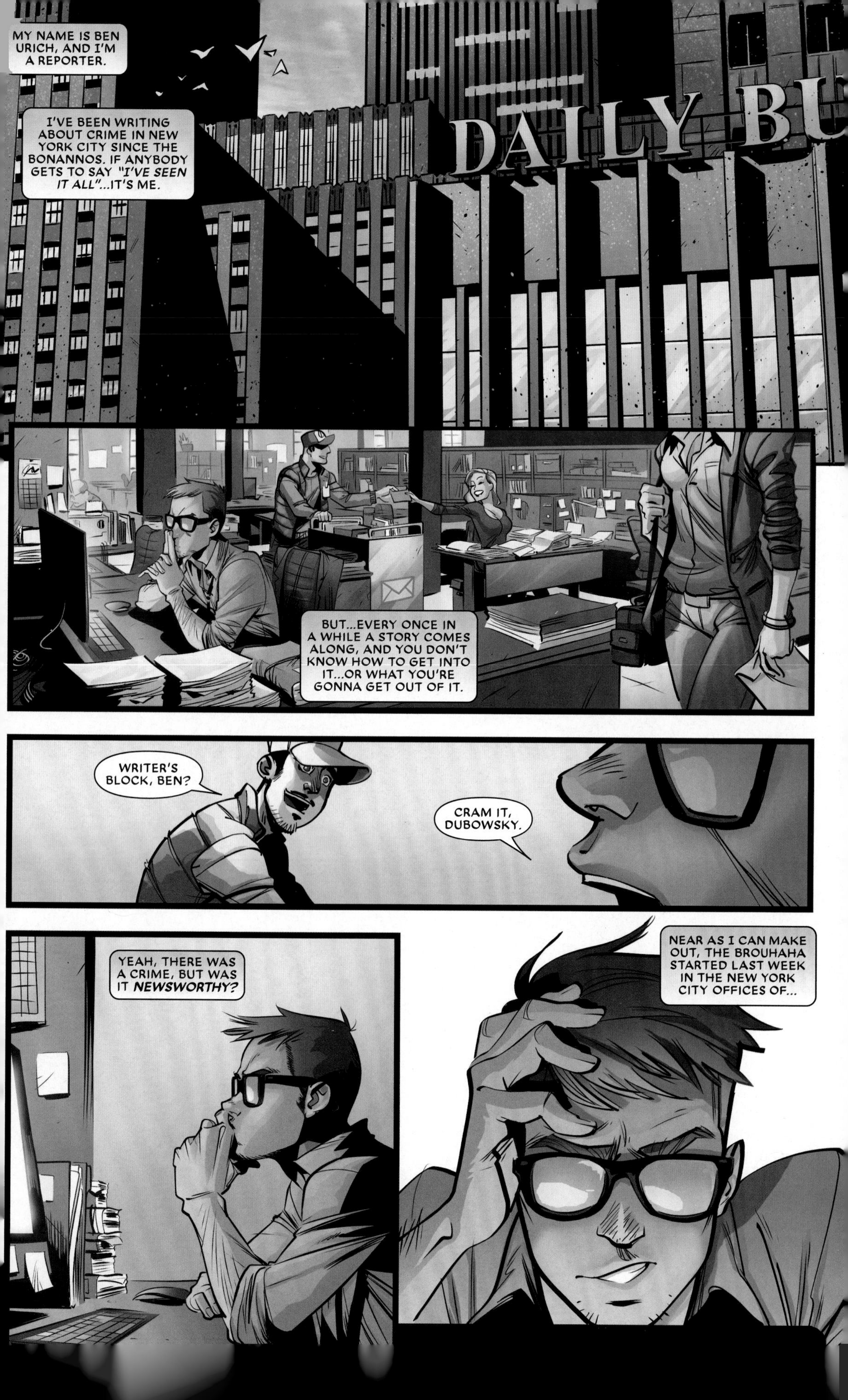
MY NAME IS BEN URICH, AND I'M A REPORTER.
I'VE BEEN WRITING ABOUT CRIME IN NEW YORK CITY SINCE THE BONANNOS. IF ANYBODY GETS TO SAY "I'VE SEEN IT ALL"...IT'S ME.
DAILY BU
BUT...EVERY ONCE IN A WHILE A STORY COMES ALONG, AND YOU DON'T KNOW HOW TO GET INTO IT...OR WHAT YOU'RE GONNA GET OUT OF IT.
WRITER'S BLOCK, BEN?
CRAM IT, DUBOWSKY.
YEAH, THERE WAS A CRIME, BUT WAS IT NEWSWORTHY?
NEAR AS I CAN MAKE OUT, THE BROUHAHA STARTED LAST WEEK IN THE NEW YORK CITY OFFICES OF...

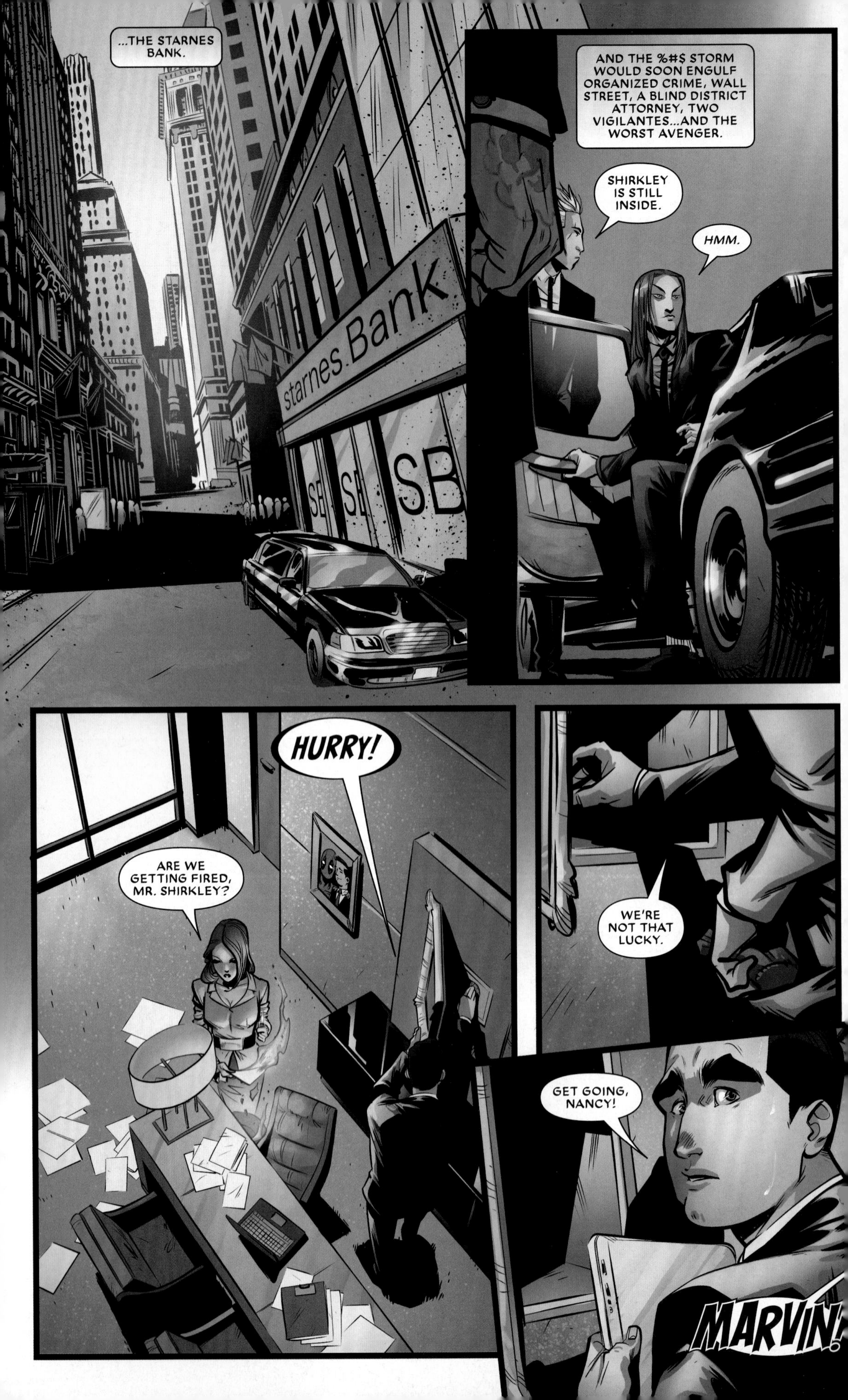
...THE STARNES BANK.
starnes.Bank
SB
AND THE %#$ STORM WOULD SOON ENGULF ORGANIZED CRIME, WALL STREET, A BLIND DISTRICT ATTORNEY, TWO VIGILANTES...AND THE WORST AVENGER.
SHIRKLEY IS STILL INSIDE.
HMM.
HURRY!
ARE WE GETTING FIRED, MR. SHIRKLEY?
WE'RE NOT THAT LUCKY.
GET GOING, NANCY!
MARVIN!

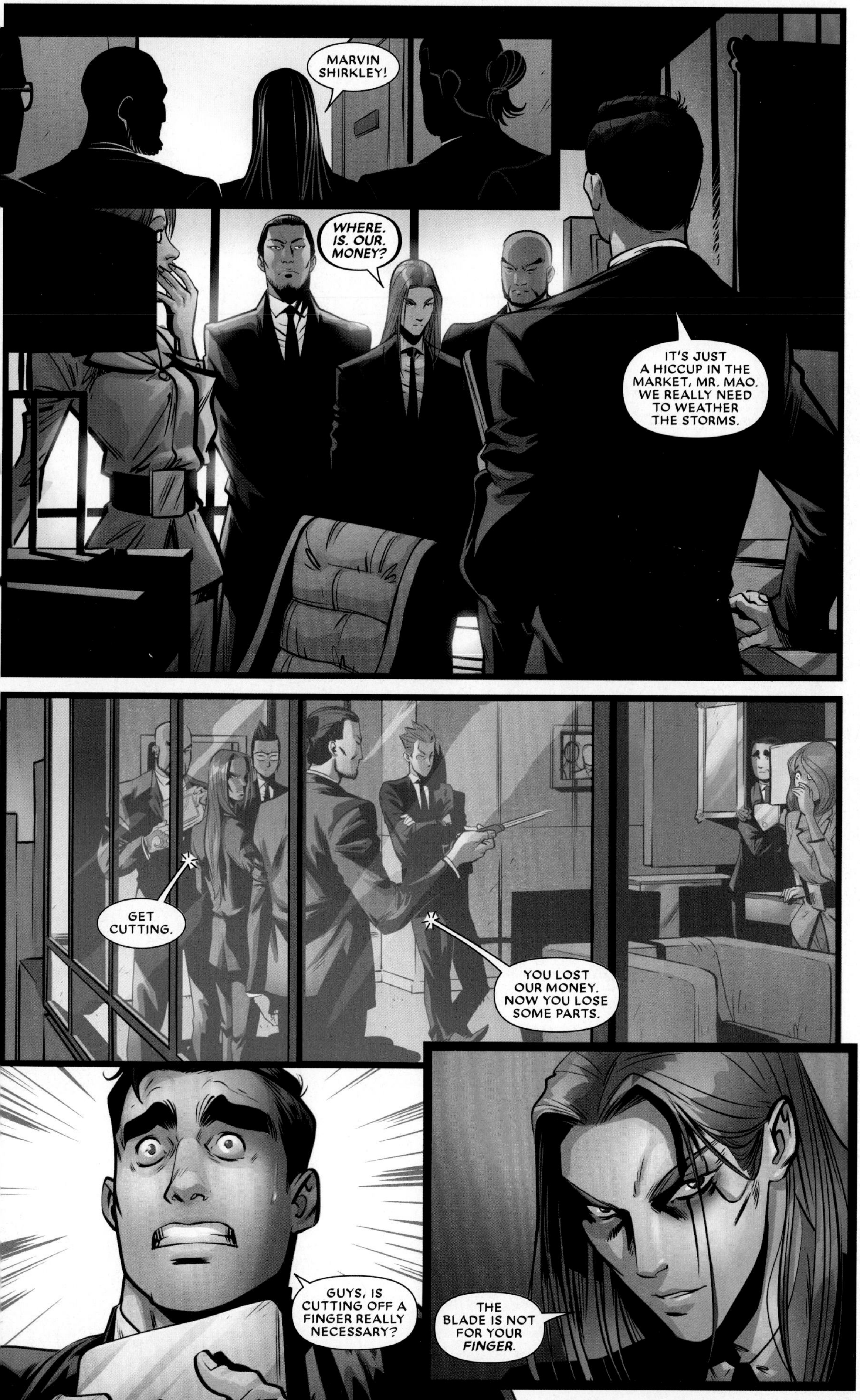
MARVIN SHIRKLEY!
WHERE. IS. OUR. MONEY?
IT'S JUST A HICCUP IN THE MARKET, MR. MAO. WE REALLY NEED TO WEATHER THE STORMS.
GET CUTTING.
YOU LOST OUR MONEY. NOW YOU LOSE SOME PARTS.
GUYS, IS CUTTING OFF A FINGER REALLY NECESSARY?
THE BLADE IS NOT FOR YOUR FINGER.

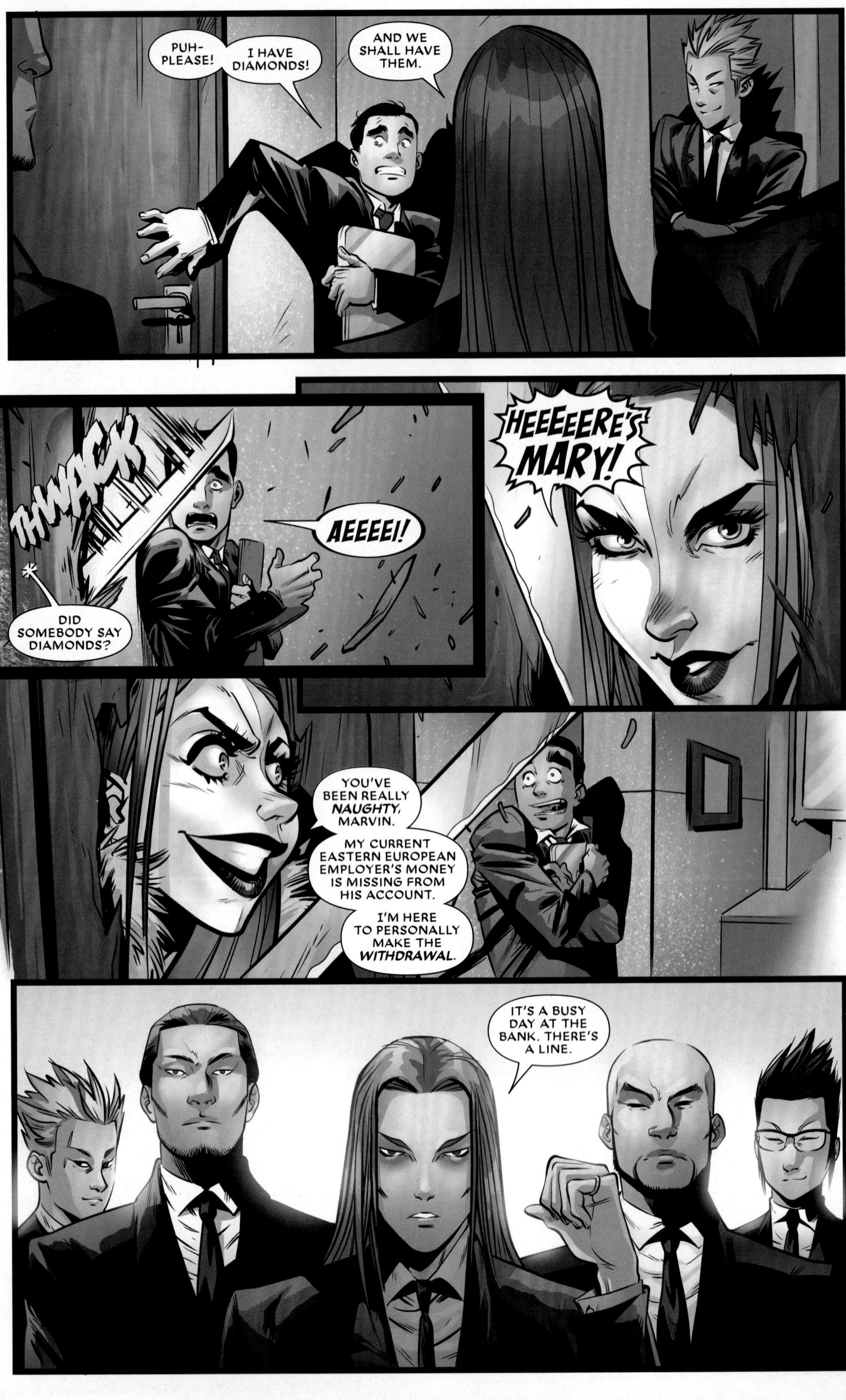

PUH-PLEASE!
I HAVE DIAMONDS!
AND WE SHALL HAVE THEM.
THWACK
AEEEEI!
DID SOMEBODY SAY DIAMONDS?
HEEEEERE'S MARY!
YOU'VE BEEN REALLY NAUGHTY, MARVIN.
MY CURRENT EASTERN EUROPEAN EMPLOYER'S MONEY IS MISSING FROM HIS ACCOUNT.
I'M HERE TO PERSONALLY MAKE THE WITHDRAWAL.
IT'S A BUSY DAY AT THE BANK. THERE'S A LINE.

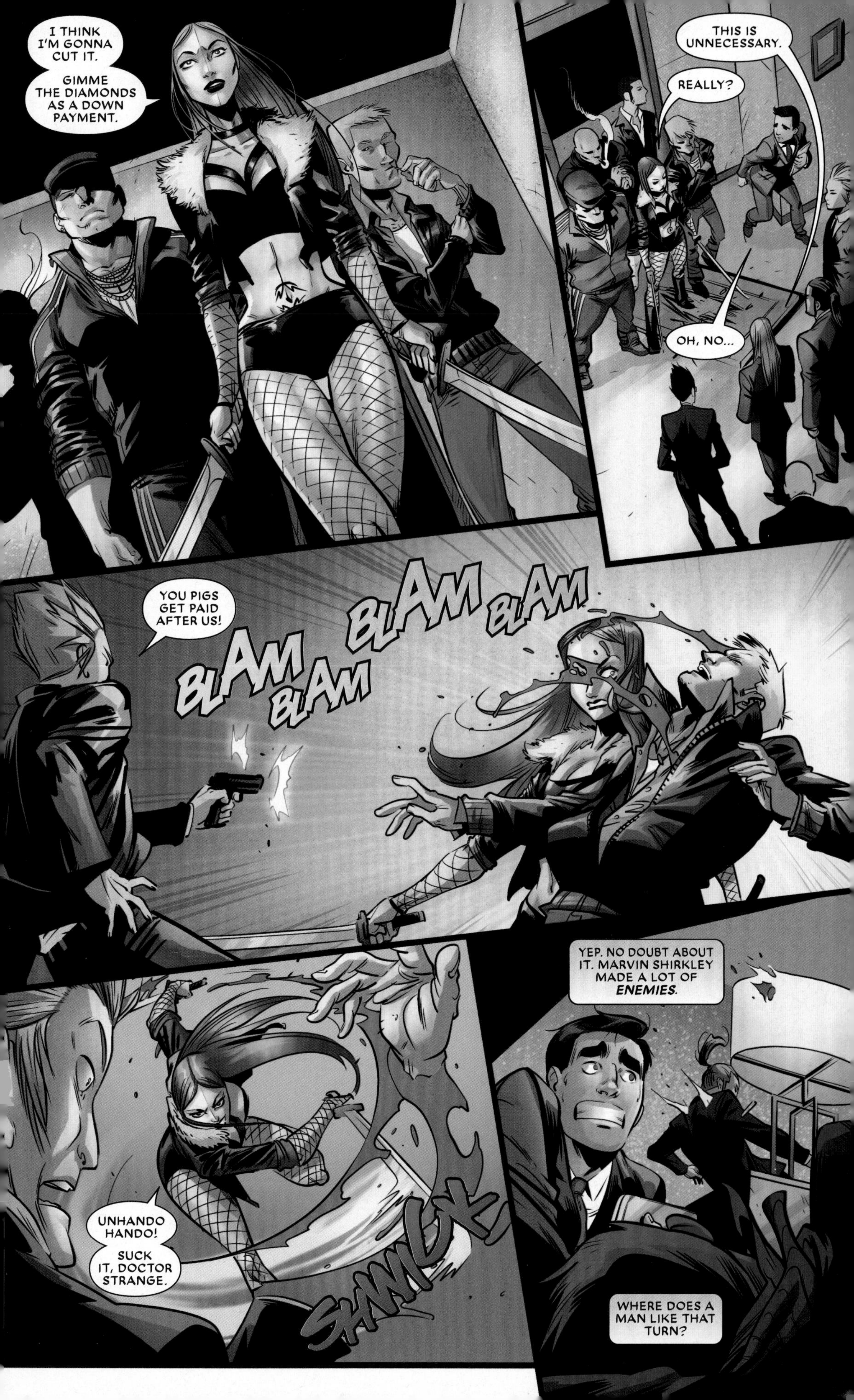
I THINK I'M GONNA CUT IT.
GIMME THE DIAMONDS AS A DOWN PAYMENT.
THIS IS UNNECESSARY.
REALLY?
OH, NO...
YOU PIGS GET PAID AFTER US!
BLAM BLAM BLAM BLAM
YEP. NO DOUBT ABOUT IT. MARVIN SHIRKLEY MADE A LOT OF ENEMIES.
UNHANDO HANDO!
SUCK IT, DOCTOR STRANGE.
SHNICK
WHERE DOES A MAN LIKE THAT TURN?

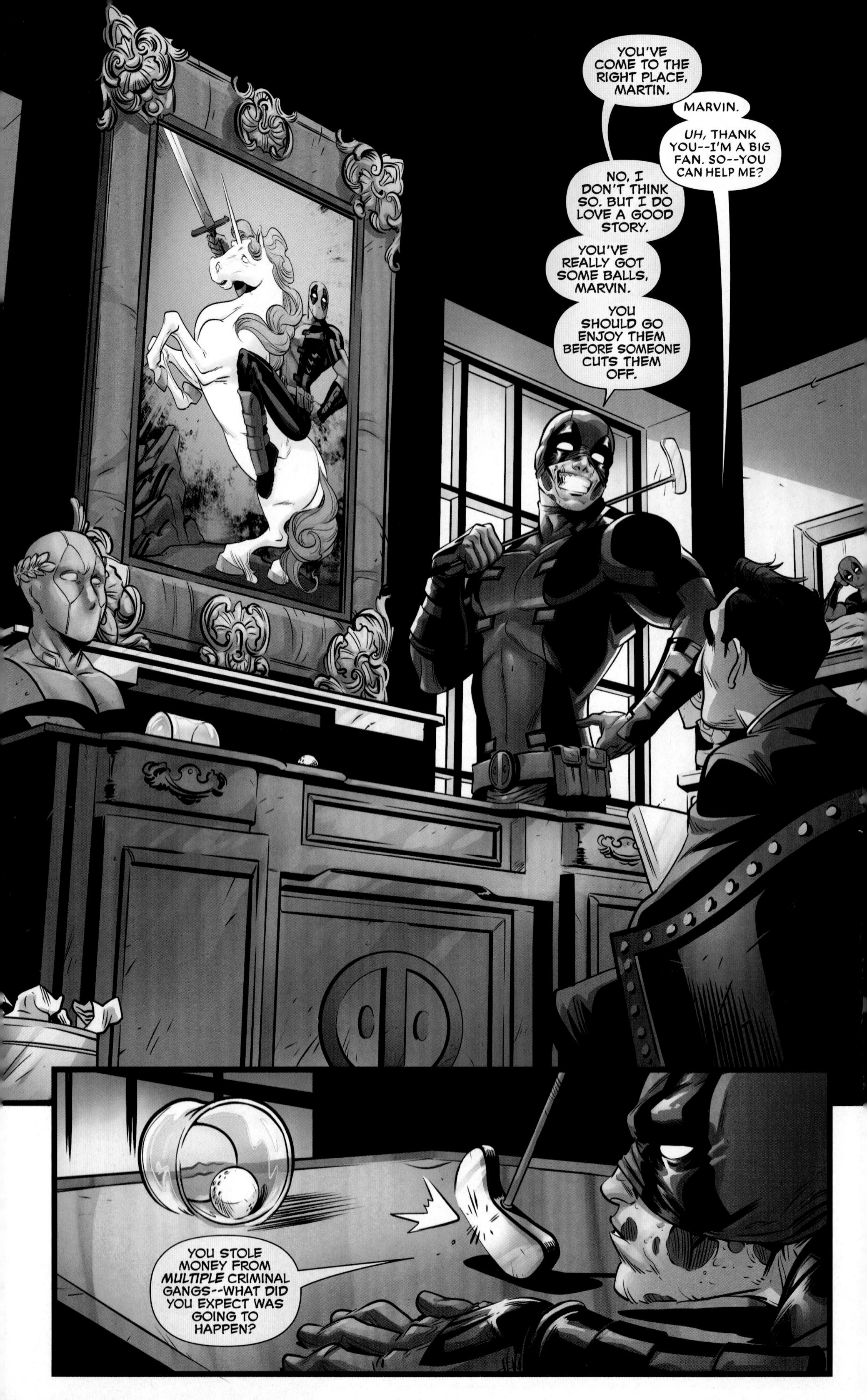
YOU'VE COME TO THE RIGHT PLACE, MARTIN.
MARVIN.
UH, THANK YOU--I'M A BIG FAN. SO--YOU CAN HELP ME?
NO, I DON'T THINK SO. BUT I DO LOVE A GOOD STORY.
YOU'VE REALLY GOT SOME BALLS, MARVIN.
YOU SHOULD GO ENJOY THEM BEFORE SOMEONE CUTS THEM OFF.
YOU STOLE MONEY FROM MULTIPLE CRIMINAL GANGS--WHAT DID YOU EXPECT WAS GOING TO HAPPEN?

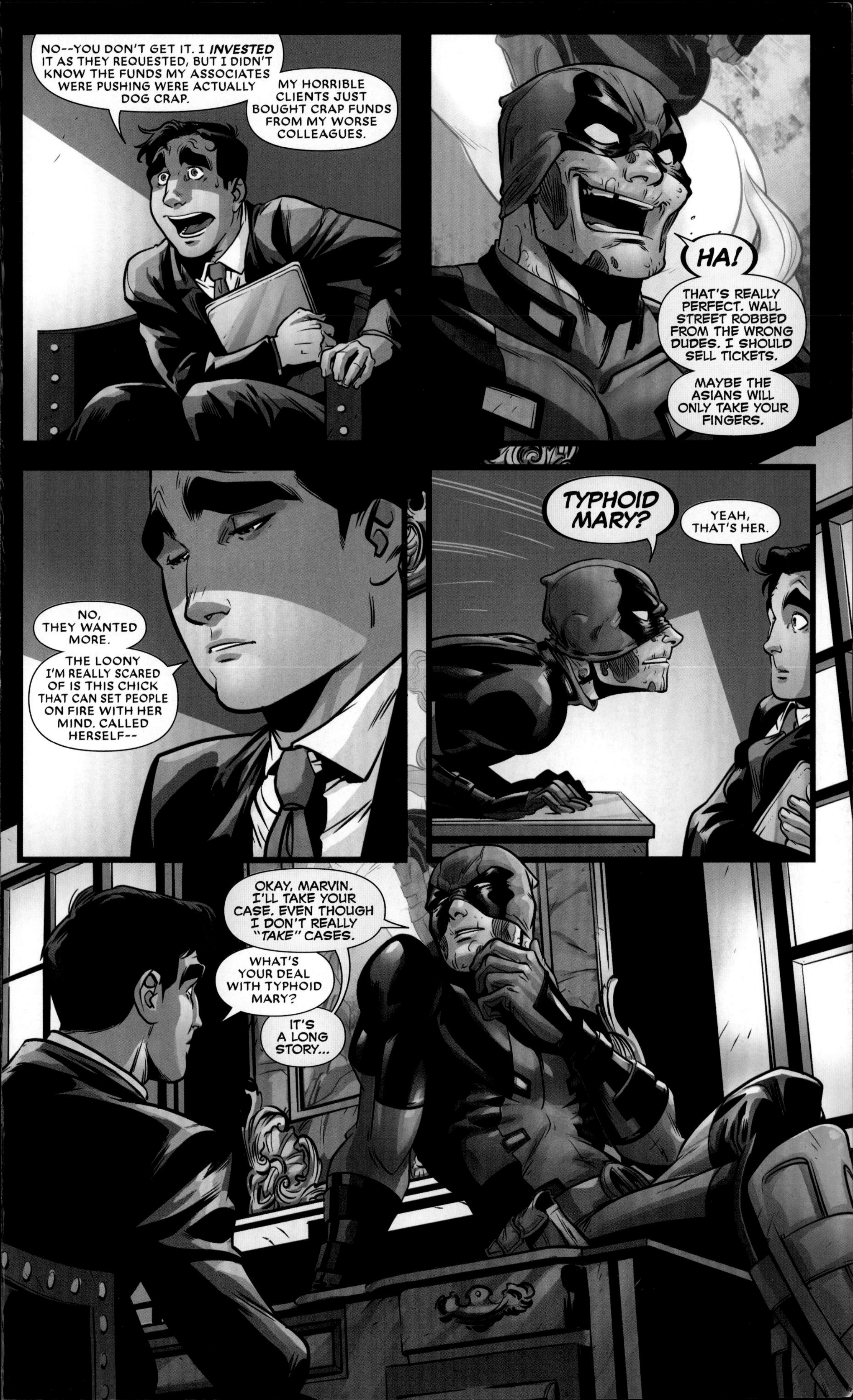
NO--YOU DON'T GET IT. I *INVESTED* IT AS THEY REQUESTED, BUT I DIDN'T KNOW THE FUNDS MY ASSOCIATES WERE PUSHING WERE ACTUALLY DOG CRAP.
MY HORRIBLE CLIENTS JUST BOUGHT CRAP FUNDS FROM MY WORSE COLLEAGUES.
HA!
THAT'S REALLY PERFECT. WALL STREET ROBBED FROM THE WRONG DUDES. I SHOULD SELL TICKETS.
MAYBE THE ASIANS WILL ONLY TAKE YOUR FINGERS.
NO, THEY WANTED MORE.
THE LOONY I'M REALLY SCARED OF IS THIS CHICK THAT CAN SET PEOPLE ON FIRE WITH HER MIND. CALLED HERSELF--
TYPHOID MARY?
YEAH, THAT'S HER.
OKAY, MARVIN. I'LL TAKE YOUR CASE. EVEN THOUGH I DON'T REALLY "*TAKE*" CASES.
WHAT'S YOUR DEAL WITH TYPHOID MARY?
IT'S A LONG STORY...

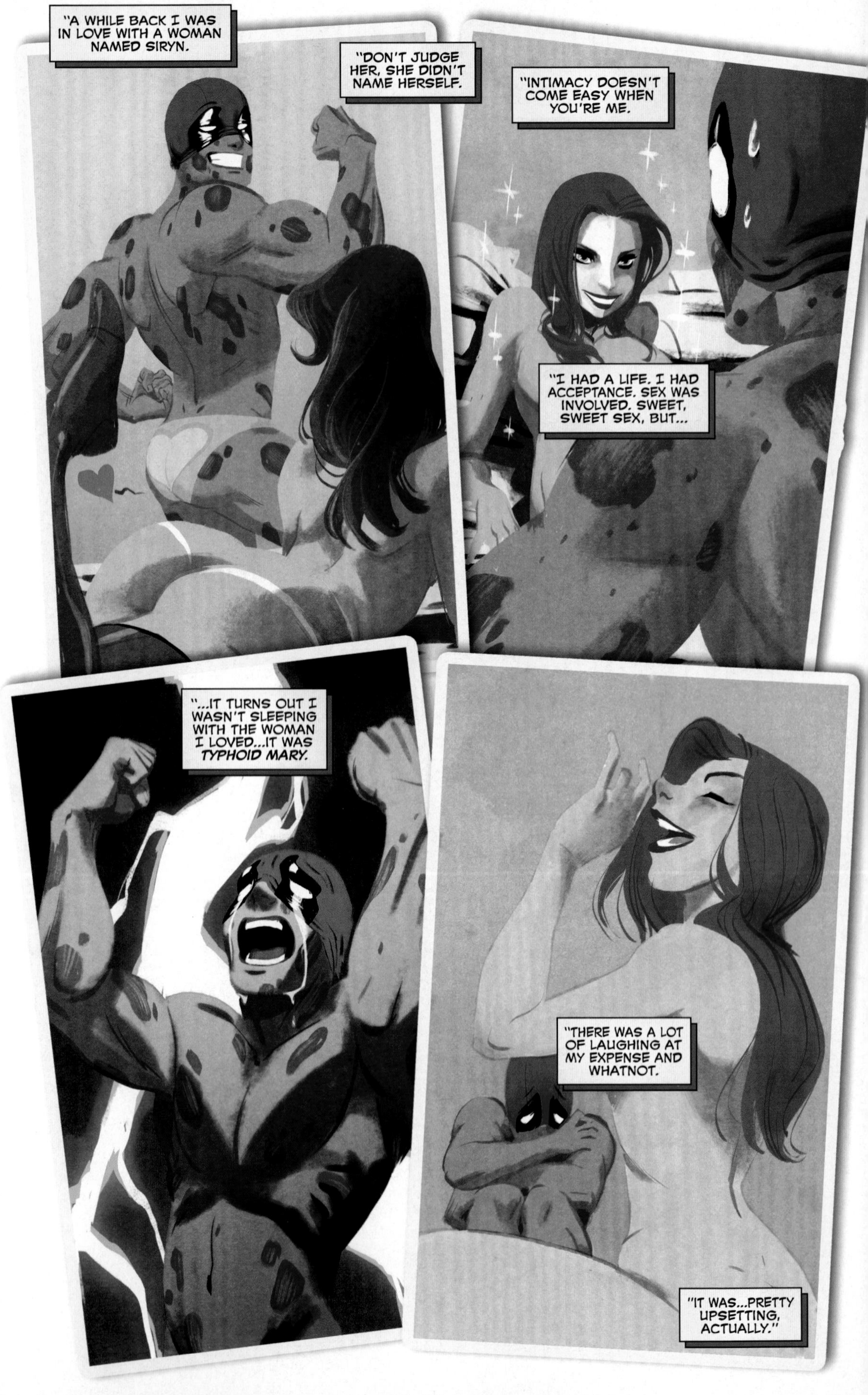
"A WHILE BACK I WAS IN LOVE WITH A WOMAN NAMED SIRYN.
"DON'T JUDGE HER, SHE DIDN'T NAME HERSELF.
"INTIMACY DOESN'T COME EASY WHEN YOU'RE ME.
"I HAD A LIFE. I HAD ACCEPTANCE. SEX WAS INVOLVED. SWEET, SWEET SEX, BUT...
"...IT TURNS OUT I WASN'T SLEEPING WITH THE WOMAN I LOVED...IT WAS *TYPHOID MARY.*
"THERE WAS A LOT OF LAUGHING AT MY EXPENSE AND WHATNOT.
"IT WAS...PRETTY UPSETTING, ACTUALLY."

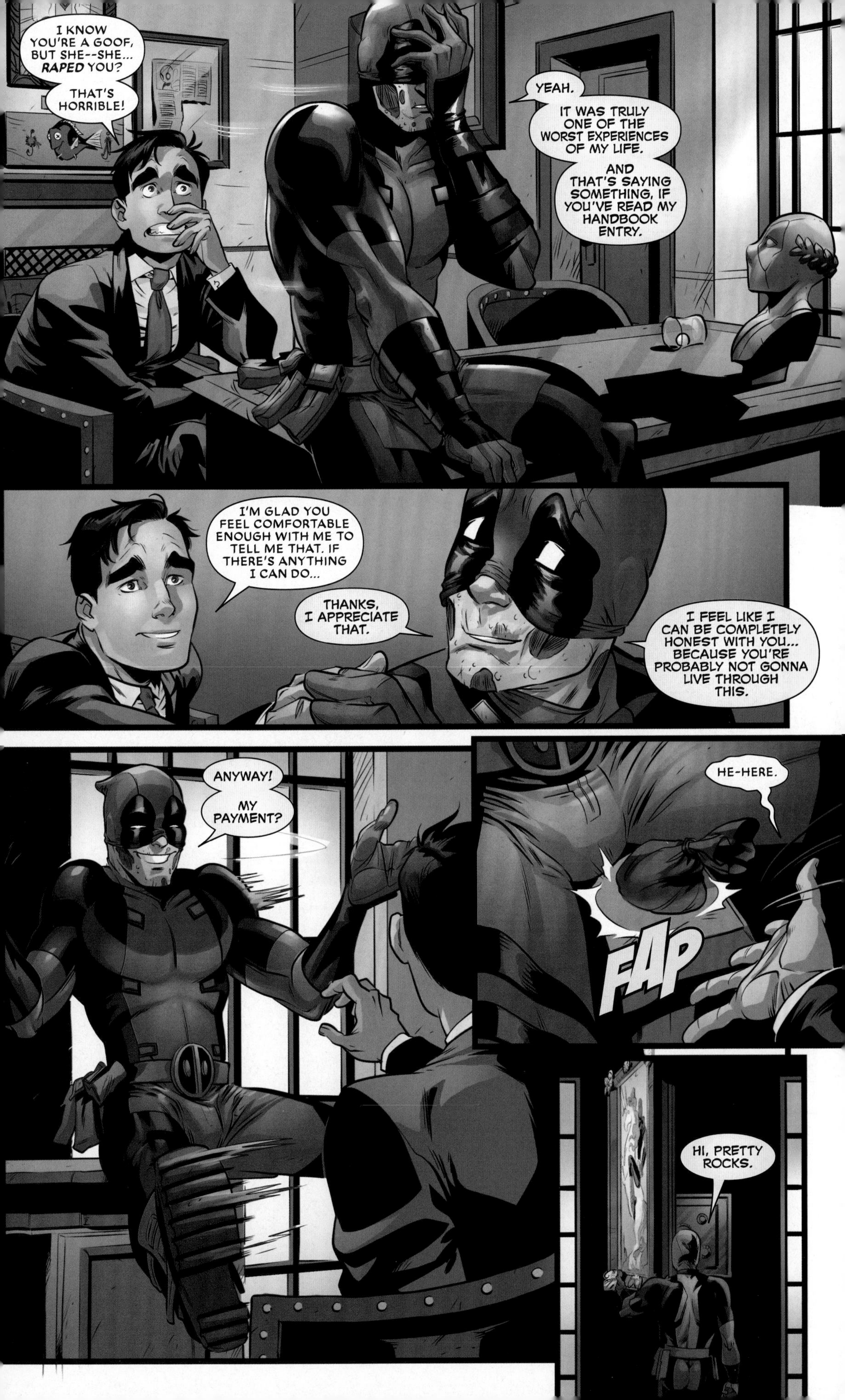
I KNOW YOU'RE A GOOF, BUT SHE--SHE... *RAPED* YOU?
THAT'S HORRIBLE!
YEAH.
IT WAS TRULY ONE OF THE WORST EXPERIENCES OF MY LIFE.
AND THAT'S SAYING SOMETHING, IF YOU'VE READ MY HANDBOOK ENTRY.
I'M GLAD YOU FEEL COMFORTABLE ENOUGH WITH ME TO TELL ME THAT. IF THERE'S ANYTHING I CAN DO...
THANKS, I APPRECIATE THAT.
I FEEL LIKE I CAN BE COMPLETELY HONEST WITH YOU... BECAUSE YOU'RE PROBABLY NOT GONNA LIVE THROUGH THIS.
ANYWAY!
MY PAYMENT?
HE-HERE.
FAP
HI, PRETTY ROCKS.

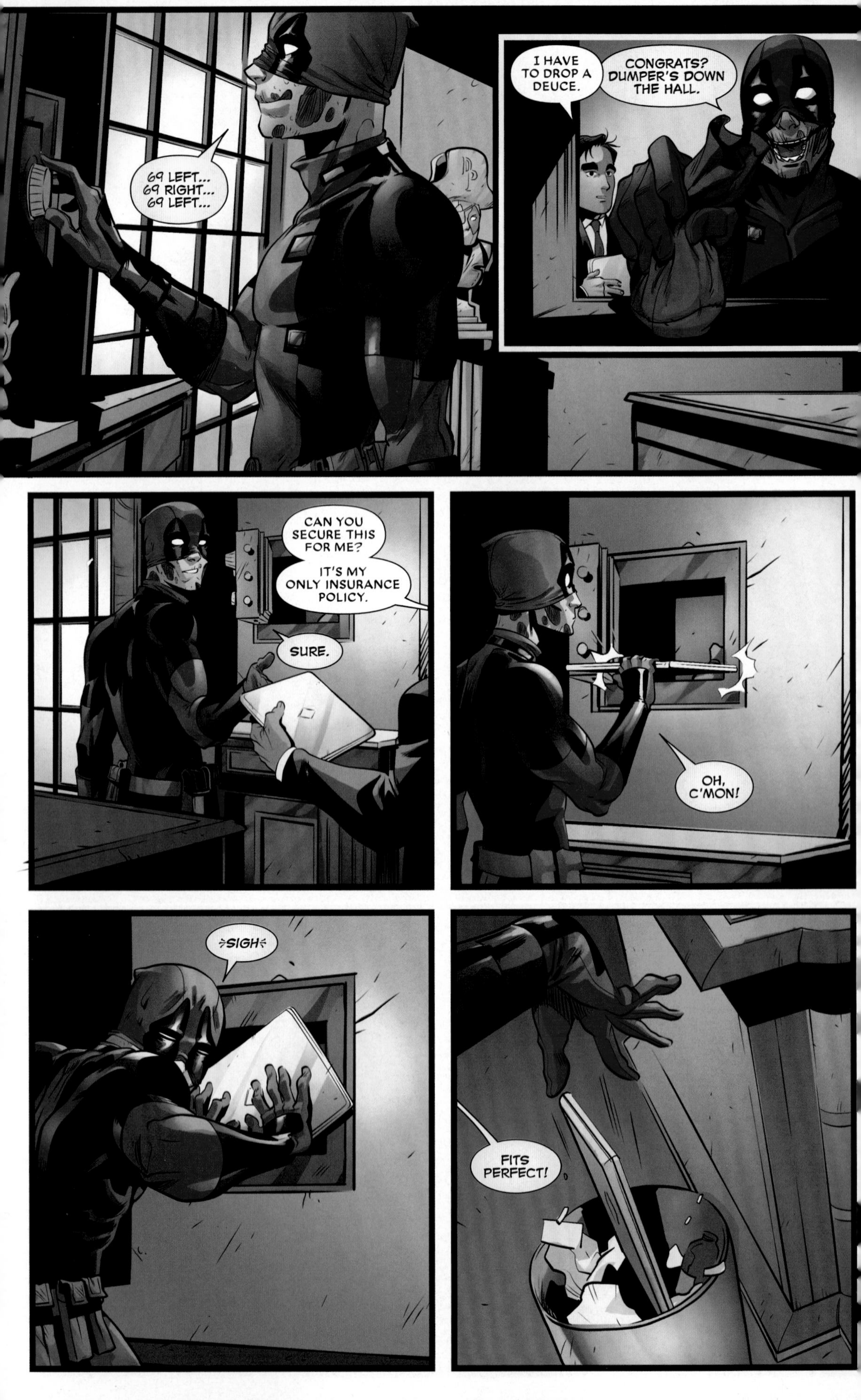
69 LEFT...
69 RIGHT...
69 LEFT...
I HAVE TO DROP A DEUCE.
CONGRATS? DUMPER'S DOWN THE HALL.
CAN YOU SECURE THIS FOR ME?
IT'S MY ONLY INSURANCE POLICY.
SURE.
OH, C'MON!
SIGH
FITS PERFECT!

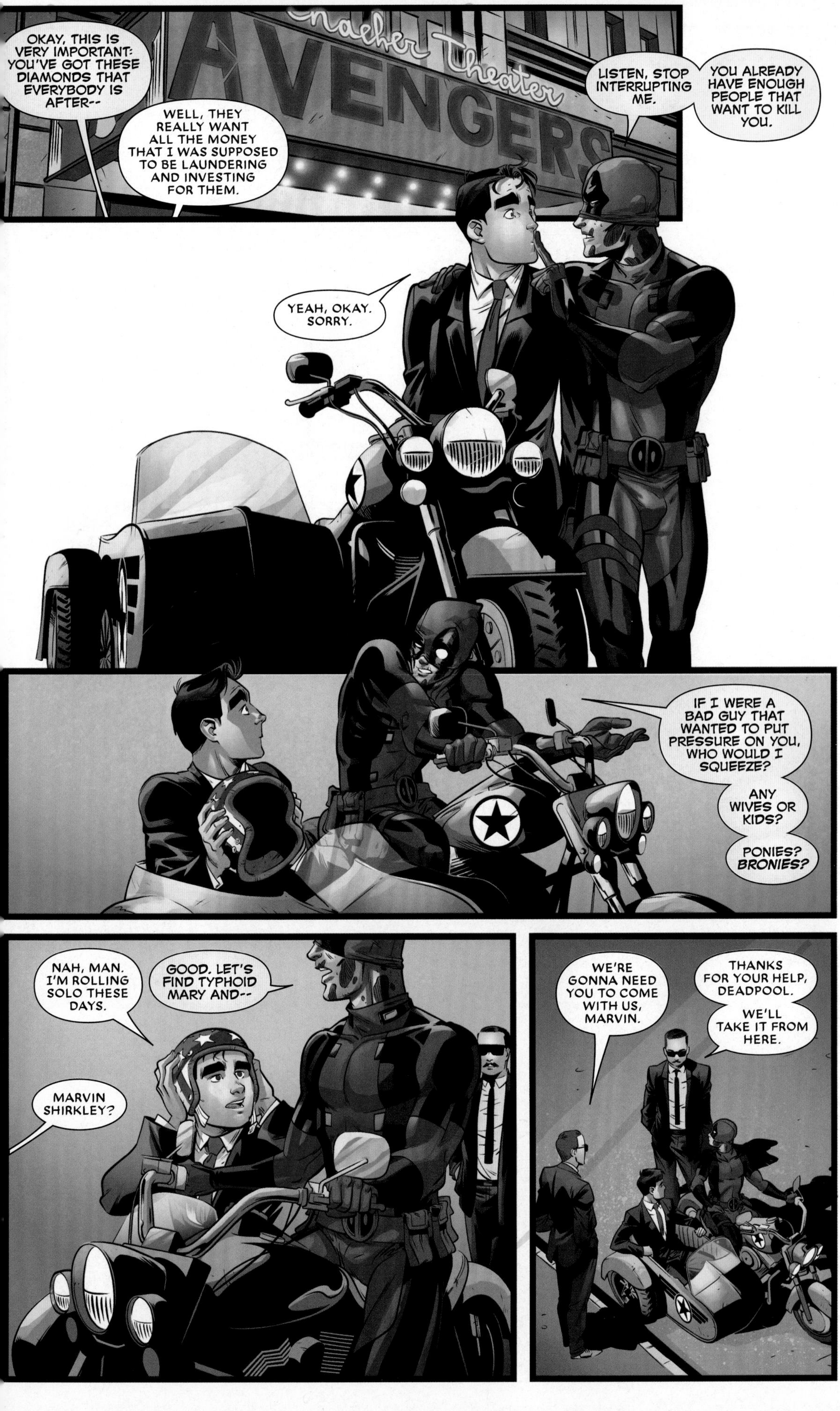
OKAY, THIS IS VERY IMPORTANT: YOU'VE GOT THESE DIAMONDS THAT EVERYBODY IS AFTER--
WELL, THEY REALLY WANT ALL THE MONEY THAT I WAS SUPPOSED TO BE LAUNDERING AND INVESTING FOR THEM.
LISTEN, STOP INTERRUPTING ME.
YOU ALREADY HAVE ENOUGH PEOPLE THAT WANT TO KILL YOU.
YEAH, OKAY. SORRY.
IF I WERE A BAD GUY THAT WANTED TO PUT PRESSURE ON YOU, WHO WOULD I SQUEEZE?
ANY WIVES OR KIDS?
PONIES? *BRONIES?*
NAH, MAN. I'M ROLLING SOLO THESE DAYS.
GOOD. LET'S FIND TYPHOID MARY AND--
MARVIN SHIRKLEY?
WE'RE GONNA NEED YOU TO COME WITH US, MARVIN.
THANKS FOR YOUR HELP, DEADPOOL.
WE'LL TAKE IT FROM HERE.

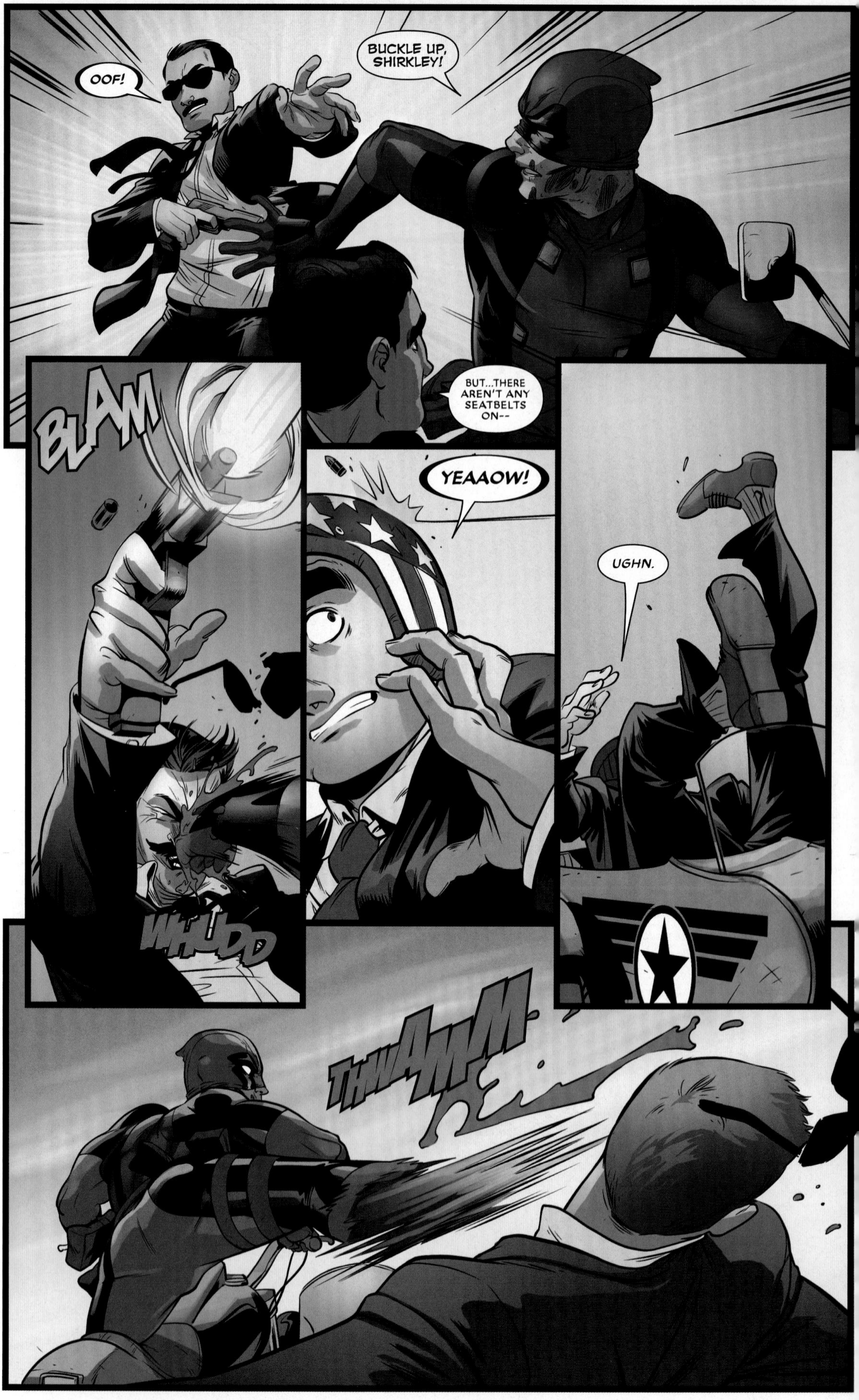
OOF!
BUCKLE UP, SHIRKLEY!
BUT...THERE AREN'T ANY SEATBELTS ON--
BLAM
WHUDD
YEAAOW!
UGHN.
THWAMM

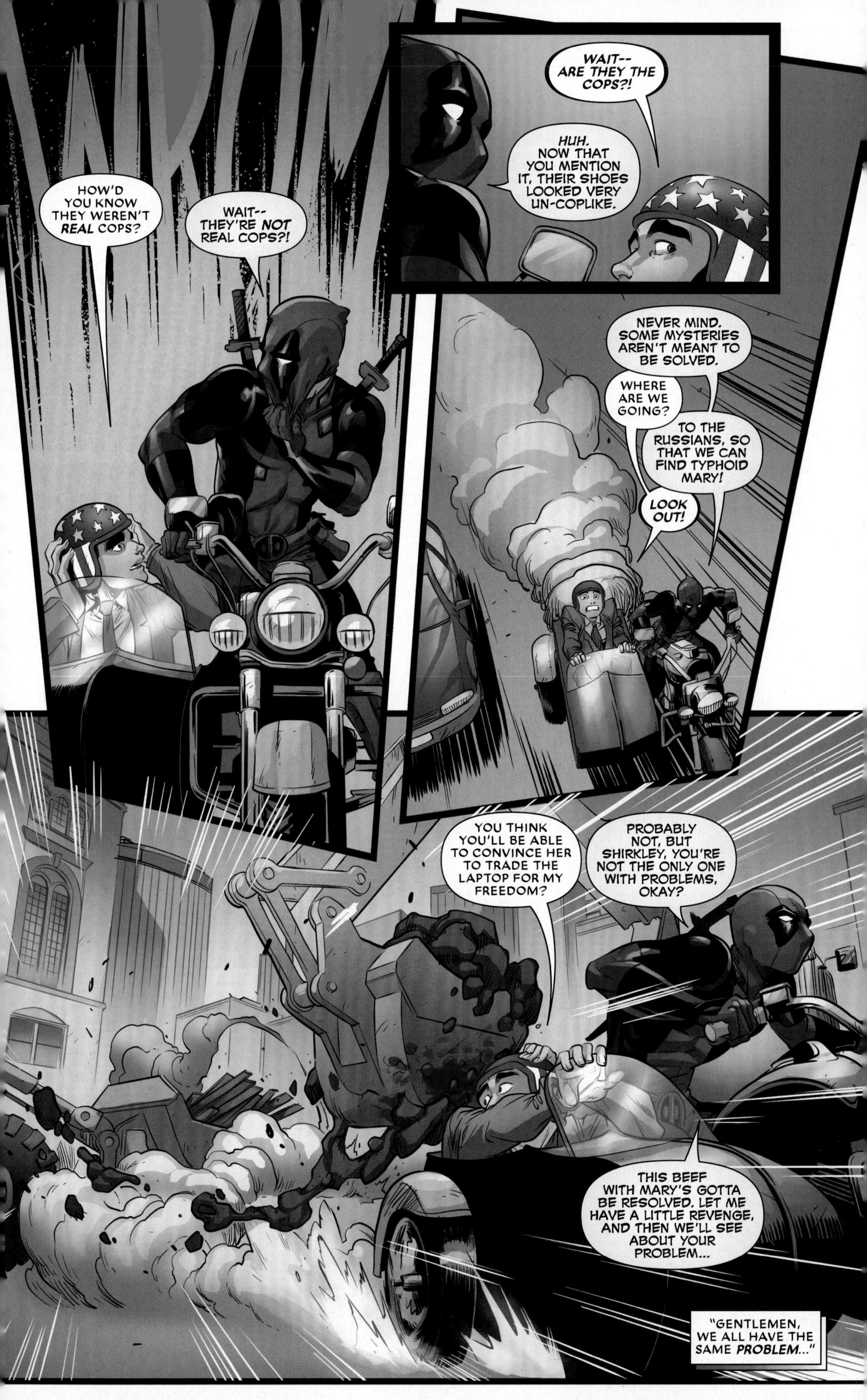

HOW'D YOU KNOW THEY WEREN'T *REAL* COPS?
WAIT-- THEY'RE *NOT* REAL COPS?!
WAIT-- ARE THEY THE COPS?!
HUH. NOW THAT YOU MENTION IT, THEIR SHOES LOOKED VERY UN-COPLIKE.
NEVER MIND. SOME MYSTERIES AREN'T MEANT TO BE SOLVED.
WHERE ARE WE GOING?
TO THE RUSSIANS, SO THAT WE CAN FIND TYPHOID MARY!
LOOK OUT!
YOU THINK YOU'LL BE ABLE TO CONVINCE HER TO TRADE THE LAPTOP FOR MY FREEDOM?
PROBABLY NOT, BUT SHIRKLEY, YOU'RE NOT THE ONLY ONE WITH PROBLEMS, OKAY?
THIS BEEF WITH MARY'S GOTTA BE RESOLVED. LET ME HAVE A LITTLE REVENGE, AND THEN WE'LL SEE ABOUT YOUR PROBLEM...
"GENTLEMEN, WE ALL HAVE THE SAME *PROBLEM...*"

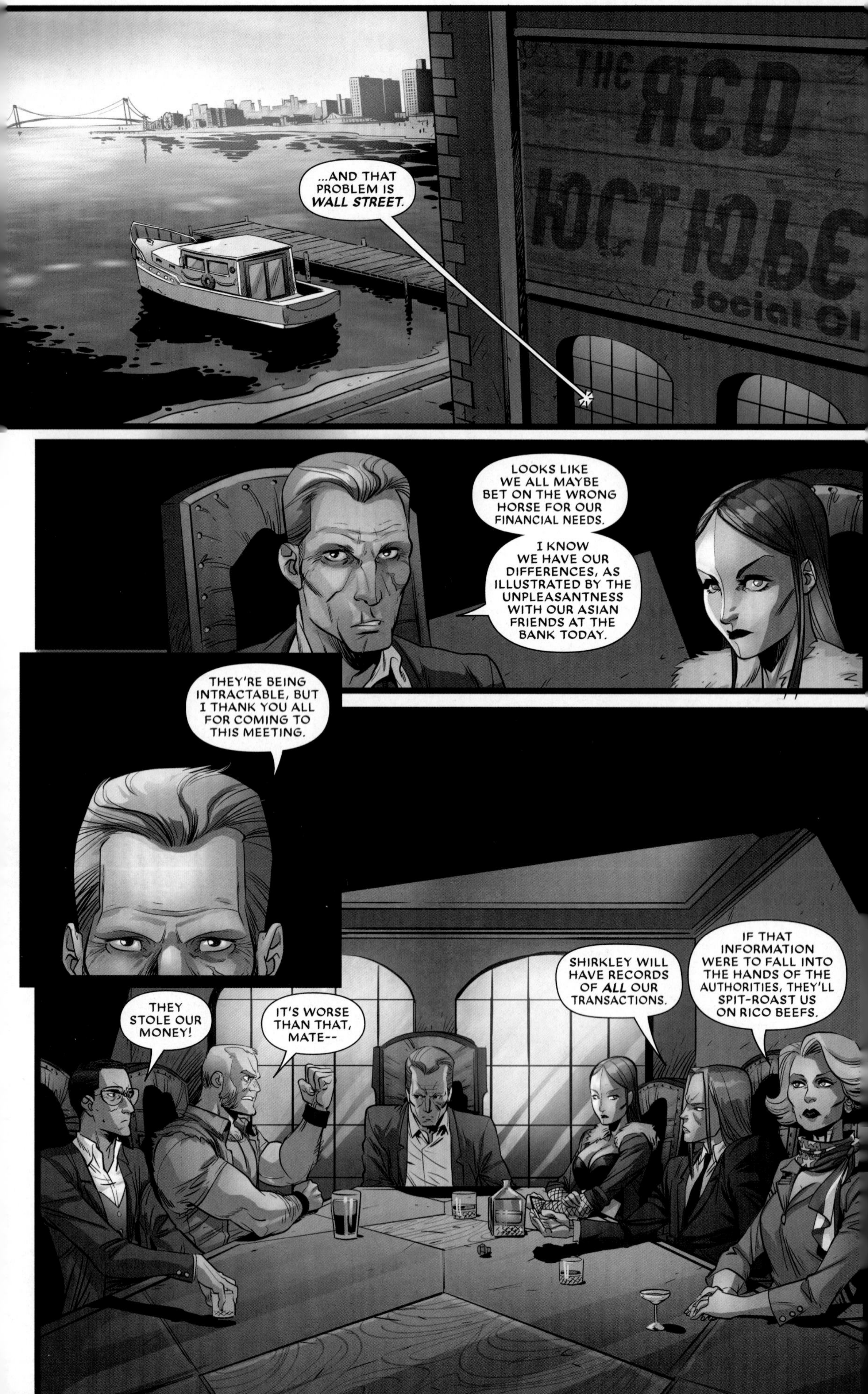

THE RED OCTOBER Social Cl
...AND THAT PROBLEM IS WALL STREET.
LOOKS LIKE WE ALL MAYBE BET ON THE WRONG HORSE FOR OUR FINANCIAL NEEDS.
I KNOW WE HAVE OUR DIFFERENCES, AS ILLUSTRATED BY THE UNPLEASANTNESS WITH OUR ASIAN FRIENDS AT THE BANK TODAY.
THEY'RE BEING INTRACTABLE, BUT I THANK YOU ALL FOR COMING TO THIS MEETING.
THEY STOLE OUR MONEY!
IT'S WORSE THAN THAT, MATE--
SHIRKLEY WILL HAVE RECORDS OF ALL OUR TRANSACTIONS.
IF THAT INFORMATION WERE TO FALL INTO THE HANDS OF THE AUTHORITIES, THEY'LL SPIT-ROAST US ON RICO BEEFS.

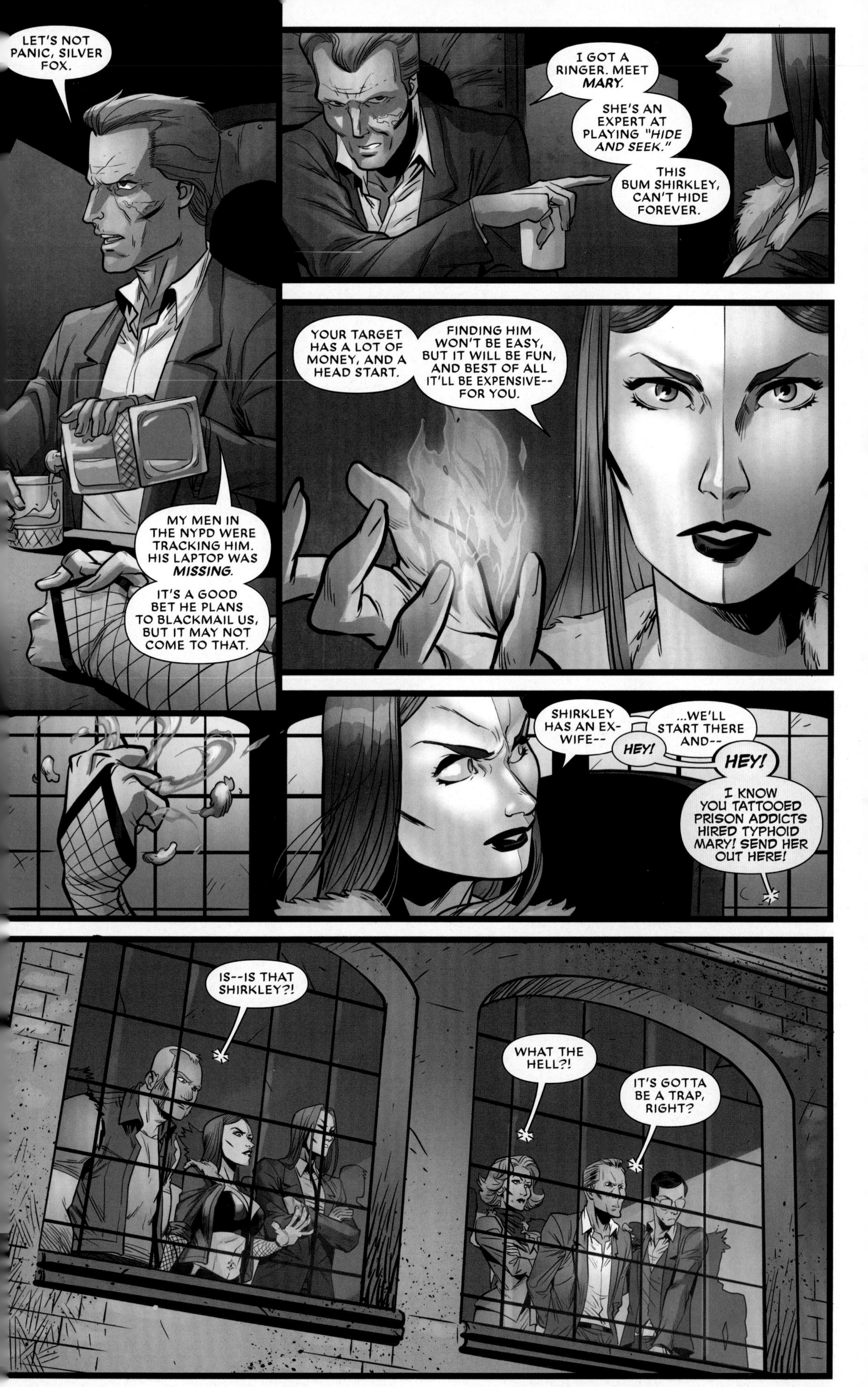
LET'S NOT PANIC, SILVER FOX.
I GOT A RINGER. MEET MARY.
SHE'S AN EXPERT AT PLAYING "HIDE AND SEEK."
THIS BUM SHIRKLEY, CAN'T HIDE FOREVER.
YOUR TARGET HAS A LOT OF MONEY, AND A HEAD START.
FINDING HIM WON'T BE EASY, BUT IT WILL BE FUN, AND BEST OF ALL IT'LL BE EXPENSIVE-- FOR YOU.
MY MEN IN THE NYPD WERE TRACKING HIM. HIS LAPTOP WAS MISSING.
IT'S A GOOD BET HE PLANS TO BLACKMAIL US, BUT IT MAY NOT COME TO THAT.
SHIRKLEY HAS AN EX-WIFE--
HEY!
...WE'LL START THERE AND--
HEY!
I KNOW YOU TATTOOED PRISON ADDICTS HIRED TYPHOID MARY! SEND HER OUT HERE!
IS--IS THAT SHIRKLEY?!
WHAT THE HELL?!
IT'S GOTTA BE A TRAP, RIGHT?

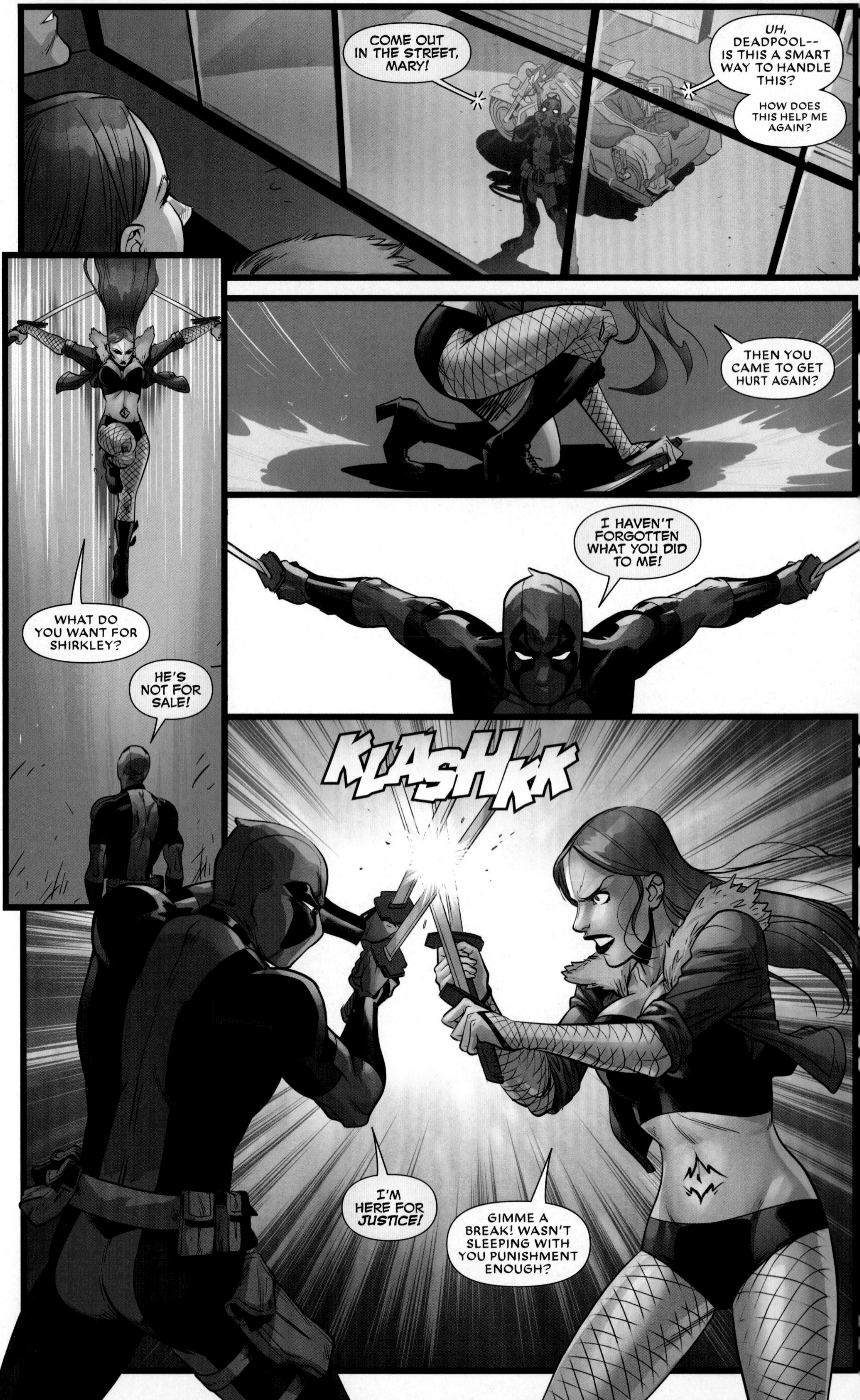
COME OUT IN THE STREET, MARY!
UH, DEADPOOL-- IS THIS A SMART WAY TO HANDLE THIS?
HOW DOES THIS HELP ME AGAIN?
WHAT DO YOU WANT FOR SHIRKLEY?
HE'S NOT FOR SALE!
THEN YOU CAME TO GET HURT AGAIN?
I HAVEN'T FORGOTTEN WHAT YOU DID TO ME!
KLASHKK
I'M HERE FOR JUSTICE!
GIMME A BREAK! WASN'T SLEEPING WITH YOU PUNISHMENT ENOUGH?

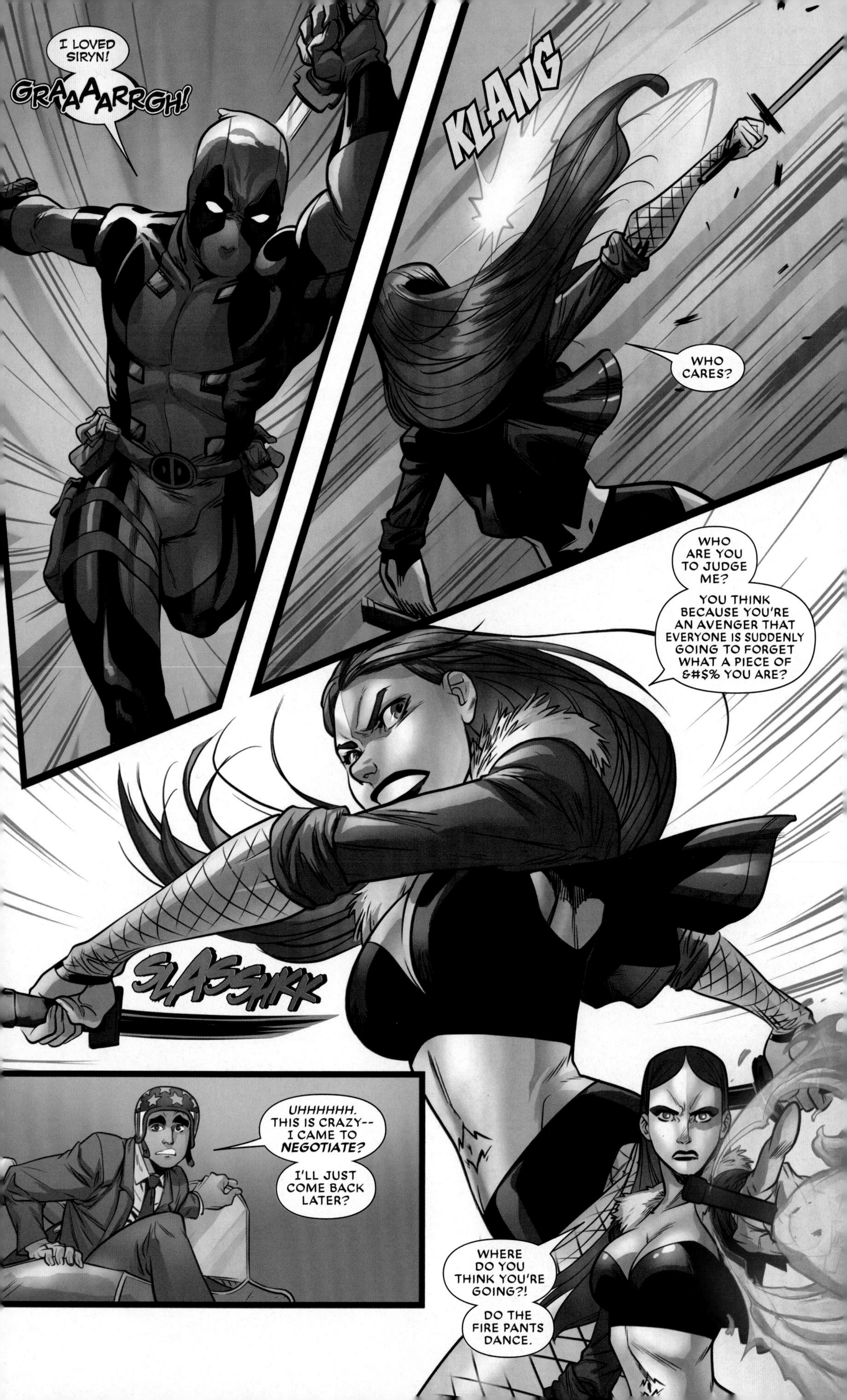
I LOVED SIRYN!
GRAAAARRGH!
KLANG
WHO CARES?
WHO ARE YOU TO JUDGE ME?
YOU THINK BECAUSE YOU'RE AN AVENGER THAT EVERYONE IS SUDDENLY GOING TO FORGET WHAT A PIECE OF &#$% YOU ARE?
SLASSHKK
UHHHHHH. THIS IS CRAZY-- I CAME TO NEGOTIATE?
I'LL JUST COME BACK LATER?
WHERE DO YOU THINK YOU'RE GOING?!
DO THE FIRE PANTS DANCE.

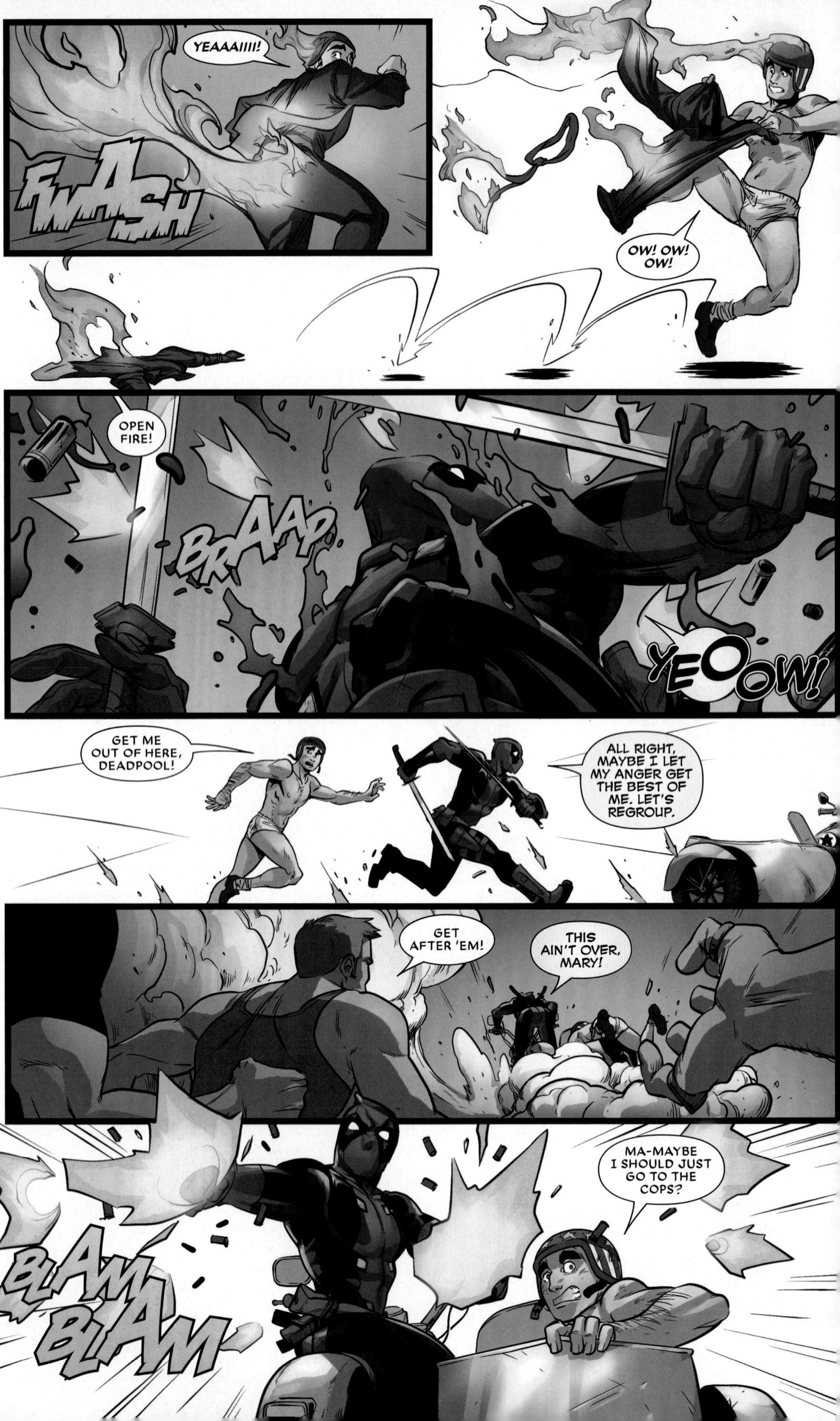
YEAAAIIII!
FWASH
OW! OW! OW!
OPEN FIRE!
BRAAAP
YEOOOW!
GET ME OUT OF HERE, DEADPOOL!
ALL RIGHT, MAYBE I LET MY ANGER GET THE BEST OF ME. LET'S REGROUP.
GET AFTER 'EM!
THIS AIN'T OVER, MARY!
BLAM BLAM
MA-MAYBE I SHOULD JUST GO TO THE COPS?

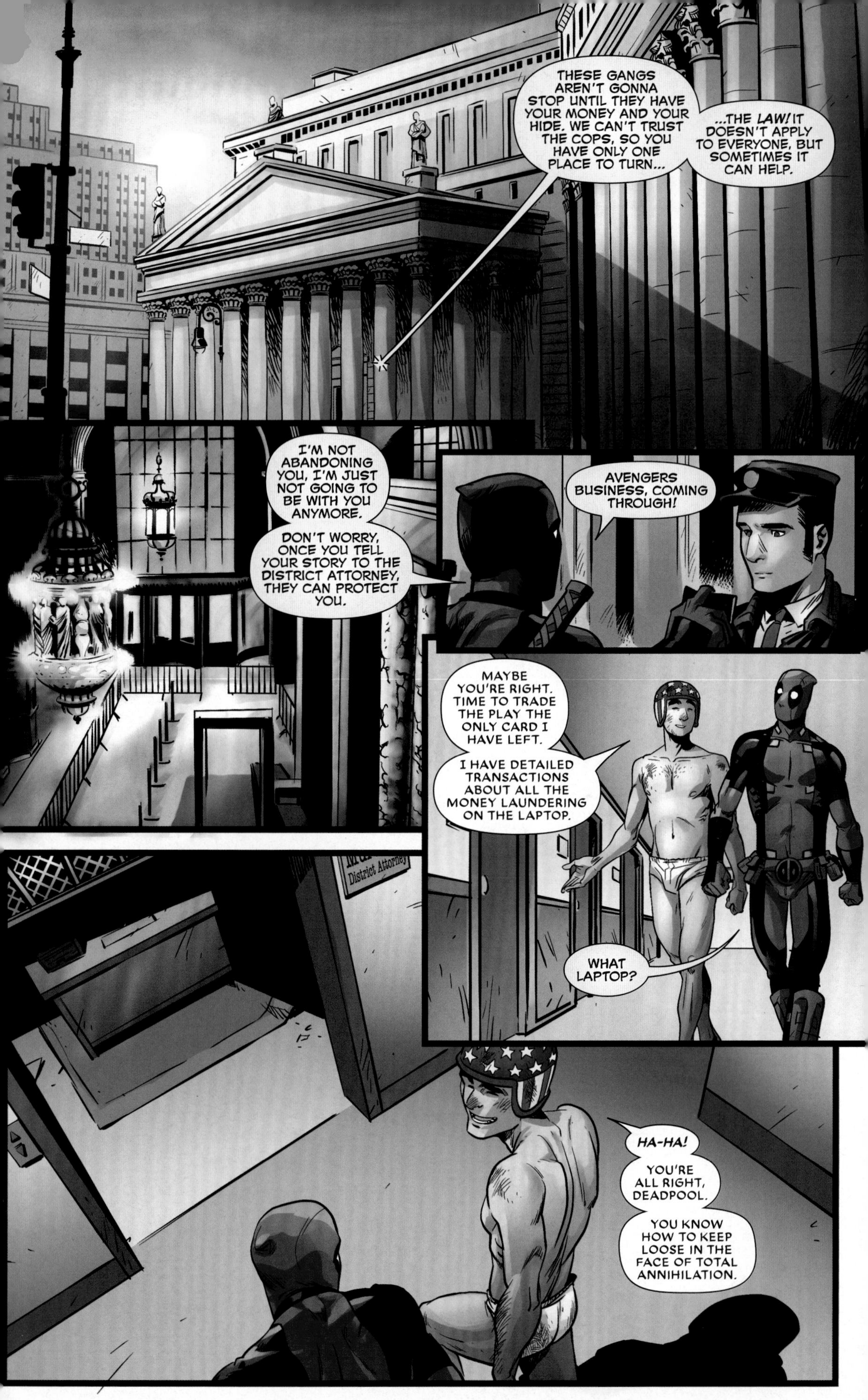
THESE GANGS AREN'T GONNA STOP UNTIL THEY HAVE YOUR MONEY AND YOUR HIDE. WE CAN'T TRUST THE COPS, SO YOU HAVE ONLY ONE PLACE TO TURN...
...THE LAW! IT DOESN'T APPLY TO EVERYONE, BUT SOMETIMES IT CAN HELP.
I'M NOT ABANDONING YOU, I'M JUST NOT GOING TO BE WITH YOU ANYMORE.
DON'T WORRY, ONCE YOU TELL YOUR STORY TO THE DISTRICT ATTORNEY, THEY CAN PROTECT YOU.
AVENGERS BUSINESS, COMING THROUGH!
MAYBE YOU'RE RIGHT. TIME TO TRADE THE PLAY THE ONLY CARD I HAVE LEFT.
I HAVE DETAILED TRANSACTIONS ABOUT ALL THE MONEY LAUNDERING ON THE LAPTOP.
WHAT LAPTOP?
District Attorney
HA-HA!
YOU'RE ALL RIGHT, DEADPOOL.
YOU KNOW HOW TO KEEP LOOSE IN THE FACE OF TOTAL ANNIHILATION.

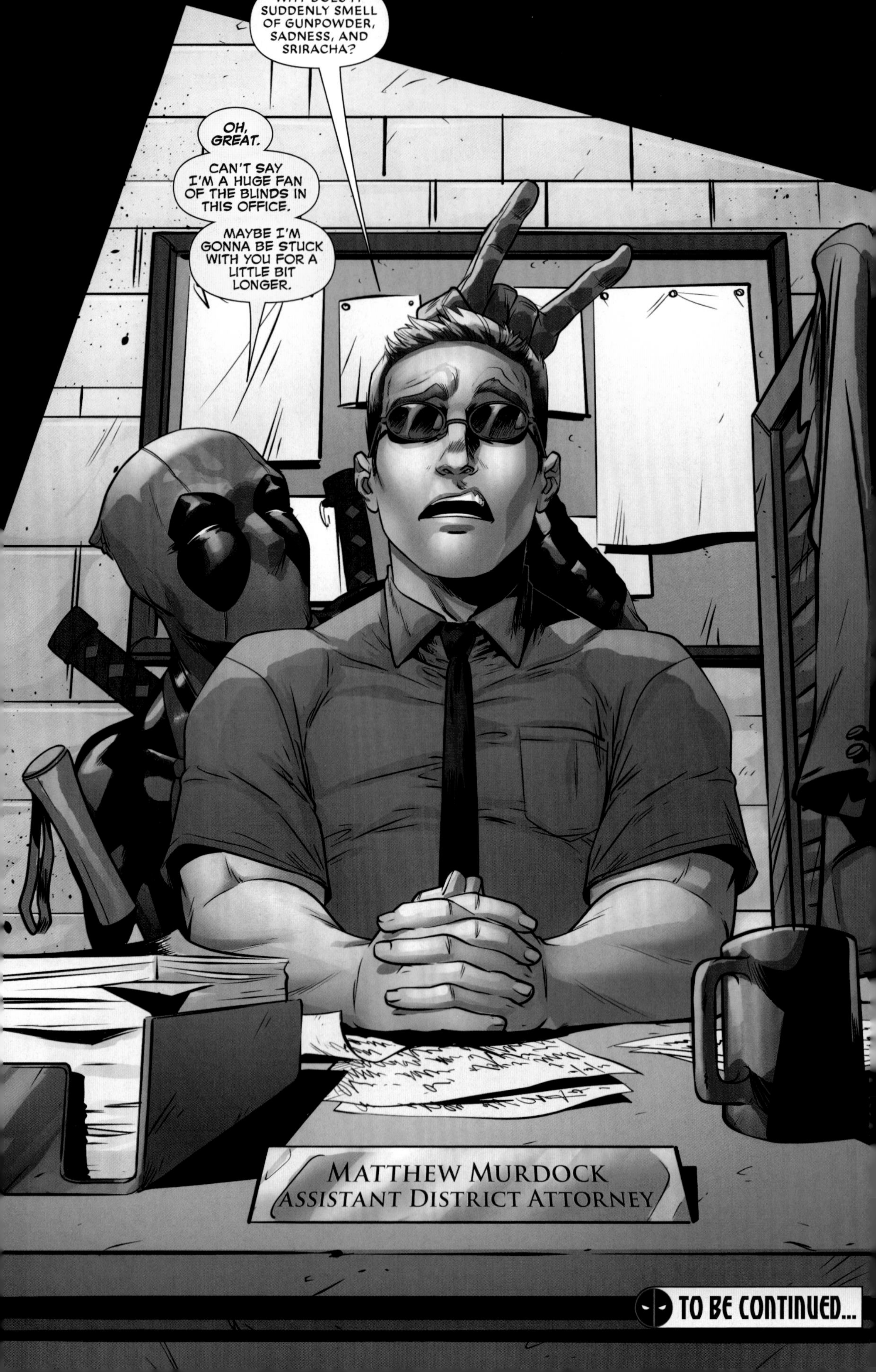
WHY DOES IT SUDDENLY SMELL OF GUNPOWDER, SADNESS, AND SRIRACHA?
OH, GREAT.
CAN'T SAY I'M A HUGE FAN OF THE BLINDS IN THIS OFFICE.
MAYBE I'M GONNA BE STUCK WITH YOU FOR A LITTLE BIT LONGER.
MATTHEW MURDOCK
ASSISTANT DISTRICT ATTORNEY
TO BE CONTINUED...

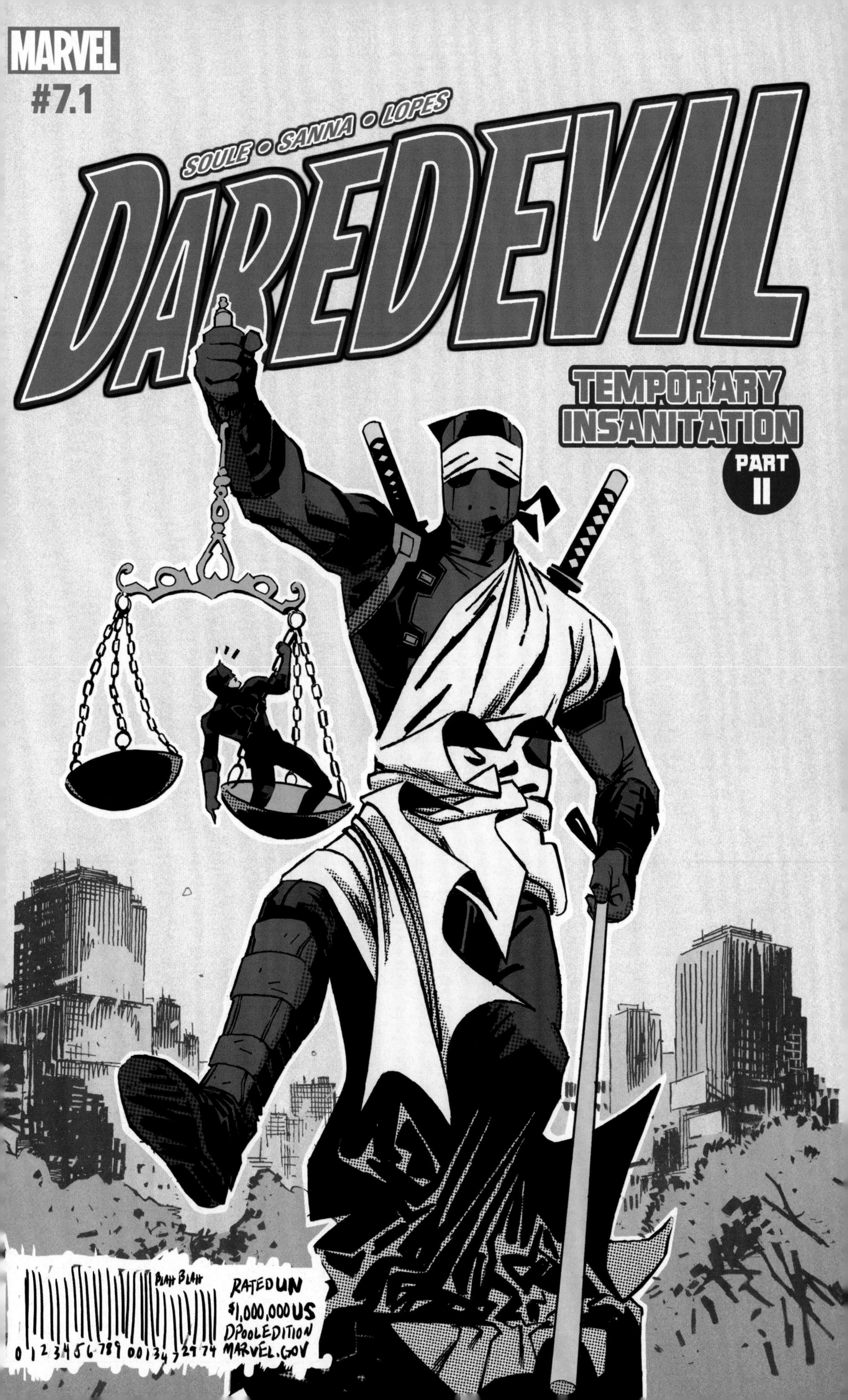

MARVEL
#7.1
SOULE • SANNA • LOPES
DAREDEVIL
TEMPORARY INSANITATION
PART II
BLAH BLAH
RATED UN
$1,000,000 US
DPOOL EDITION
MARVEL.GOV

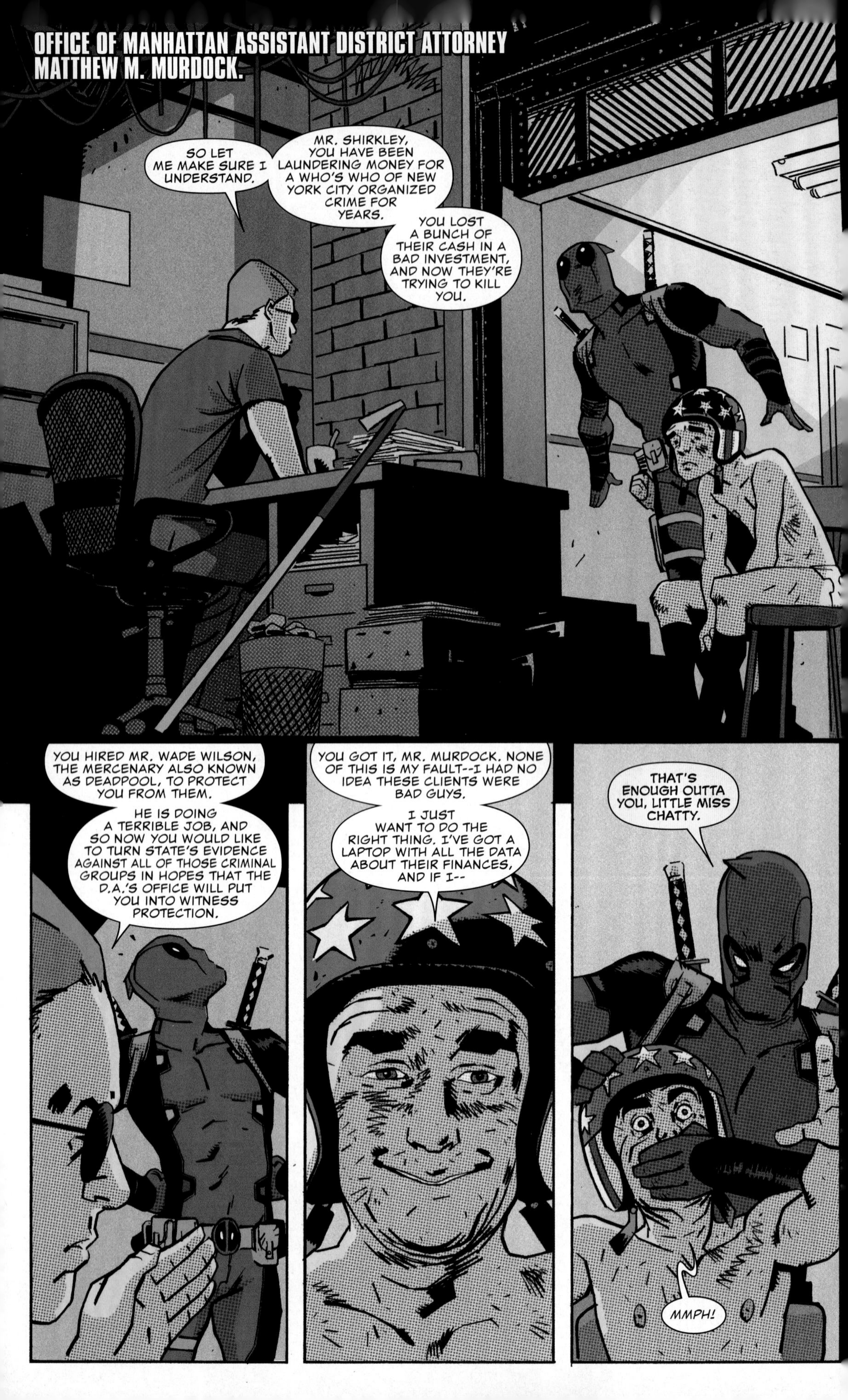
OFFICE OF MANHATTAN ASSISTANT DISTRICT ATTORNEY MATTHEW M. MURDOCK.
SO LET ME MAKE SURE I UNDERSTAND.
MR. SHIRKLEY, YOU HAVE BEEN LAUNDERING MONEY FOR A WHO'S WHO OF NEW YORK CITY ORGANIZED CRIME FOR YEARS.
YOU LOST A BUNCH OF THEIR CASH IN A BAD INVESTMENT, AND NOW THEY'RE TRYING TO KILL YOU.
YOU HIRED MR. WADE WILSON, THE MERCENARY ALSO KNOWN AS DEADPOOL, TO PROTECT YOU FROM THEM.
HE IS DOING A TERRIBLE JOB, AND SO NOW YOU WOULD LIKE TO TURN STATE'S EVIDENCE AGAINST ALL OF THOSE CRIMINAL GROUPS IN HOPES THAT THE D.A.'S OFFICE WILL PUT YOU INTO WITNESS PROTECTION.
YOU GOT IT, MR. MURDOCK. NONE OF THIS IS MY FAULT--I HAD NO IDEA THESE CLIENTS WERE BAD GUYS.
I JUST WANT TO DO THE RIGHT THING. I'VE GOT A LAPTOP WITH ALL THE DATA ABOUT THEIR FINANCES, AND IF I--
THAT'S ENOUGH OUTTA YOU, LITTLE MISS CHATTY.
MMPH!

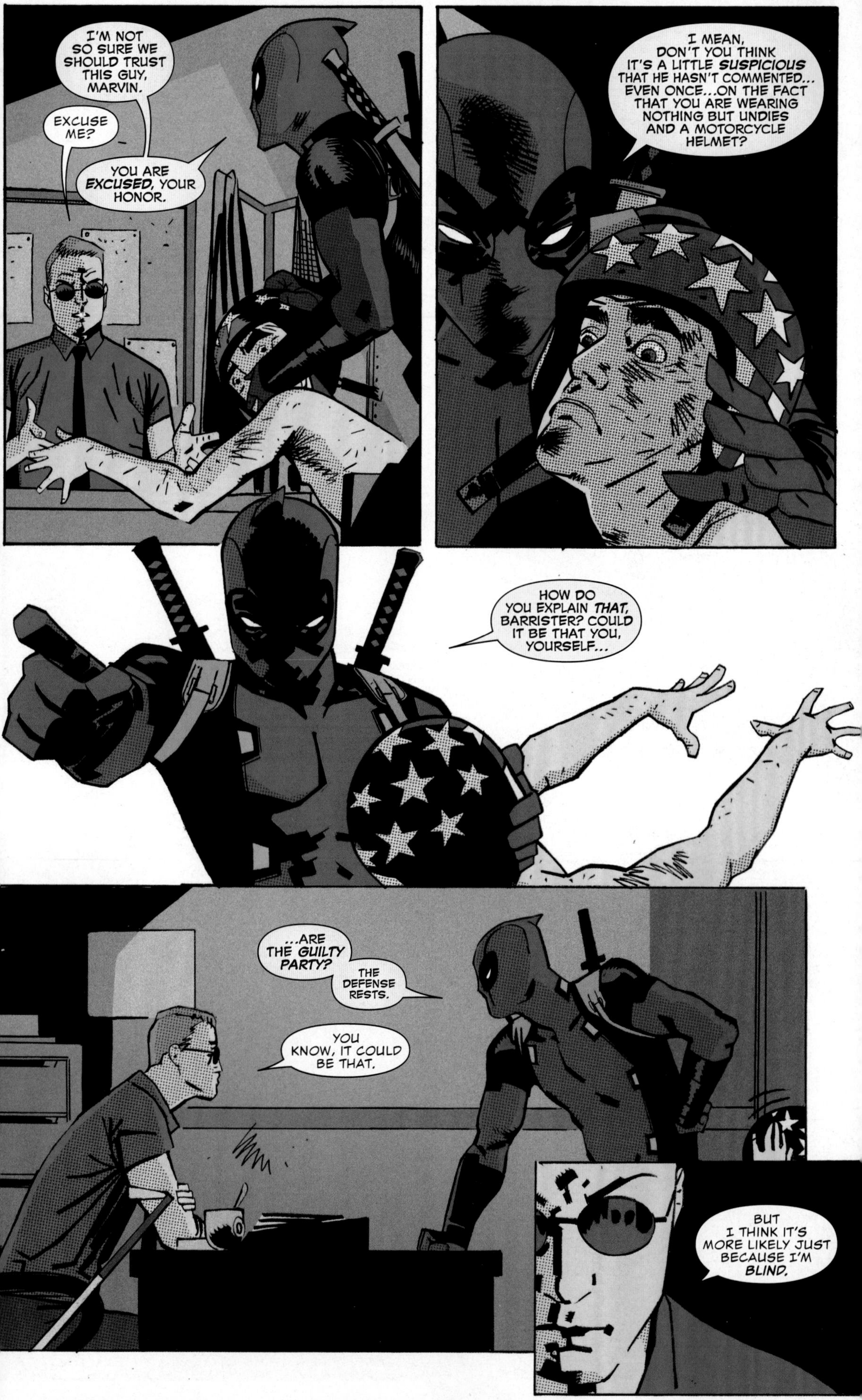
I'M NOT SO SURE WE SHOULD TRUST THIS GUY, MARVIN.
EXCUSE ME?
YOU ARE EXCUSED, YOUR HONOR.
I MEAN, DON'T YOU THINK IT'S A LITTLE SUSPICIOUS THAT HE HASN'T COMMENTED... EVEN ONCE...ON THE FACT THAT YOU ARE WEARING NOTHING BUT UNDIES AND A MOTORCYCLE HELMET?
HOW DO YOU EXPLAIN THAT, BARRISTER? COULD IT BE THAT YOU, YOURSELF...
...ARE THE GUILTY PARTY?
THE DEFENSE RESTS.
YOU KNOW, IT COULD BE THAT.
BUT I THINK IT'S MORE LIKELY JUST BECAUSE I'M BLIND.

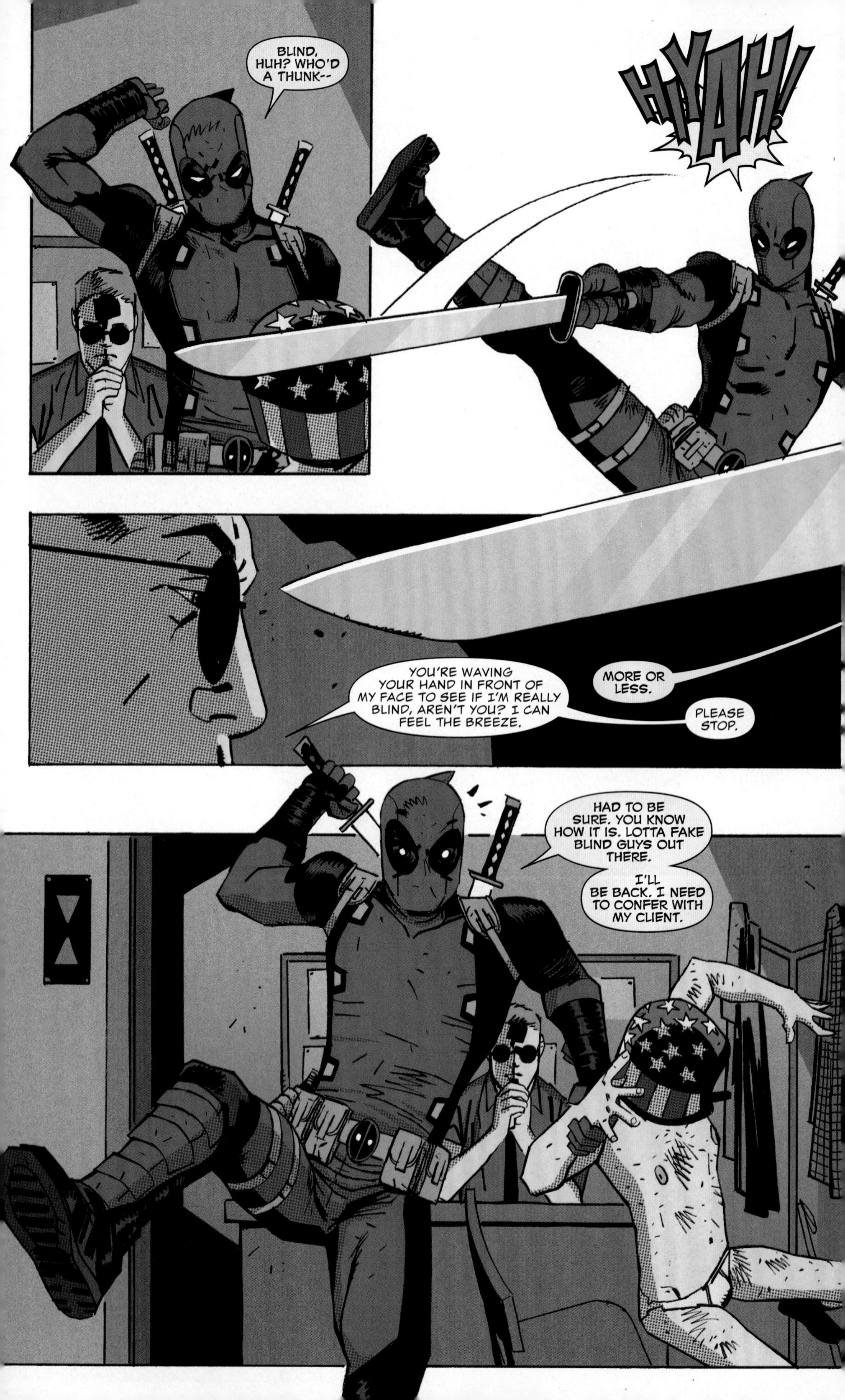
BLIND, HUH? WHO'D A THUNK--
HIYAH!
YOU'RE WAVING YOUR HAND IN FRONT OF MY FACE TO SEE IF I'M REALLY BLIND, AREN'T YOU? I CAN FEEL THE BREEZE.
MORE OR LESS.
PLEASE STOP.
HAD TO BE SURE. YOU KNOW HOW IT IS. LOTTA FAKE BLIND GUYS OUT THERE.
I'LL BE BACK. I NEED TO CONFER WITH MY CLIENT.

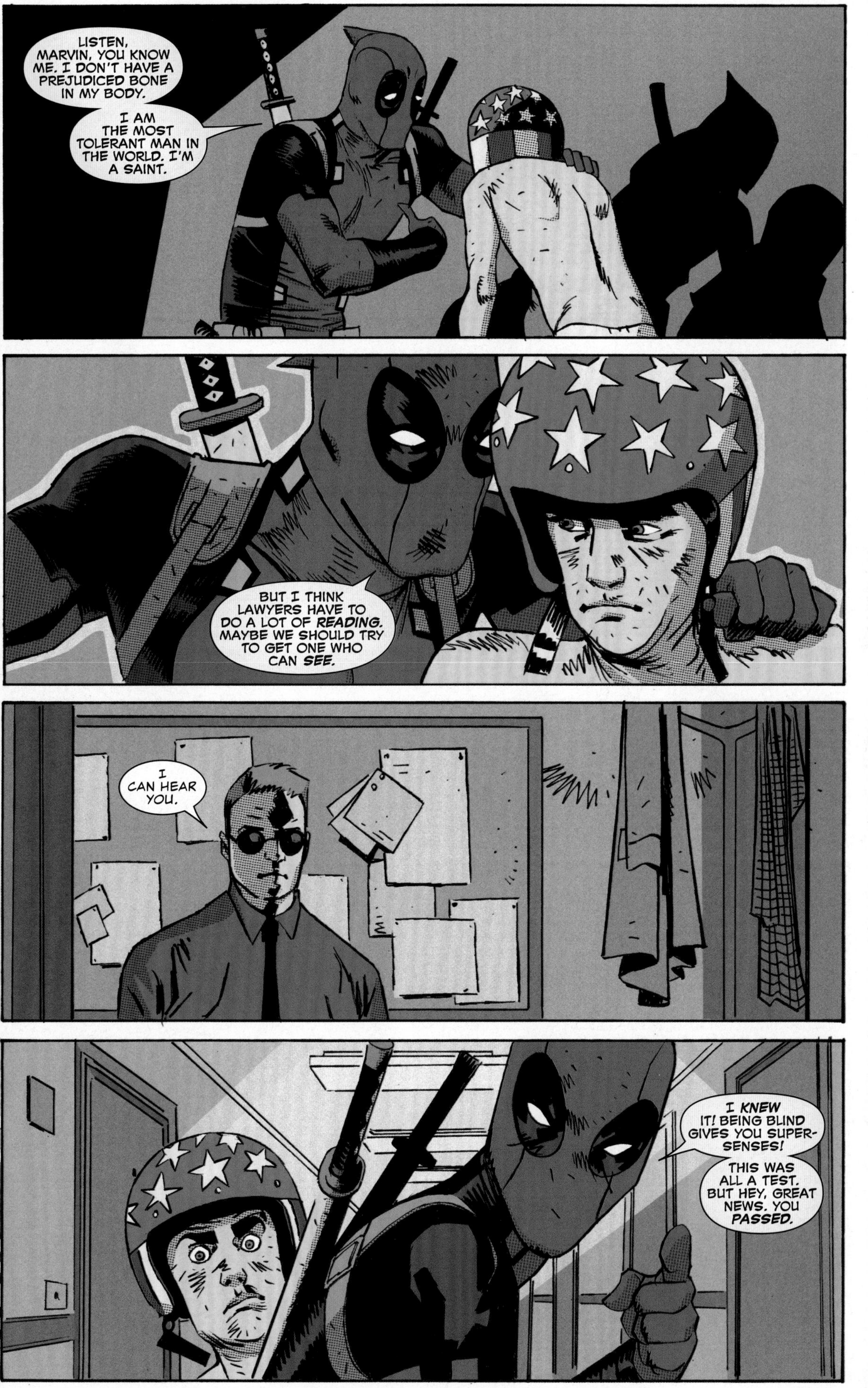
LISTEN, MARVIN, YOU KNOW ME. I DON'T HAVE A PREJUDICED BONE IN MY BODY.
I AM THE MOST TOLERANT MAN IN THE WORLD. I'M A SAINT.
BUT I THINK LAWYERS HAVE TO DO A LOT OF *READING*. MAYBE WE SHOULD TRY TO GET ONE WHO CAN *SEE*.
I CAN HEAR YOU.
I *KNEW* IT! BEING BLIND GIVES YOU SUPER-SENSES!
THIS WAS ALL A TEST. BUT HEY, GREAT NEWS. YOU *PASSED*.

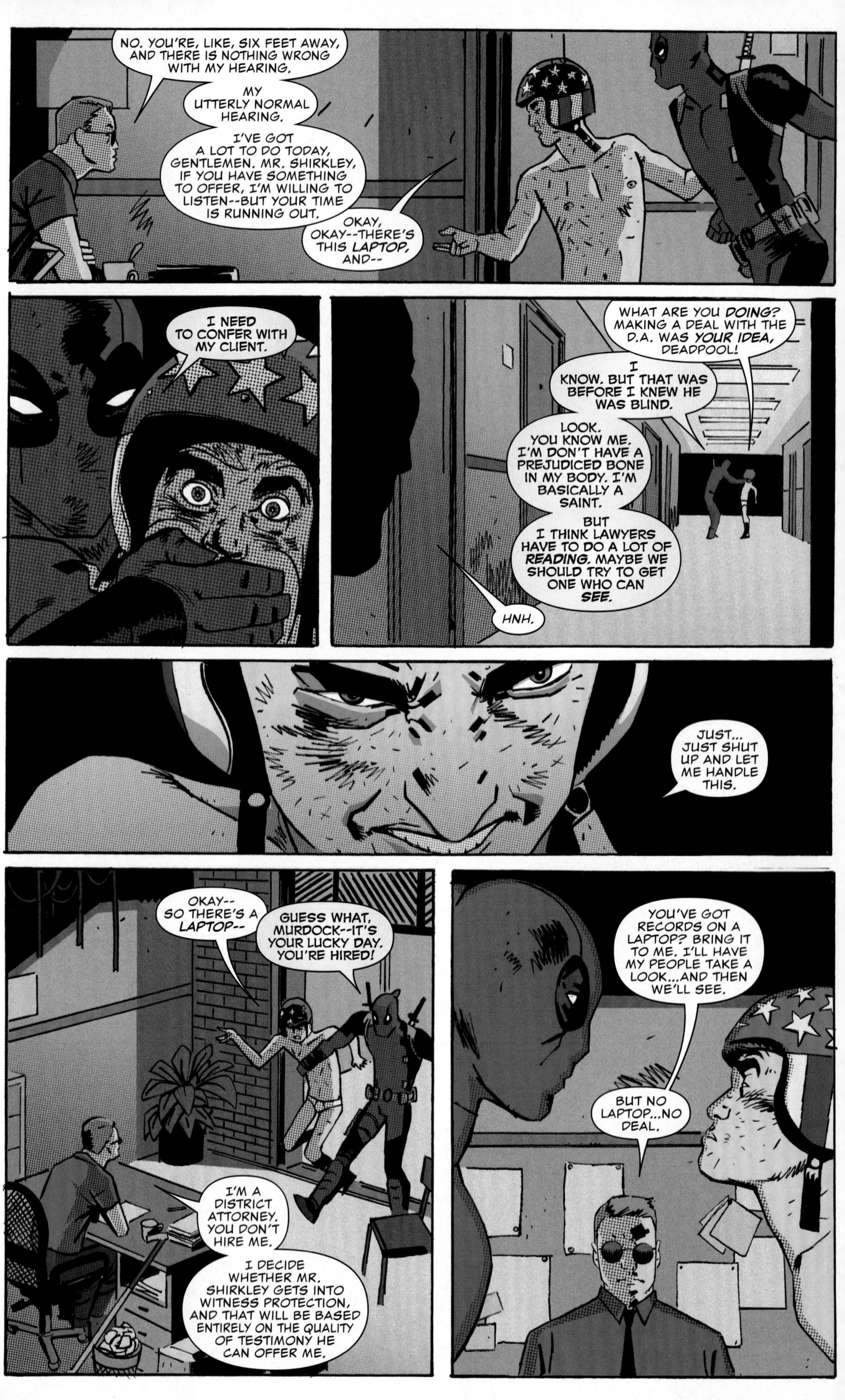
NO. YOU'RE, LIKE, SIX FEET AWAY, AND THERE IS NOTHING WRONG WITH MY HEARING.
MY UTTERLY NORMAL HEARING.
I'VE GOT A LOT TO DO TODAY, GENTLEMEN. MR. SHIRKLEY, IF YOU HAVE SOMETHING TO OFFER, I'M WILLING TO LISTEN--BUT YOUR TIME IS RUNNING OUT.
OKAY, OKAY--THERE'S THIS LAPTOP, AND--
I NEED TO CONFER WITH MY CLIENT.
WHAT ARE YOU DOING? MAKING A DEAL WITH THE D.A. WAS YOUR IDEA, DEADPOOL!
I KNOW. BUT THAT WAS BEFORE I KNEW HE WAS BLIND.
LOOK. YOU KNOW ME. I'M DON'T HAVE A PREJUDICED BONE IN MY BODY. I'M BASICALLY A SAINT.
BUT I THINK LAWYERS HAVE TO DO A LOT OF READING. MAYBE WE SHOULD TRY TO GET ONE WHO CAN SEE.
HNH.
JUST... JUST SHUT UP AND LET ME HANDLE THIS.
OKAY-- SO THERE'S A LAPTOP--
GUESS WHAT, MURDOCK--IT'S YOUR LUCKY DAY. YOU'RE HIRED!
I'M A DISTRICT ATTORNEY. YOU DON'T HIRE ME.
I DECIDE WHETHER MR. SHIRKLEY GETS INTO WITNESS PROTECTION, AND THAT WILL BE BASED ENTIRELY ON THE QUALITY OF TESTIMONY HE CAN OFFER ME.
YOU'VE GOT RECORDS ON A LAPTOP? BRING IT TO ME. I'LL HAVE MY PEOPLE TAKE A LOOK...AND THEN WE'LL SEE.
BUT NO LAPTOP...NO DEAL.

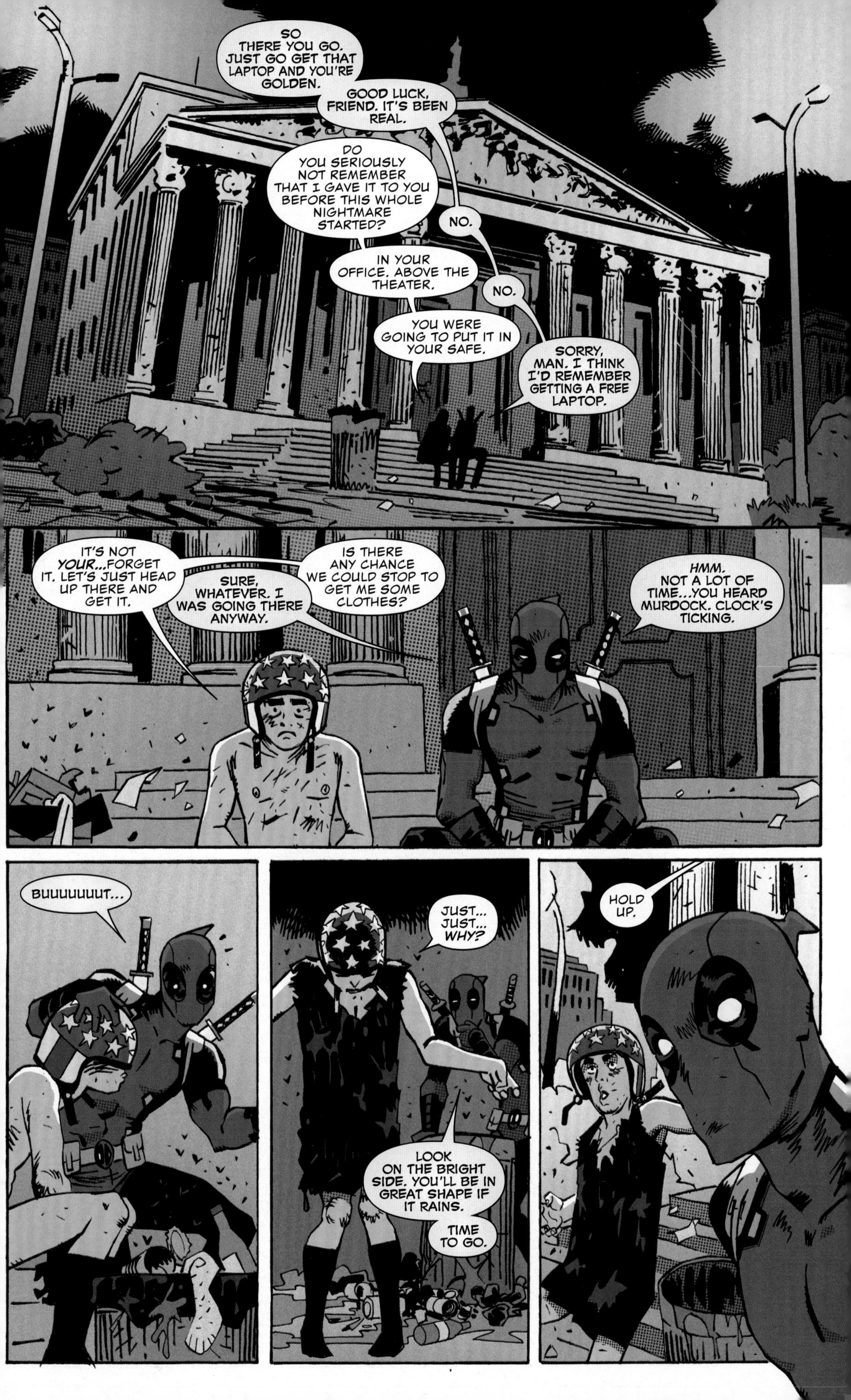

SO THERE YOU GO. JUST GO GET THAT LAPTOP AND YOU'RE GOLDEN.
GOOD LUCK, FRIEND. IT'S BEEN REAL.
DO YOU SERIOUSLY NOT REMEMBER THAT I GAVE IT TO YOU BEFORE THIS WHOLE NIGHTMARE STARTED?
NO.
IN YOUR OFFICE. ABOVE THE THEATER.
NO.
YOU WERE GOING TO PUT IT IN YOUR SAFE.
SORRY, MAN. I THINK I'D REMEMBER GETTING A FREE LAPTOP.
IT'S NOT *YOUR*...FORGET IT. LET'S JUST HEAD UP THERE AND GET IT.
SURE, WHATEVER. I WAS GOING THERE ANYWAY.
IS THERE ANY CHANCE WE COULD STOP TO GET ME SOME CLOTHES?
HMM. NOT A LOT OF TIME...YOU HEARD MURDOCK. CLOCK'S TICKING.
BUUUUUUUT...
JUST... JUST... *WHY?*
LOOK ON THE BRIGHT SIDE. YOU'LL BE IN GREAT SHAPE IF IT RAINS.
TIME TO GO.
HOLD UP.

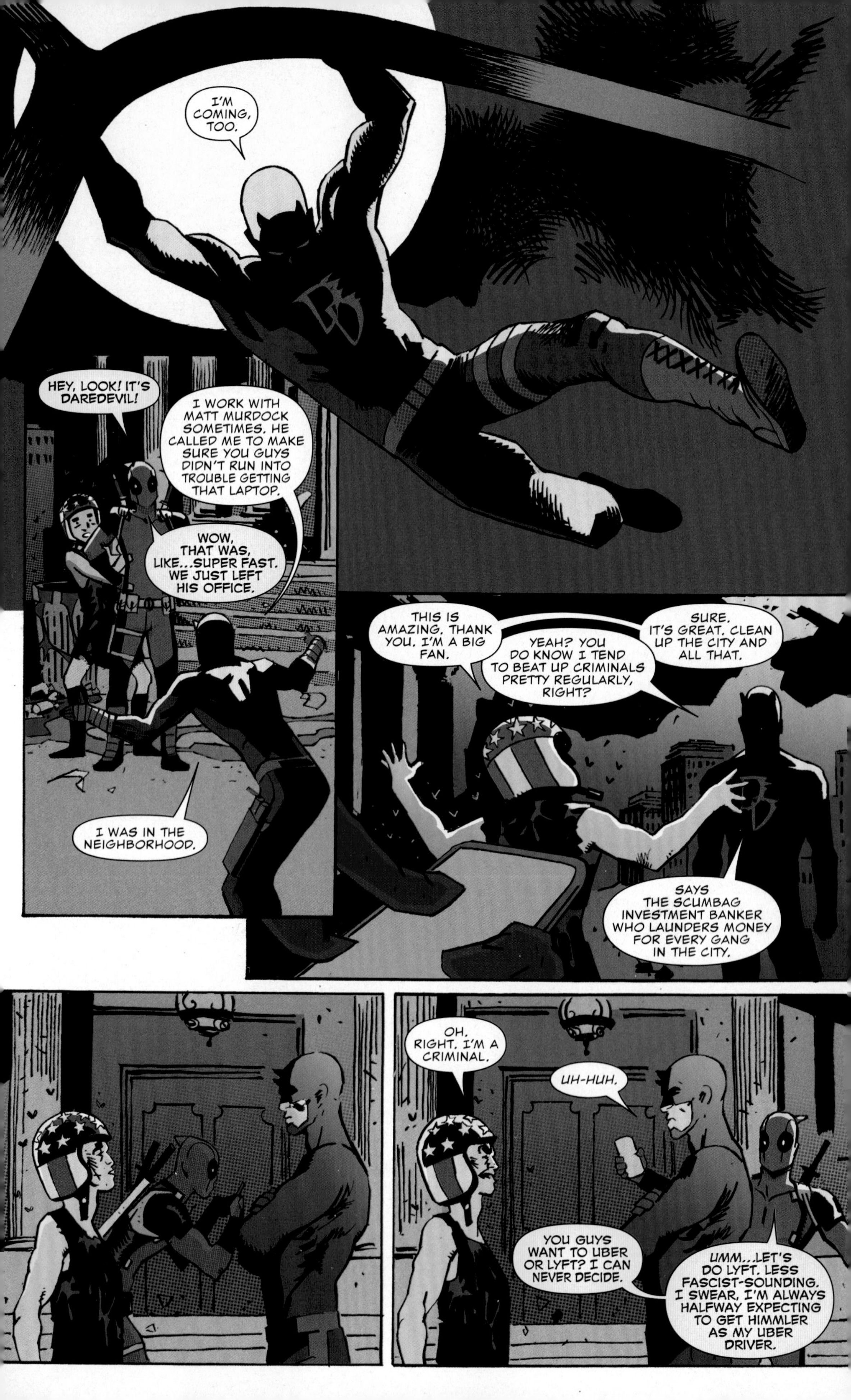
I'M COMING, TOO.
HEY, LOOK! IT'S DAREDEVIL!
I WORK WITH MATT MURDOCK SOMETIMES. HE CALLED ME TO MAKE SURE YOU GUYS DIDN'T RUN INTO TROUBLE GETTING THAT LAPTOP.
WOW, THAT WAS, LIKE...SUPER FAST. WE JUST LEFT HIS OFFICE.
I WAS IN THE NEIGHBORHOOD.
THIS IS AMAZING. THANK YOU. I'M A BIG FAN.
YEAH? YOU DO KNOW I TEND TO BEAT UP CRIMINALS PRETTY REGULARLY, RIGHT?
SURE. IT'S GREAT. CLEAN UP THE CITY AND ALL THAT.
SAYS THE SCUMBAG INVESTMENT BANKER WHO LAUNDERS MONEY FOR EVERY GANG IN THE CITY.
OH. RIGHT. I'M A CRIMINAL.
UH-HUH.
YOU GUYS WANT TO UBER OR LYFT? I CAN NEVER DECIDE.
UMM...LET'S DO LYFT. LESS FASCIST-SOUNDING. I SWEAR, I'M ALWAYS HALFWAY EXPECTING TO GET HIMMLER AS MY UBER DRIVER.

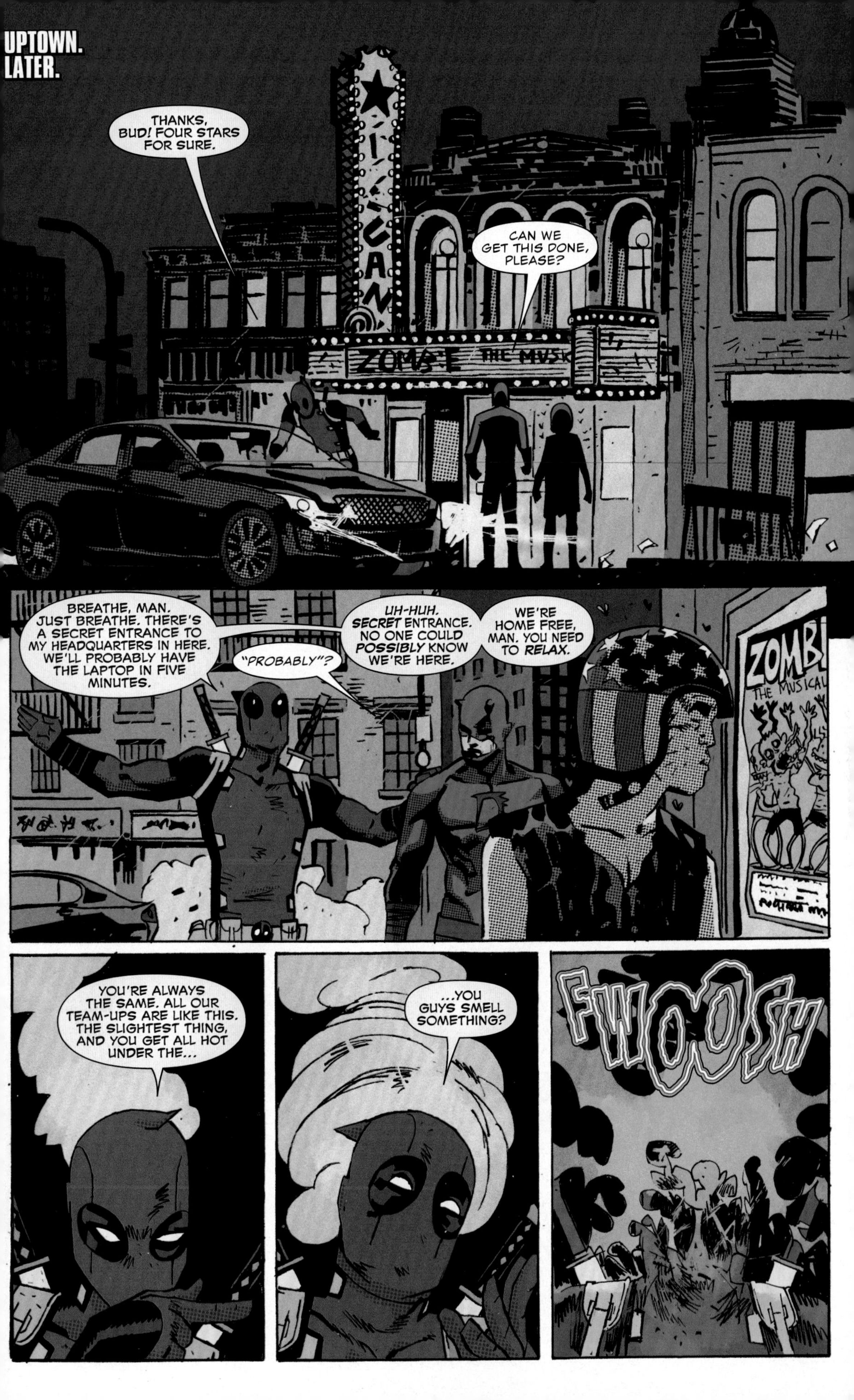
UPTOWN. LATER.
THANKS, BUD! FOUR STARS FOR SURE.
CAN WE GET THIS DONE, PLEASE?
ZOMBIE THE MUSICAL
BREATHE, MAN. JUST BREATHE. THERE'S A SECRET ENTRANCE TO MY HEADQUARTERS IN HERE. WE'LL PROBABLY HAVE THE LAPTOP IN FIVE MINUTES.
"PROBABLY"?
UH-HUH. SECRET ENTRANCE. NO ONE COULD POSSIBLY KNOW WE'RE HERE.
WE'RE HOME FREE, MAN. YOU NEED TO RELAX.
ZOMBI THE MUSICAL
YOU'RE ALWAYS THE SAME. ALL OUR TEAM-UPS ARE LIKE THIS. THE SLIGHTEST THING, AND YOU GET ALL HOT UNDER THE...
...YOU GUYS SMELL SOMETHING?
FWOOSH

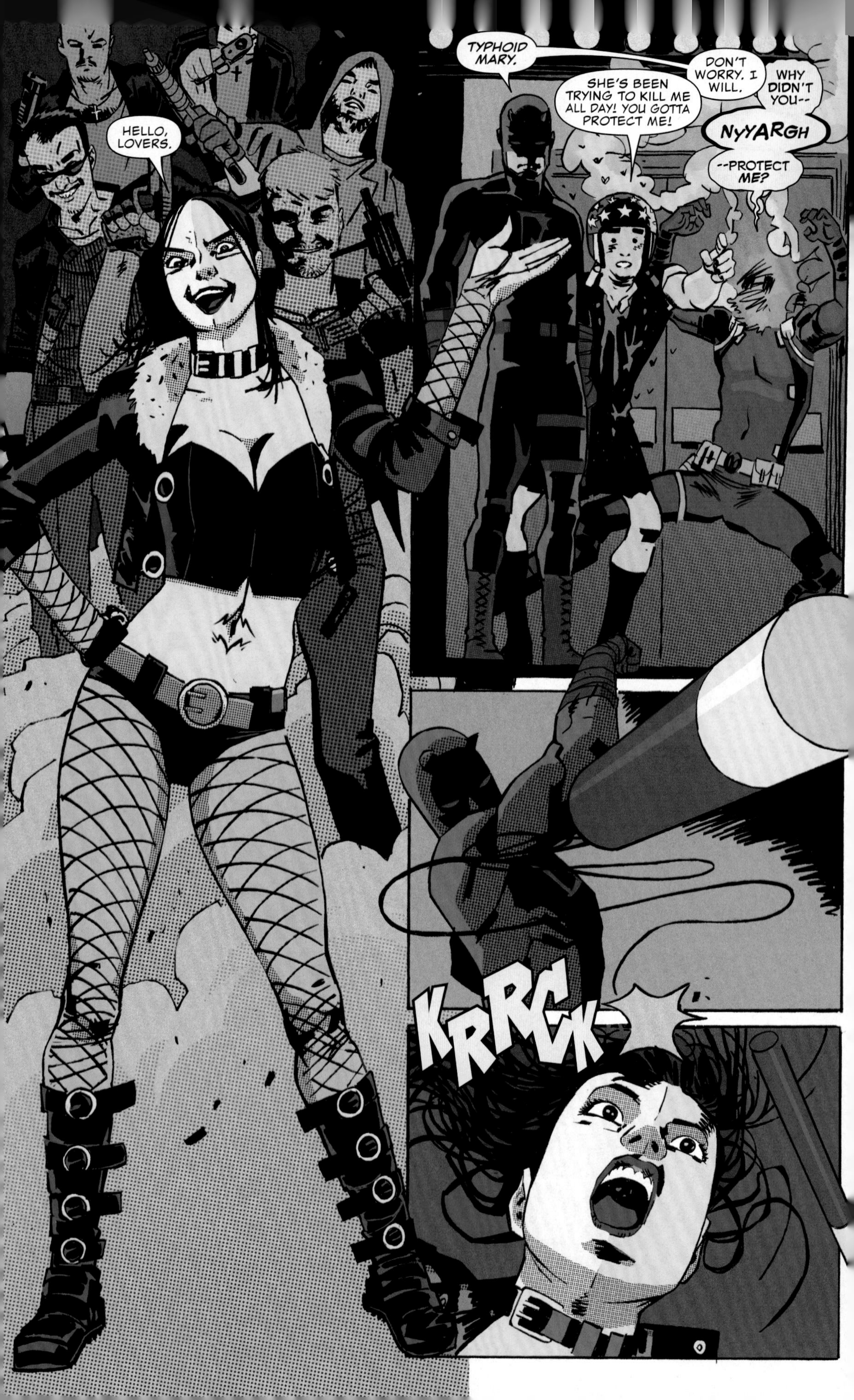
HELLO, LOVERS.
TYPHOID MARY.
SHE'S BEEN TRYING TO KILL ME ALL DAY! YOU GOTTA PROTECT ME!
DON'T WORRY. I WILL.
WHY DIDN'T YOU--
NyYARGH
--PROTECT ME?
KRRCK

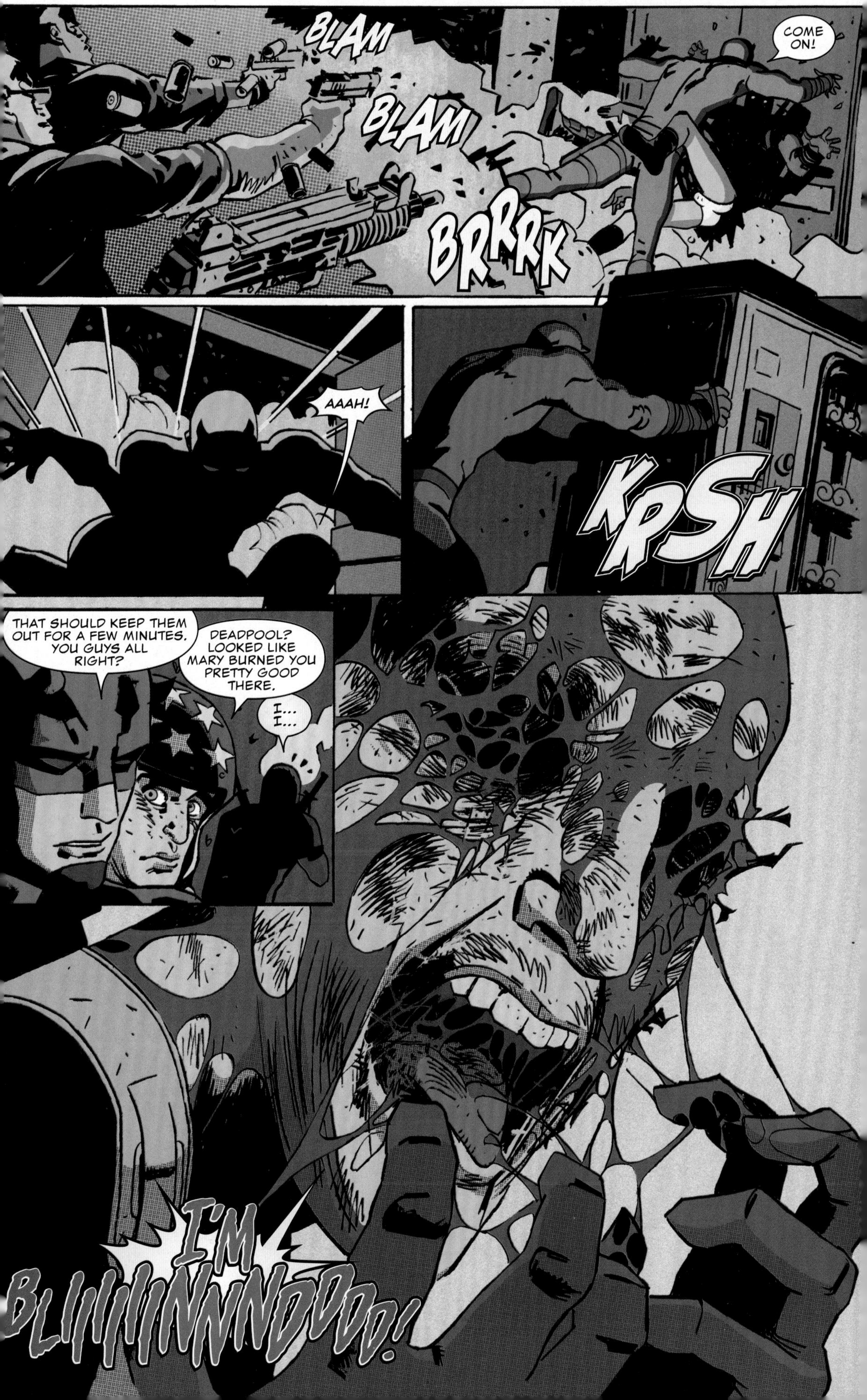
BLAM
BLAM
BRRRK
COME ON!
AAAH!
KRSH
THAT SHOULD KEEP THEM OUT FOR A FEW MINUTES. YOU GUYS ALL RIGHT?
DEADPOOL? LOOKED LIKE MARY BURNED YOU PRETTY GOOD THERE.
I... I...
I'M BLIIIIINNNDDDD!

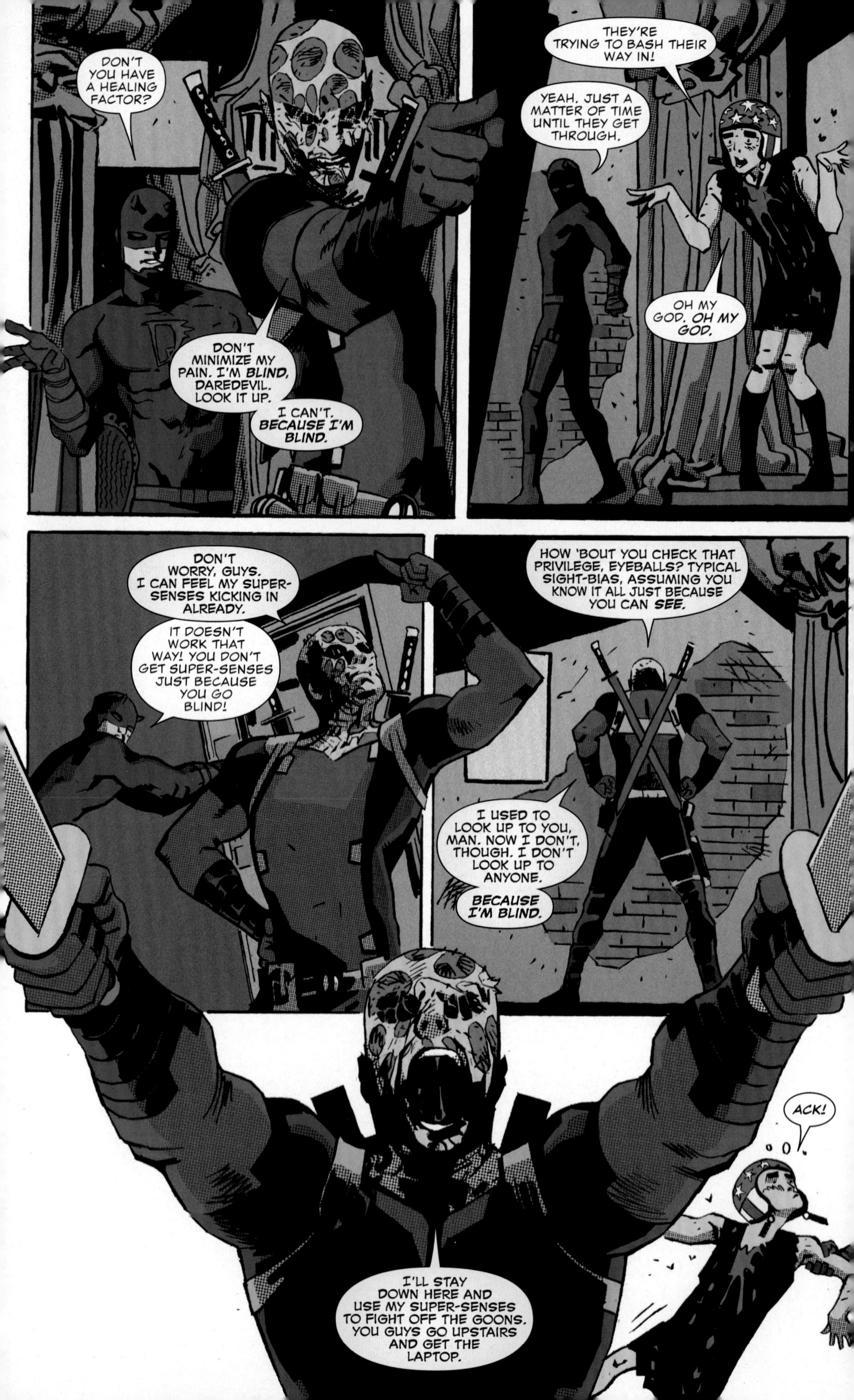
DON'T YOU HAVE A HEALING FACTOR?
DON'T MINIMIZE MY PAIN. I'M BLIND, DAREDEVIL. LOOK IT UP.
I CAN'T. BECAUSE I'M BLIND.
THEY'RE TRYING TO BASH THEIR WAY IN!
YEAH. JUST A MATTER OF TIME UNTIL THEY GET THROUGH.
OH MY GOD. OH MY GOD.
DON'T WORRY, GUYS. I CAN FEEL MY SUPER-SENSES KICKING IN ALREADY.
IT DOESN'T WORK THAT WAY! YOU DON'T GET SUPER-SENSES JUST BECAUSE YOU GO BLIND!
HOW 'BOUT YOU CHECK THAT PRIVILEGE, EYEBALLS? TYPICAL SIGHT-BIAS, ASSUMING YOU KNOW IT ALL JUST BECAUSE YOU CAN SEE.
I USED TO LOOK UP TO YOU, MAN. NOW I DON'T, THOUGH. I DON'T LOOK UP TO ANYONE.
BECAUSE I'M BLIND.
ACK!
I'LL STAY DOWN HERE AND USE MY SUPER-SENSES TO FIGHT OFF THE GOONS. YOU GUYS GO UPSTAIRS AND GET THE LAPTOP.

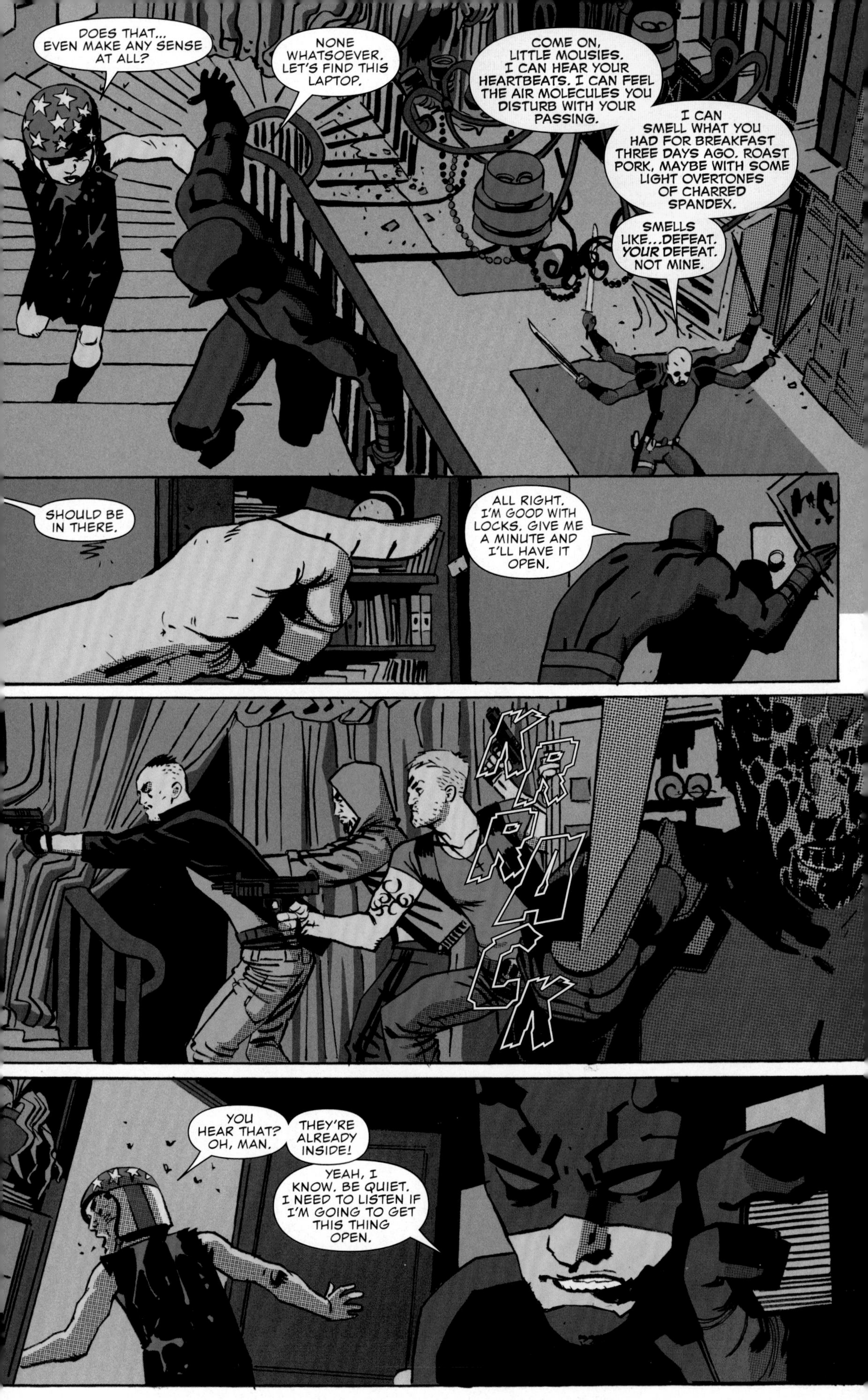

DOES THAT... EVEN MAKE ANY SENSE AT ALL?
NONE WHATSOEVER. LET'S FIND THIS LAPTOP.
COME ON, LITTLE MOUSIES. I CAN HEAR YOUR HEARTBEATS. I CAN FEEL THE AIR MOLECULES YOU DISTURB WITH YOUR PASSING.
I CAN SMELL WHAT YOU HAD FOR BREAKFAST THREE DAYS AGO. ROAST PORK, MAYBE WITH SOME LIGHT OVERTONES OF CHARRED SPANDEX.
SMELLS LIKE...DEFEAT. *YOUR* DEFEAT. NOT MINE.
SHOULD BE IN THERE.
ALL RIGHT. I'M GOOD WITH LOCKS. GIVE ME A MINUTE AND I'LL HAVE IT OPEN.
KRRAACK
YOU HEAR THAT? OH, MAN.
THEY'RE ALREADY INSIDE!
YEAH, I KNOW. BE QUIET. I NEED TO LISTEN IF I'M GOING TO GET THIS THING OPEN.

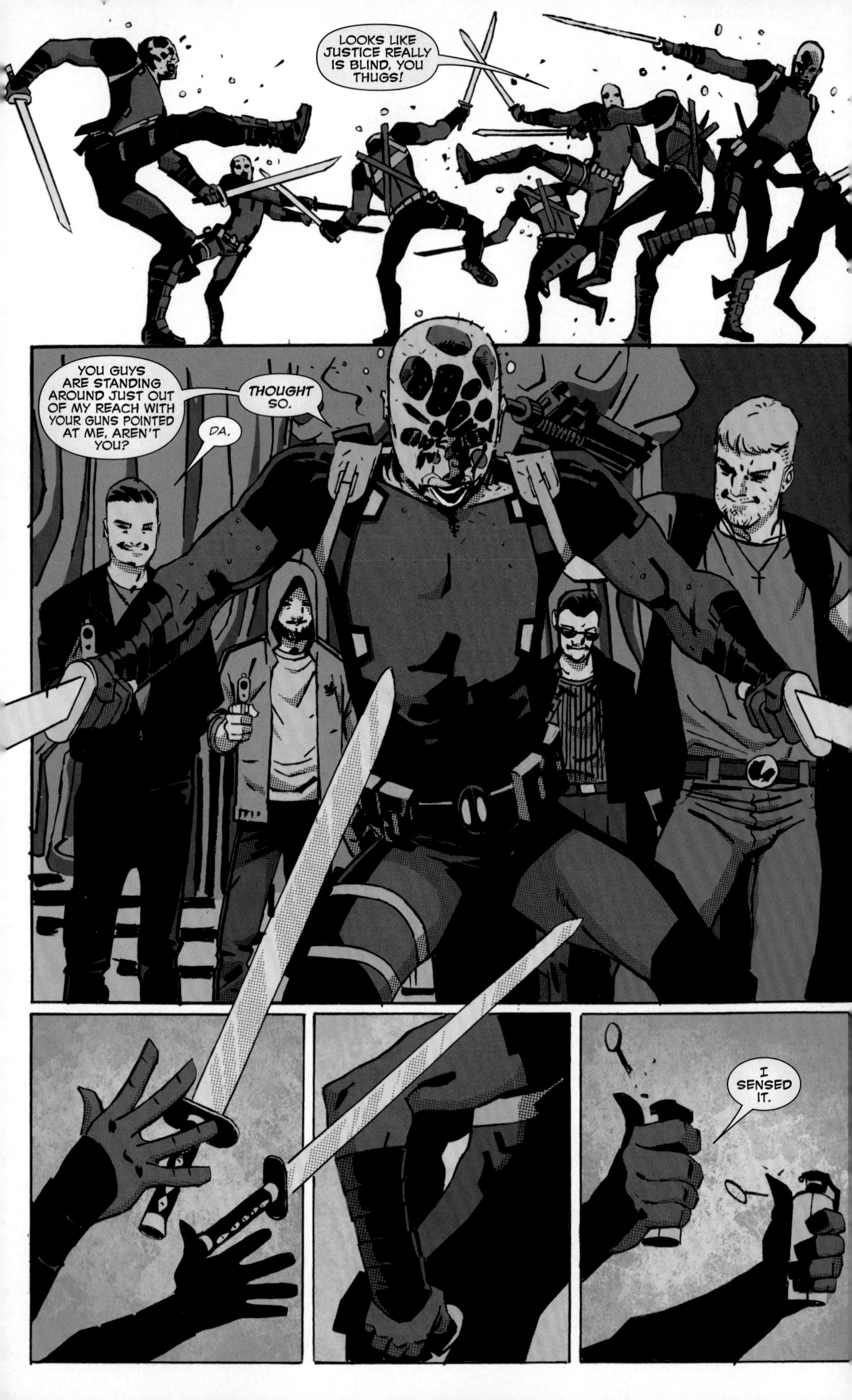
LOOKS LIKE JUSTICE REALLY IS BLIND, YOU THUGS!
YOU GUYS ARE STANDING AROUND JUST OUT OF MY REACH WITH YOUR GUNS POINTED AT ME, AREN'T YOU?
DA.
THOUGHT SO.
I SENSED IT.

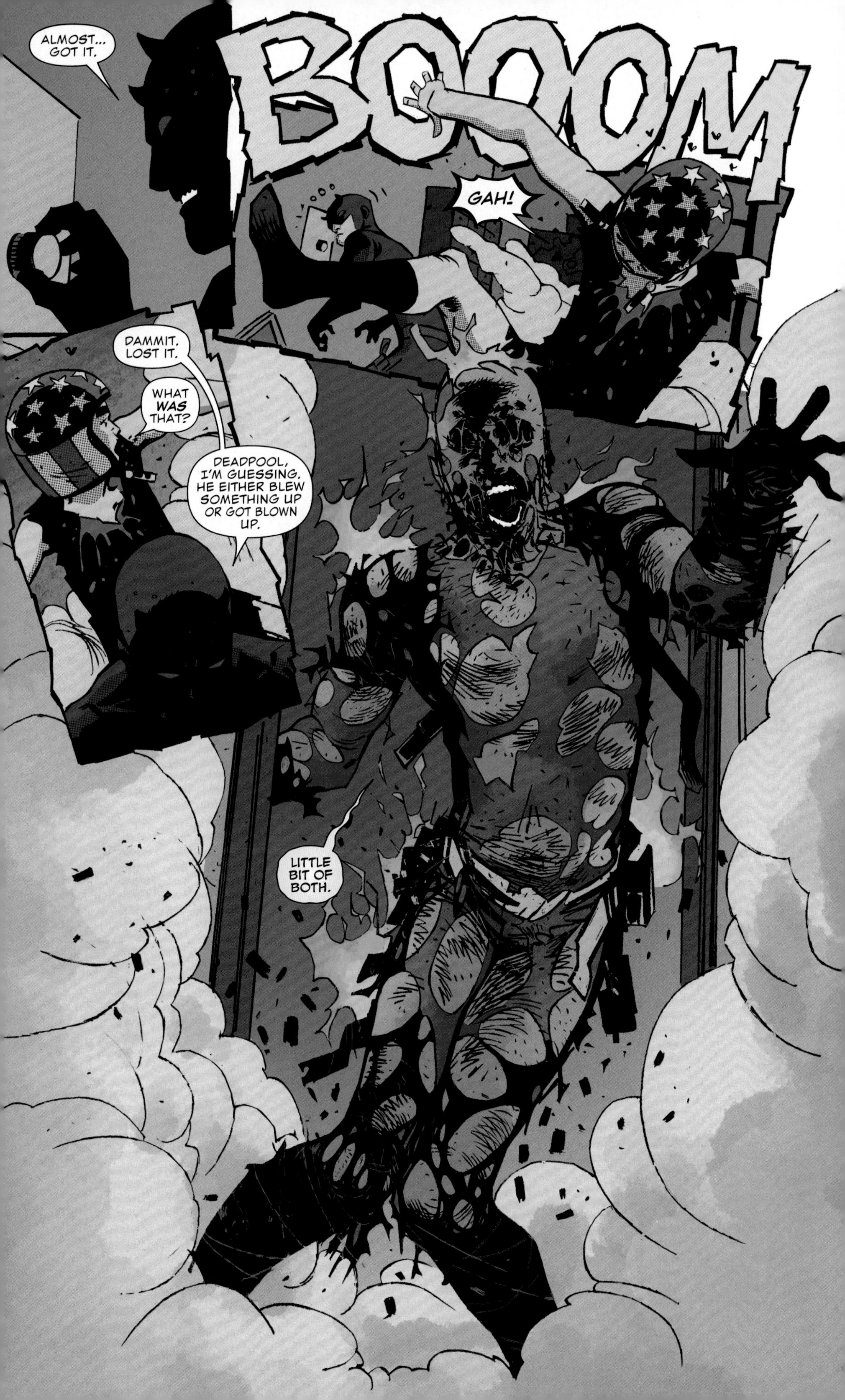
ALMOST... GOT IT.
BOOOM
GAH!
DAMMIT. LOST IT.
WHAT WAS THAT?
DEADPOOL, I'M GUESSING. HE EITHER BLEW SOMETHING UP OR GOT BLOWN UP.
LITTLE BIT OF BOTH.

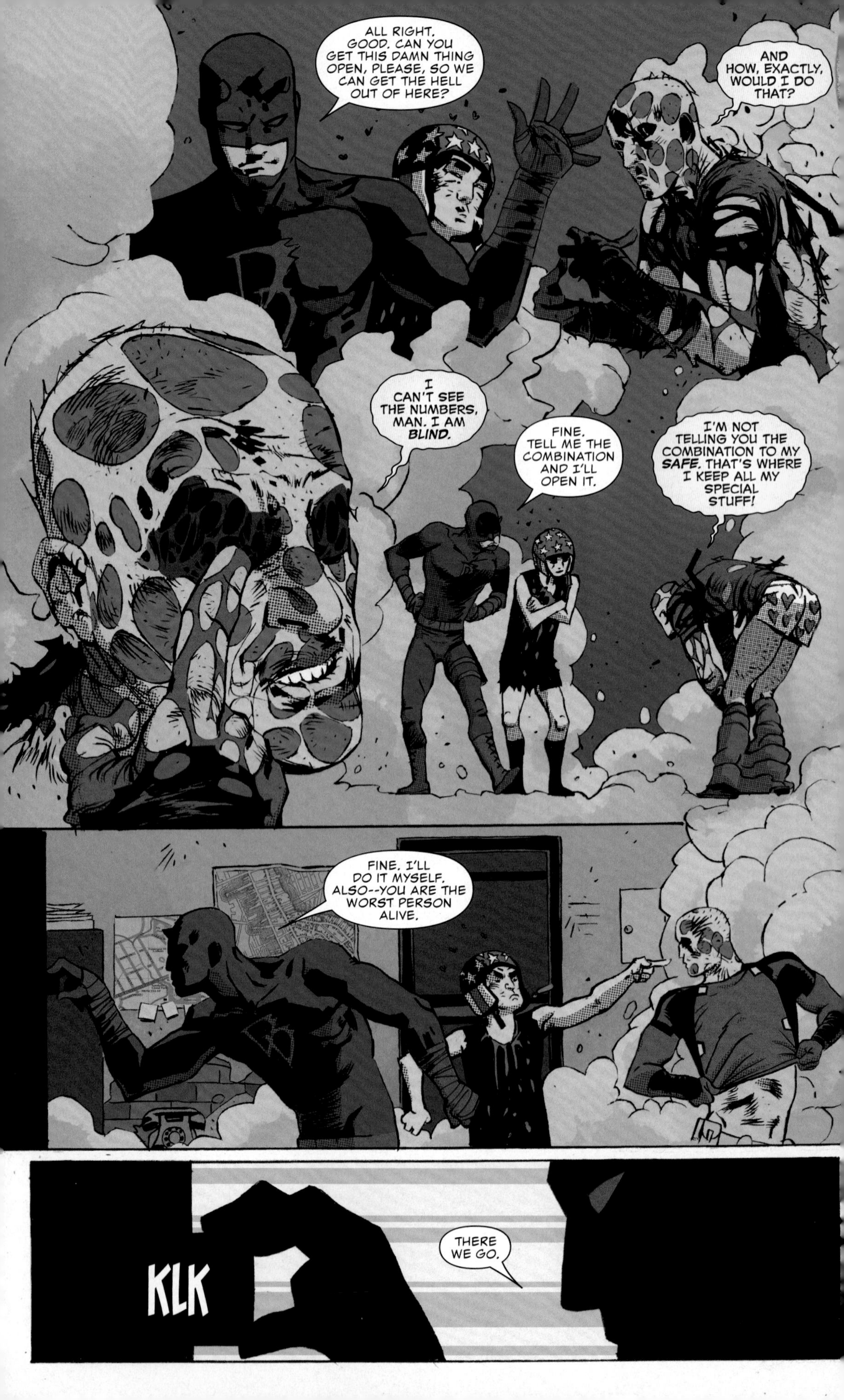
ALL RIGHT. GOOD. CAN YOU GET THIS DAMN THING OPEN, PLEASE, SO WE CAN GET THE HELL OUT OF HERE?
AND HOW, EXACTLY, WOULD I DO THAT?
I CAN'T SEE THE NUMBERS, MAN. I AM BLIND.
FINE. TELL ME THE COMBINATION AND I'LL OPEN IT.
I'M NOT TELLING YOU THE COMBINATION TO MY SAFE. THAT'S WHERE I KEEP ALL MY SPECIAL STUFF!
FINE. I'LL DO IT MYSELF. ALSO--YOU ARE THE WORST PERSON ALIVE.
KLK
THERE WE GO.

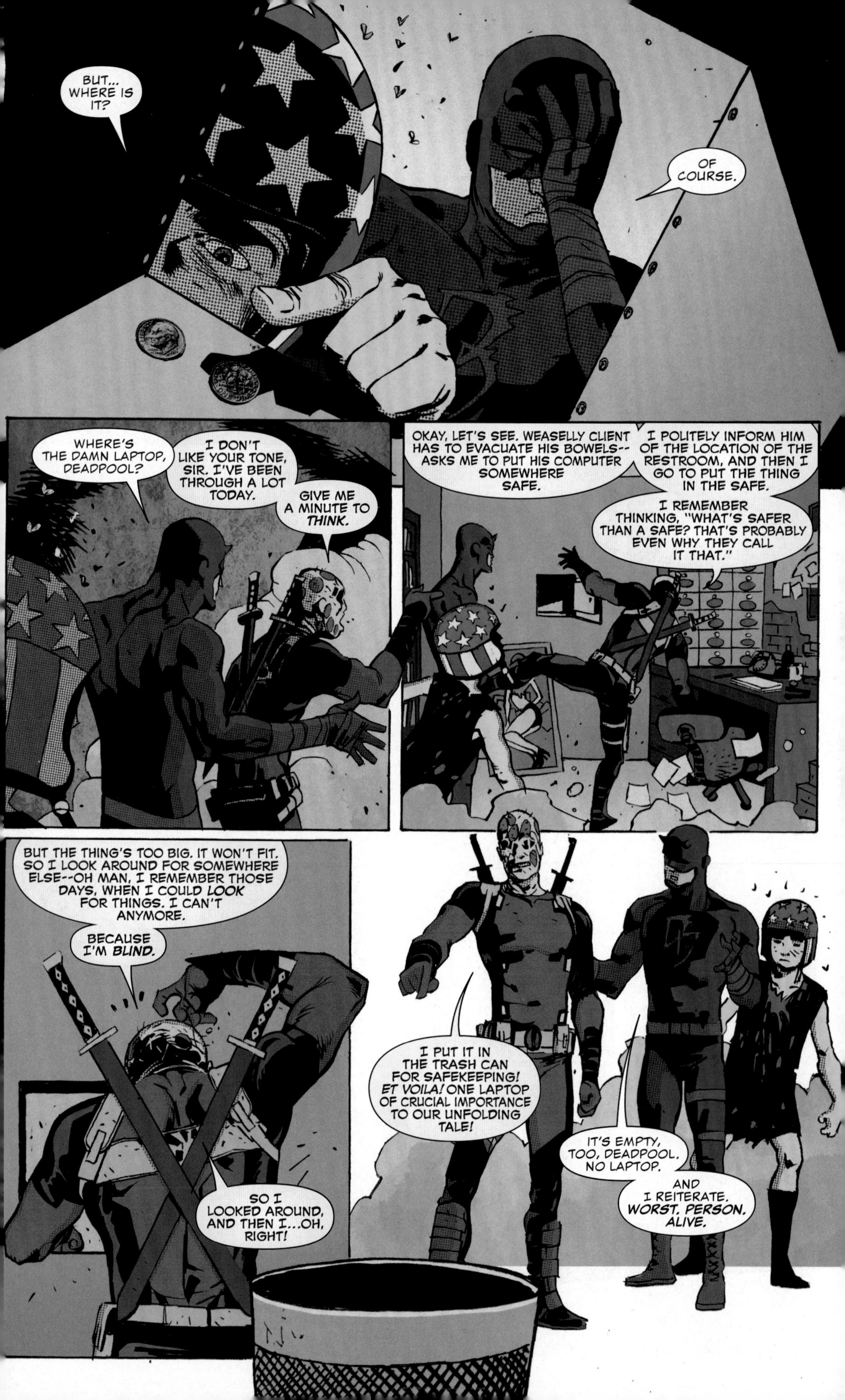
BUT... WHERE IS IT?
OF COURSE.
WHERE'S THE DAMN LAPTOP, DEADPOOL?
I DON'T LIKE YOUR TONE, SIR. I'VE BEEN THROUGH A LOT TODAY.
GIVE ME A MINUTE TO THINK.
OKAY, LET'S SEE. WEASELLY CLIENT HAS TO EVACUATE HIS BOWELS--ASKS ME TO PUT HIS COMPUTER SOMEWHERE SAFE.
I POLITELY INFORM HIM OF THE LOCATION OF THE RESTROOM, AND THEN I GO TO PUT THE THING IN THE SAFE.
I REMEMBER THINKING, "WHAT'S SAFER THAN A SAFE? THAT'S PROBABLY EVEN WHY THEY CALL IT THAT."
BUT THE THING'S TOO BIG. IT WON'T FIT. SO I LOOK AROUND FOR SOMEWHERE ELSE--OH MAN, I REMEMBER THOSE DAYS, WHEN I COULD LOOK FOR THINGS. I CAN'T ANYMORE.
BECAUSE I'M BLIND.
SO I LOOKED AROUND, AND THEN I...OH, RIGHT!
I PUT IT IN THE TRASH CAN FOR SAFEKEEPING! ET VOILA! ONE LAPTOP OF CRUCIAL IMPORTANCE TO OUR UNFOLDING TALE!
IT'S EMPTY, TOO, DEADPOOL. NO LAPTOP.
AND I REITERATE. WORST. PERSON. ALIVE.

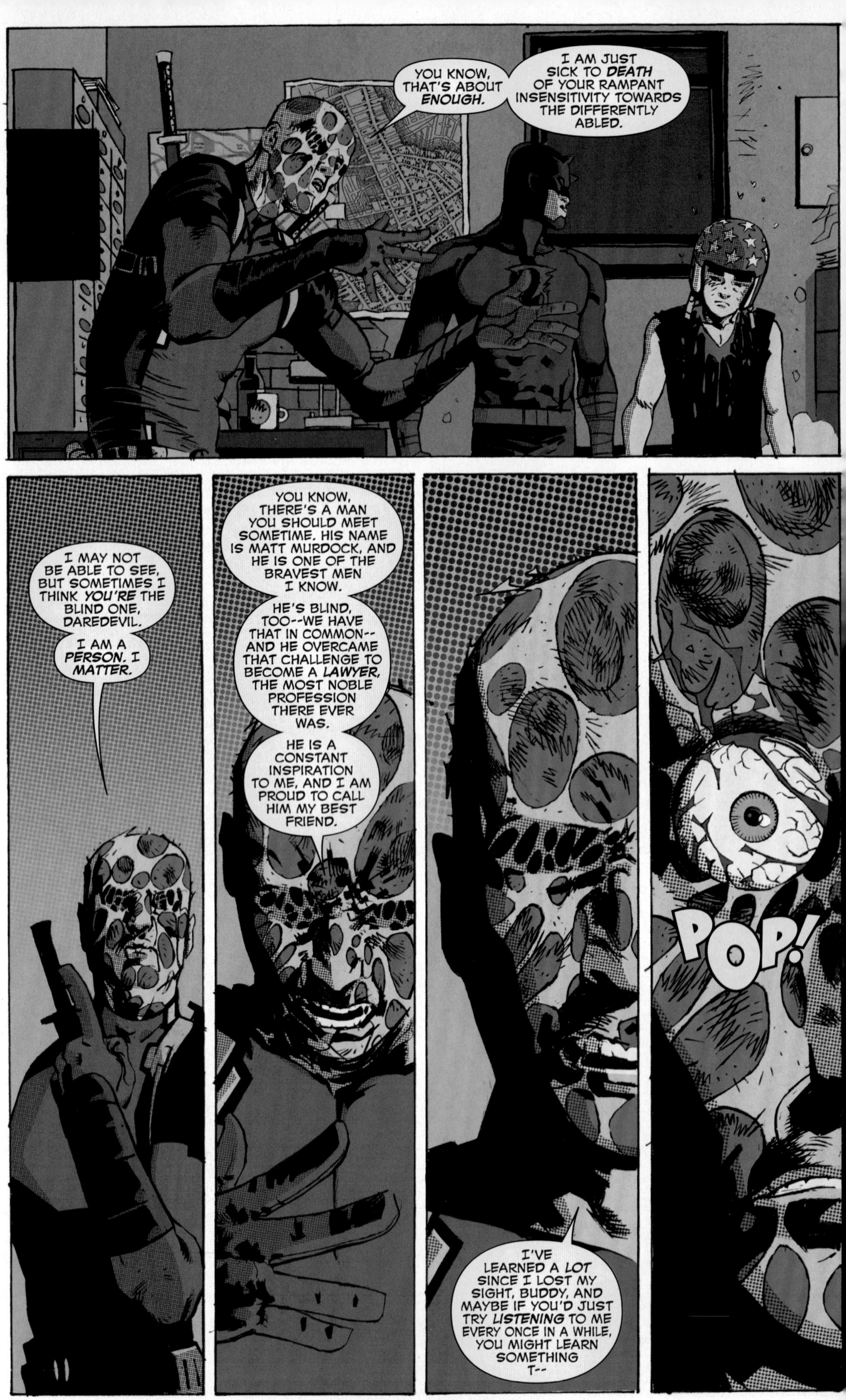
YOU KNOW, THAT'S ABOUT *ENOUGH.*
I AM JUST SICK TO *DEATH* OF YOUR RAMPANT INSENSITIVITY TOWARDS THE DIFFERENTLY ABLED.
I MAY NOT BE ABLE TO SEE, BUT SOMETIMES I THINK *YOU'RE* THE BLIND ONE, DAREDEVIL.
I AM A *PERSON.* I *MATTER.*
YOU KNOW, THERE'S A MAN YOU SHOULD MEET SOMETIME. HIS NAME IS MATT MURDOCK, AND HE IS ONE OF THE BRAVEST MEN I KNOW.
HE'S BLIND, TOO--WE HAVE THAT IN COMMON--AND HE OVERCAME THAT CHALLENGE TO BECOME A *LAWYER,* THE MOST NOBLE PROFESSION THERE EVER WAS.
HE IS A CONSTANT INSPIRATION TO ME, AND I AM PROUD TO CALL HIM MY BEST FRIEND.
I'VE LEARNED A *LOT* SINCE I LOST MY SIGHT, BUDDY, AND MAYBE IF YOU'D JUST TRY *LISTENING* TO ME EVERY ONCE IN A WHILE, YOU MIGHT LEARN SOMETHING T--
POP!

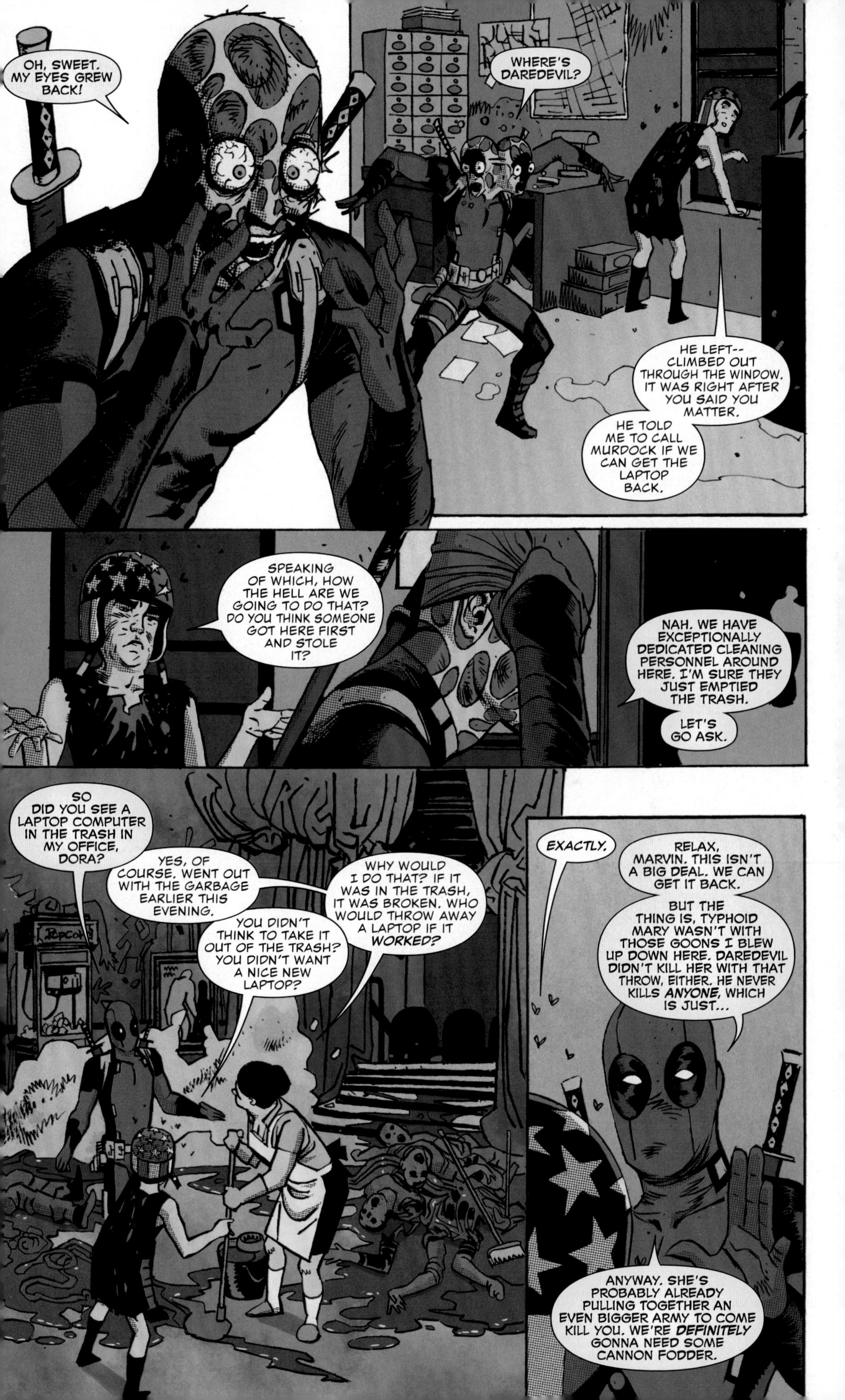
OH, SWEET. MY EYES GREW BACK!
WHERE'S DAREDEVIL?
HE LEFT-- CLIMBED OUT THROUGH THE WINDOW. IT WAS RIGHT AFTER YOU SAID YOU MATTER.
HE TOLD ME TO CALL MURDOCK IF WE CAN GET THE LAPTOP BACK.
SPEAKING OF WHICH, HOW THE HELL ARE WE GOING TO DO THAT? DO YOU THINK SOMEONE GOT HERE FIRST AND STOLE IT?
NAH. WE HAVE EXCEPTIONALLY DEDICATED CLEANING PERSONNEL AROUND HERE. I'M SURE THEY JUST EMPTIED THE TRASH.
LET'S GO ASK.
SO DID YOU SEE A LAPTOP COMPUTER IN THE TRASH IN MY OFFICE, DORA?
YES, OF COURSE. WENT OUT WITH THE GARBAGE EARLIER THIS EVENING.
YOU DIDN'T THINK TO TAKE IT OUT OF THE TRASH? YOU DIDN'T WANT A NICE NEW LAPTOP?
WHY WOULD I DO THAT? IF IT WAS IN THE TRASH, IT WAS BROKEN. WHO WOULD THROW AWAY A LAPTOP IF IT *WORKED?*
EXACTLY.
RELAX, MARVIN. THIS ISN'T A BIG DEAL. WE CAN GET IT BACK.
BUT THE THING IS, TYPHOID MARY WASN'T WITH THOSE GOONS I BLEW UP DOWN HERE. DAREDEVIL DIDN'T KILL HER WITH THAT THROW, EITHER. HE NEVER KILLS *ANYONE*, WHICH IS JUST...
ANYWAY. SHE'S PROBABLY ALREADY PULLING TOGETHER AN EVEN BIGGER ARMY TO COME KILL YOU. WE'RE *DEFINITELY* GONNA NEED SOME CANNON FODDER.

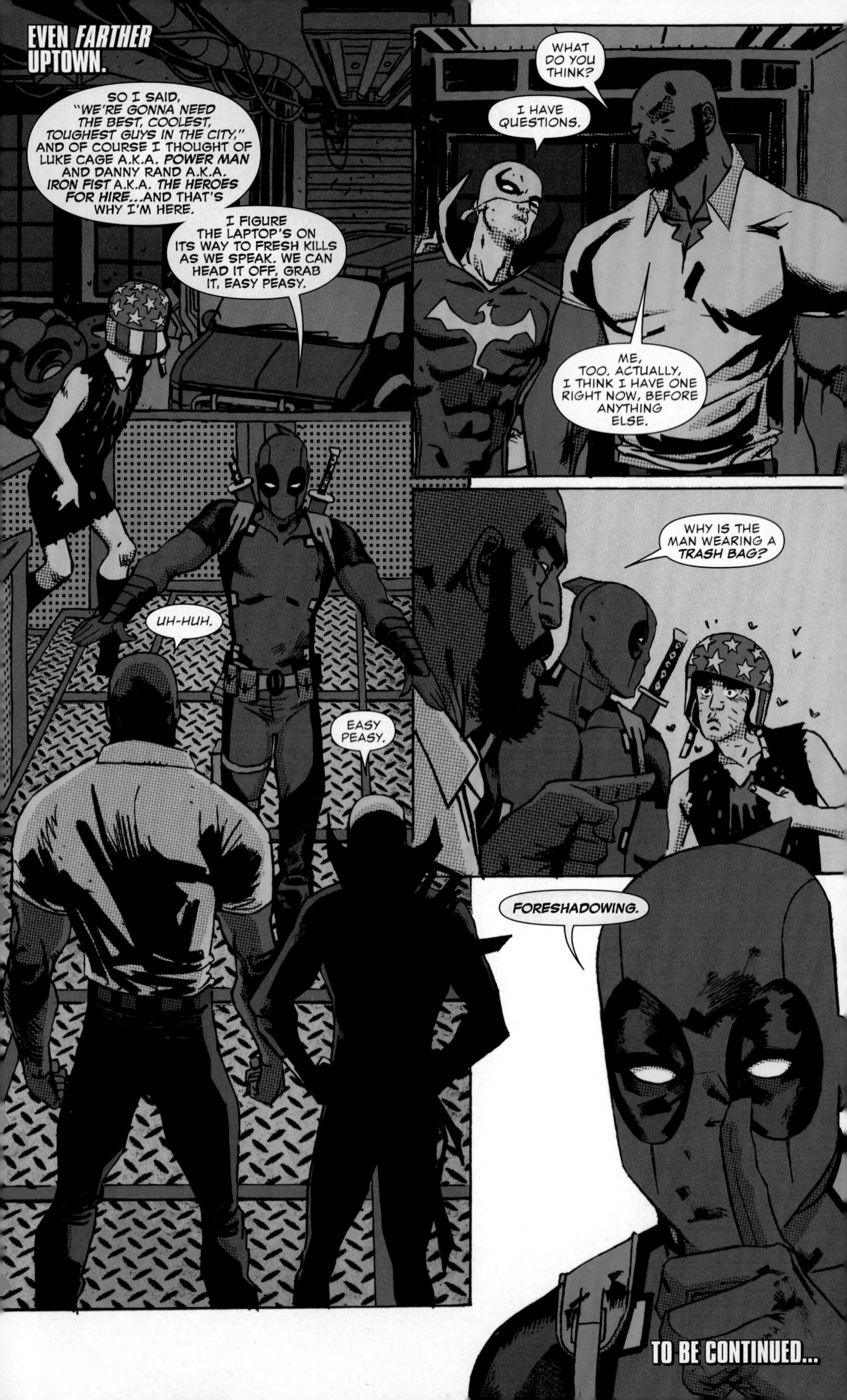
EVEN FARTHER UPTOWN.
SO I SAID, "WE'RE GONNA NEED THE BEST, COOLEST, TOUGHEST GUYS IN THE CITY," AND OF COURSE I THOUGHT OF LUKE CAGE A.K.A. POWER MAN AND DANNY RAND A.K.A. IRON FIST A.K.A. THE HEROES FOR HIRE...AND THAT'S WHY I'M HERE.
I FIGURE THE LAPTOP'S ON ITS WAY TO FRESH KILLS AS WE SPEAK. WE CAN HEAD IT OFF, GRAB IT, EASY PEASY.
UH-HUH.
EASY PEASY.
WHAT DO YOU THINK?
I HAVE QUESTIONS.
ME, TOO. ACTUALLY, I THINK I HAVE ONE RIGHT NOW, BEFORE ANYTHING ELSE.
WHY IS THE MAN WEARING A TRASH BAG?
FORESHADOWING.
TO BE CONTINUED...

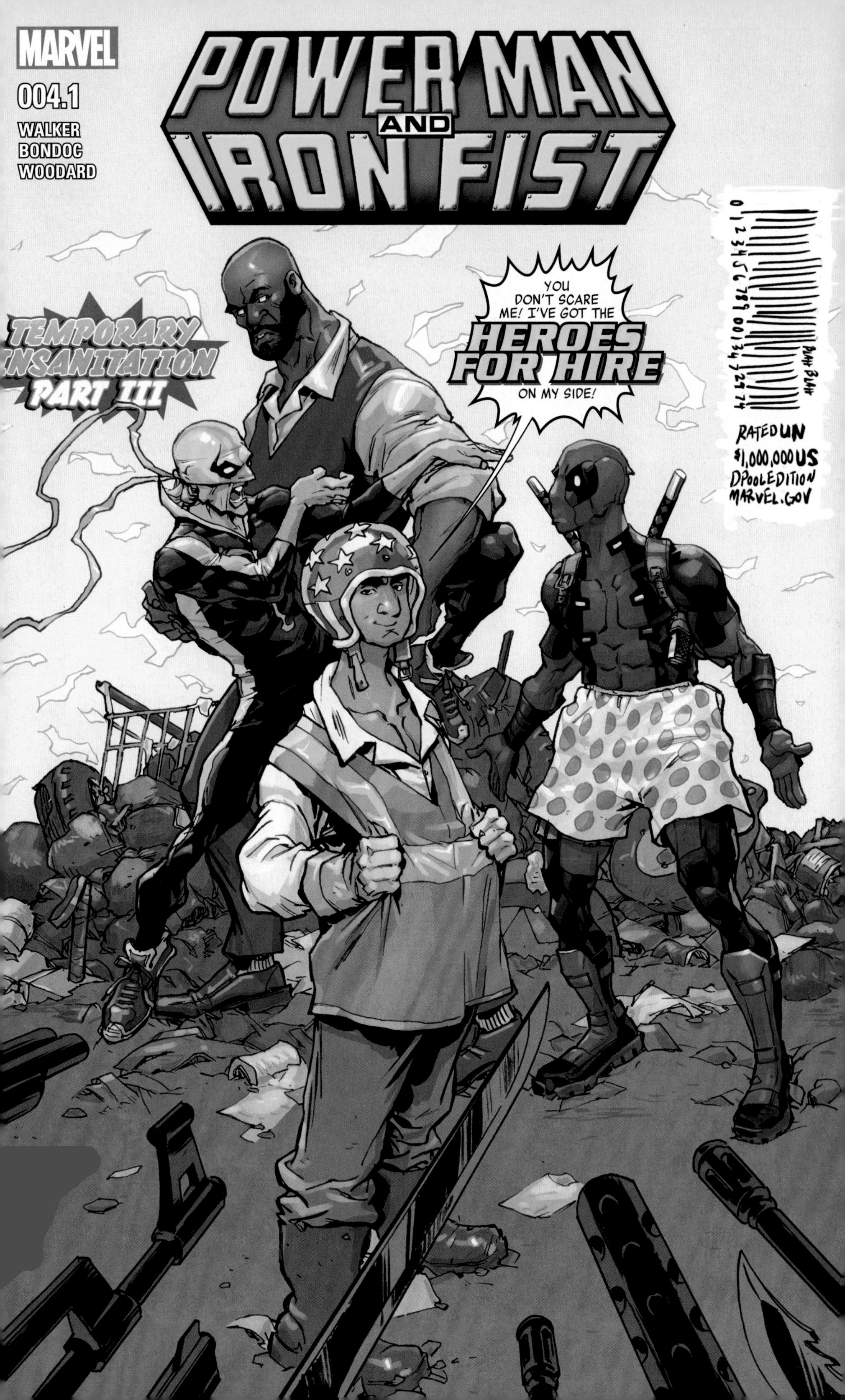
MARVEL
004.1
WALKER
BONDOC
WOODARD
POWER MAN AND IRON FIST
TEMPORARY INSANITATION PART III
YOU DON'T SCARE ME! I'VE GOT THE HEROES FOR HIRE ON MY SIDE!
RATED UN
$1,000,000 US
DPOOL EDITION
MARVEL.GOV

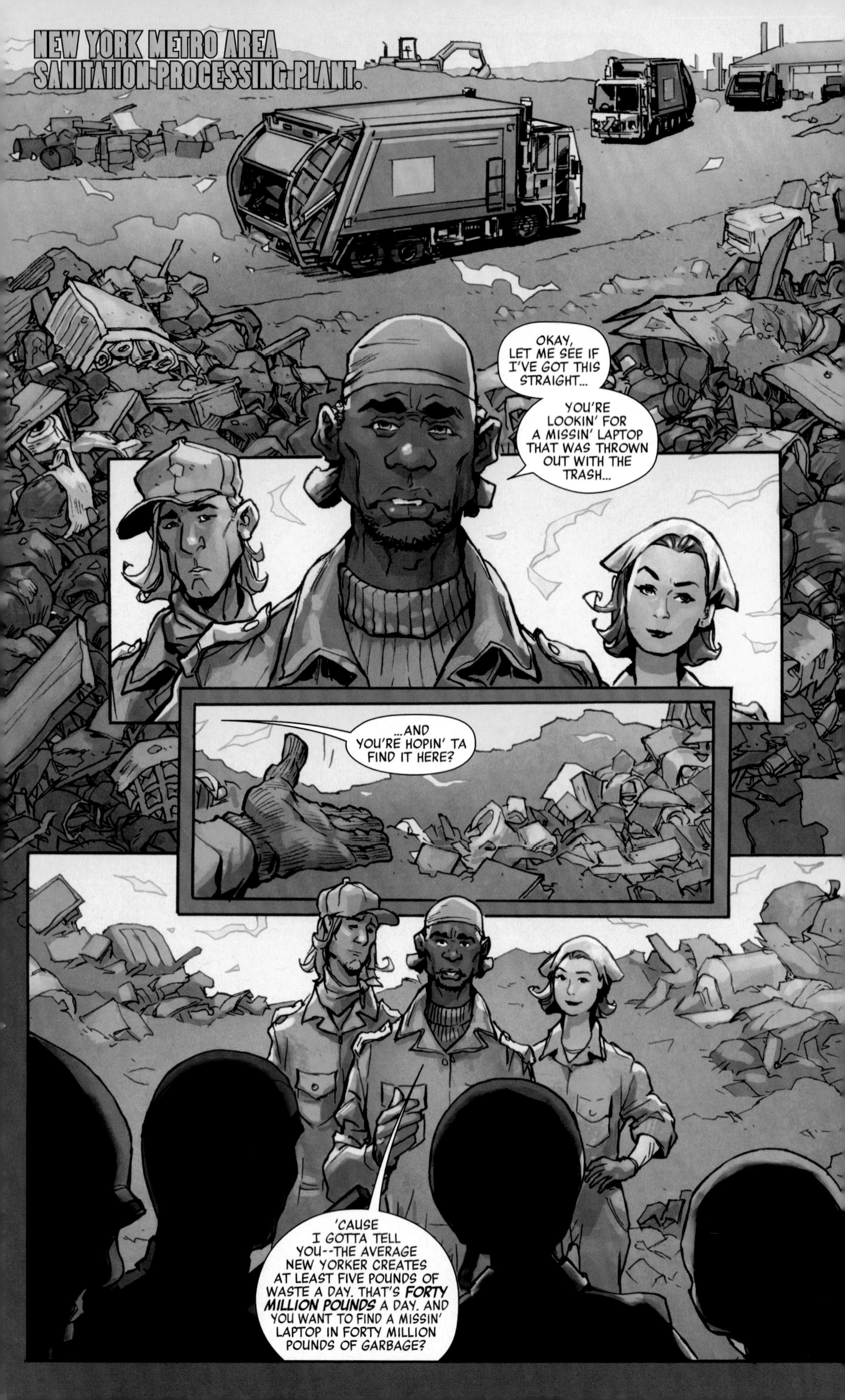
NEW YORK METRO AREA
SANITATION PROCESSING PLANT.
OKAY, LET ME SEE IF I'VE GOT THIS STRAIGHT...
YOU'RE LOOKIN' FOR A MISSIN' LAPTOP THAT WAS THROWN OUT WITH THE TRASH...
...AND YOU'RE HOPIN' TA FIND IT HERE?
'CAUSE I GOTTA TELL YOU--THE AVERAGE NEW YORKER CREATES AT LEAST FIVE POUNDS OF WASTE A DAY. THAT'S ***FORTY MILLION POUNDS*** A DAY. AND YOU WANT TO FIND A MISSIN' LAPTOP IN FORTY MILLION POUNDS OF GARBAGE?

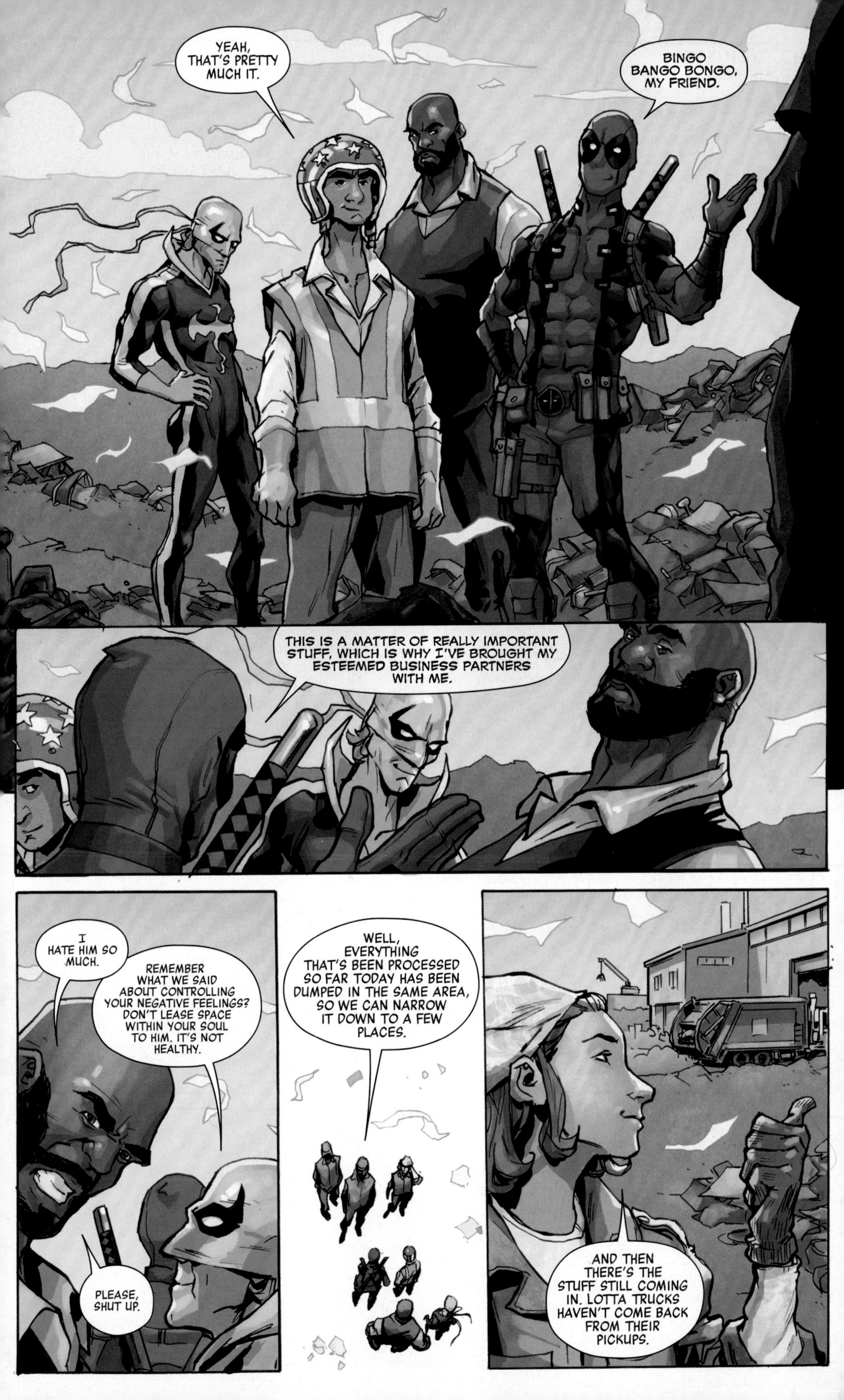
YEAH, THAT'S PRETTY MUCH IT.
BINGO BANGO BONGO, MY FRIEND.
THIS IS A MATTER OF REALLY IMPORTANT STUFF, WHICH IS WHY I'VE BROUGHT MY ESTEEMED BUSINESS PARTNERS WITH ME.
I HATE HIM SO MUCH.
REMEMBER WHAT WE SAID ABOUT CONTROLLING YOUR NEGATIVE FEELINGS? DON'T LEASE SPACE WITHIN YOUR SOUL TO HIM. IT'S NOT HEALTHY.
PLEASE, SHUT UP.
WELL, EVERYTHING THAT'S BEEN PROCESSED SO FAR TODAY HAS BEEN DUMPED IN THE SAME AREA, SO WE CAN NARROW IT DOWN TO A FEW PLACES.
AND THEN THERE'S THE STUFF STILL COMING IN. LOTTA TRUCKS HAVEN'T COME BACK FROM THEIR PICKUPS.

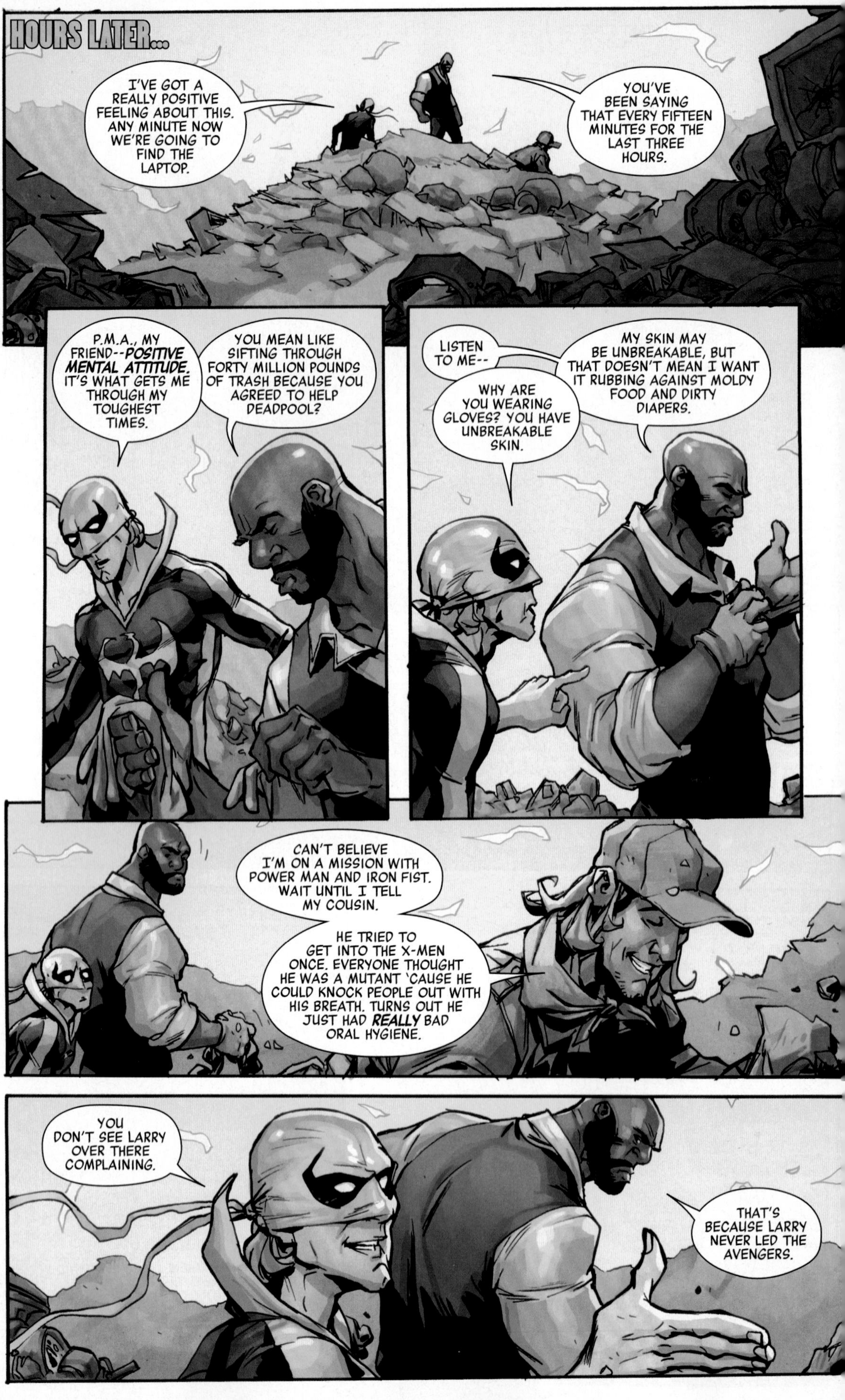
HOURS LATER...
I'VE GOT A REALLY POSITIVE FEELING ABOUT THIS. ANY MINUTE NOW WE'RE GOING TO FIND THE LAPTOP.
YOU'VE BEEN SAYING THAT EVERY FIFTEEN MINUTES FOR THE LAST THREE HOURS.
P.M.A., MY FRIEND--POSITIVE MENTAL ATTITUDE. IT'S WHAT GETS ME THROUGH MY TOUGHEST TIMES.
YOU MEAN LIKE SIFTING THROUGH FORTY MILLION POUNDS OF TRASH BECAUSE YOU AGREED TO HELP DEADPOOL?
LISTEN TO ME--
WHY ARE YOU WEARING GLOVES? YOU HAVE UNBREAKABLE SKIN.
MY SKIN MAY BE UNBREAKABLE, BUT THAT DOESN'T MEAN I WANT IT RUBBING AGAINST MOLDY FOOD AND DIRTY DIAPERS.
CAN'T BELIEVE I'M ON A MISSION WITH POWER MAN AND IRON FIST. WAIT UNTIL I TELL MY COUSIN.
HE TRIED TO GET INTO THE X-MEN ONCE. EVERYONE THOUGHT HE WAS A MUTANT 'CAUSE HE COULD KNOCK PEOPLE OUT WITH HIS BREATH. TURNS OUT HE JUST HAD REALLY BAD ORAL HYGIENE.
YOU DON'T SEE LARRY OVER THERE COMPLAINING.
THAT'S BECAUSE LARRY NEVER LED THE AVENGERS.

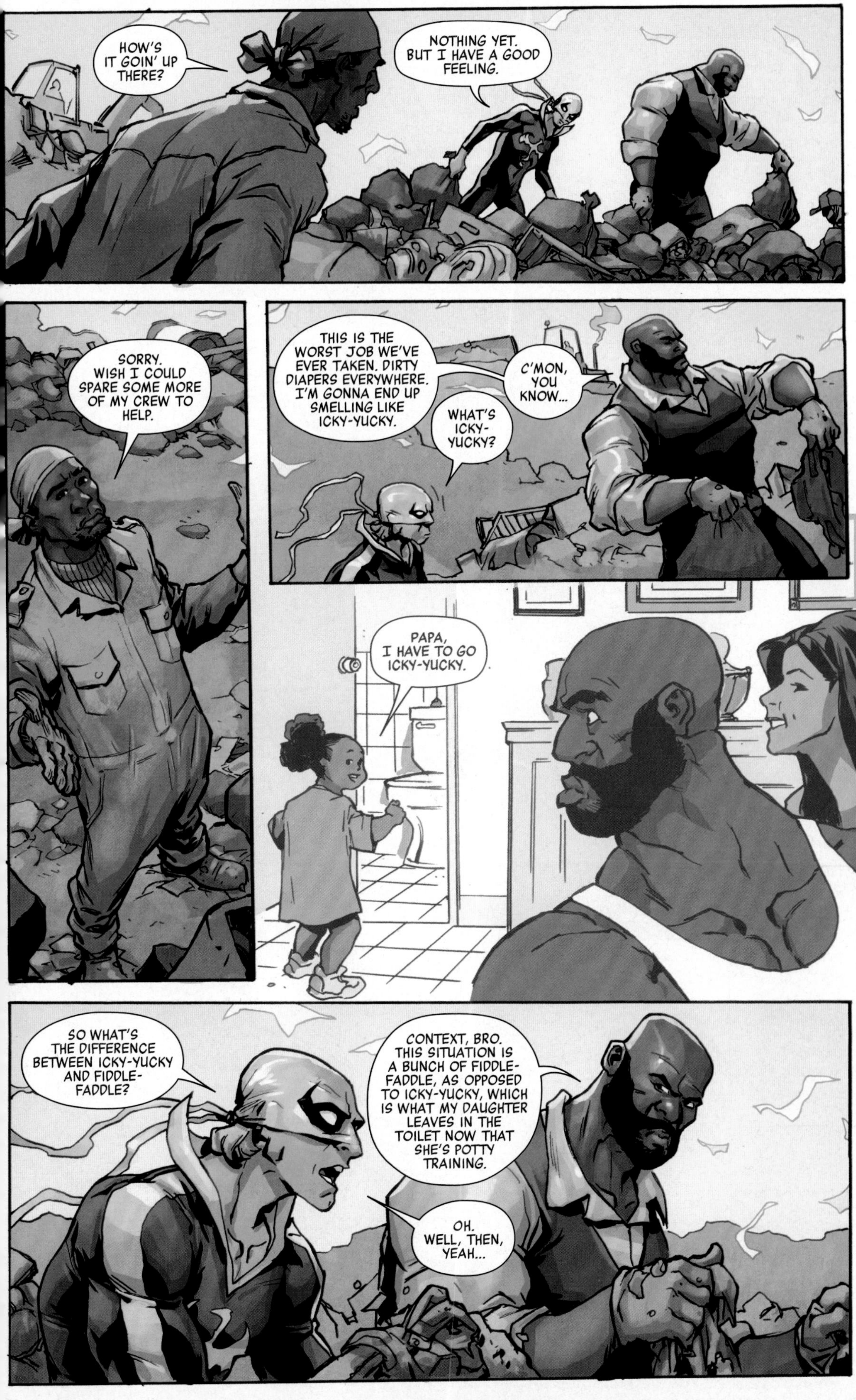

HOW'S IT GOIN' UP THERE?
NOTHING YET. BUT I HAVE A GOOD FEELING.
SORRY. WISH I COULD SPARE SOME MORE OF MY CREW TO HELP.
THIS IS THE WORST JOB WE'VE EVER TAKEN. DIRTY DIAPERS EVERYWHERE. I'M GONNA END UP SMELLING LIKE ICKY-YUCKY.
WHAT'S ICKY-YUCKY?
C'MON, YOU KNOW...
PAPA, I HAVE TO GO ICKY-YUCKY.
SO WHAT'S THE DIFFERENCE BETWEEN ICKY-YUCKY AND FIDDLE-FADDLE?
CONTEXT, BRO. THIS SITUATION IS A BUNCH OF FIDDLE-FADDLE, AS OPPOSED TO ICKY-YUCKY, WHICH IS WHAT MY DAUGHTER LEAVES IN THE TOILET NOW THAT SHE'S POTTY TRAINING.
OH. WELL, THEN, YEAH...

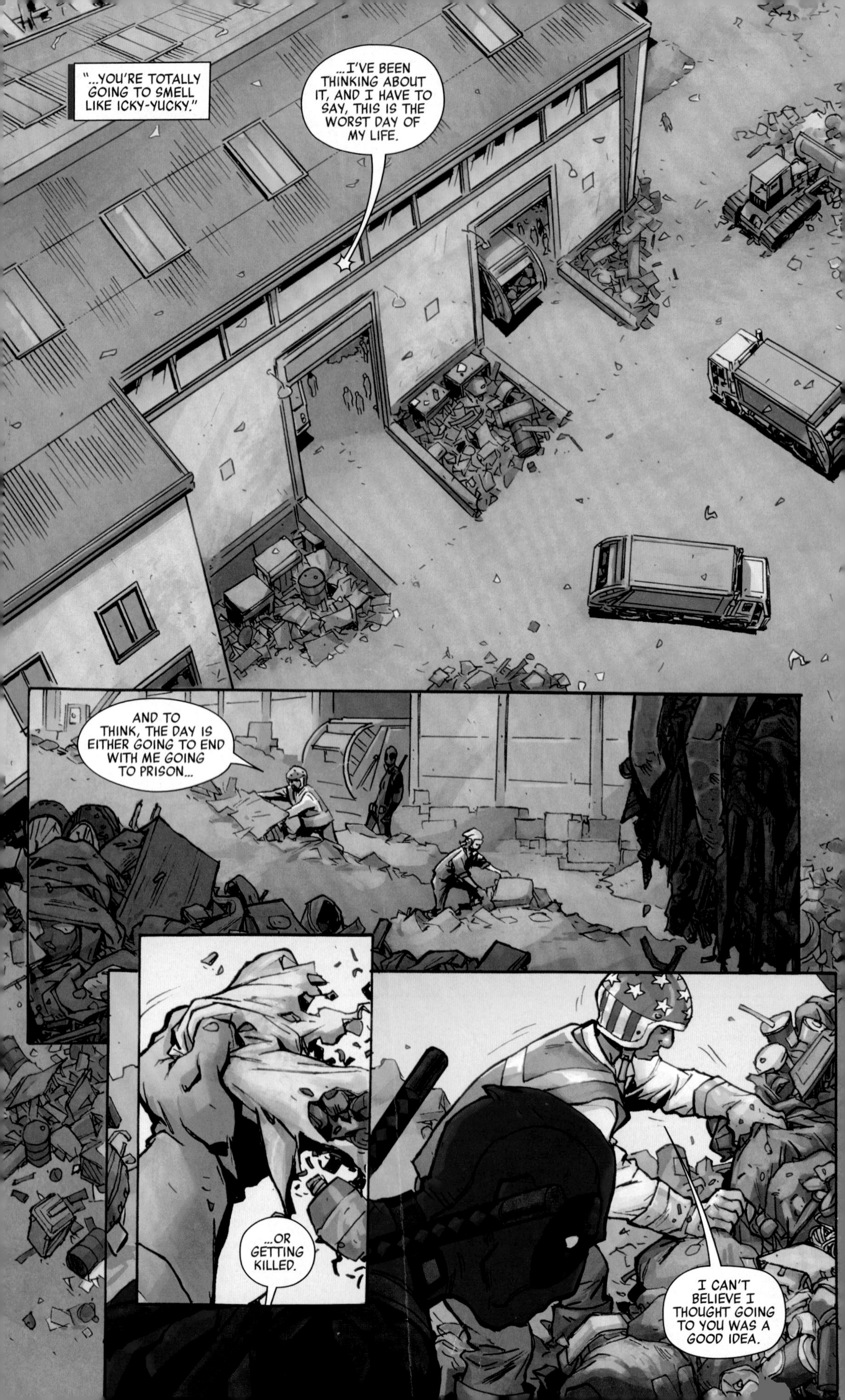
"...YOU'RE TOTALLY GOING TO SMELL LIKE ICKY-YUCKY."
...I'VE BEEN THINKING ABOUT IT, AND I HAVE TO SAY, THIS IS THE WORST DAY OF MY LIFE.
AND TO THINK, THE DAY IS EITHER GOING TO END WITH ME GOING TO PRISON...
...OR GETTING KILLED.
I CAN'T BELIEVE I THOUGHT GOING TO YOU WAS A GOOD IDEA.

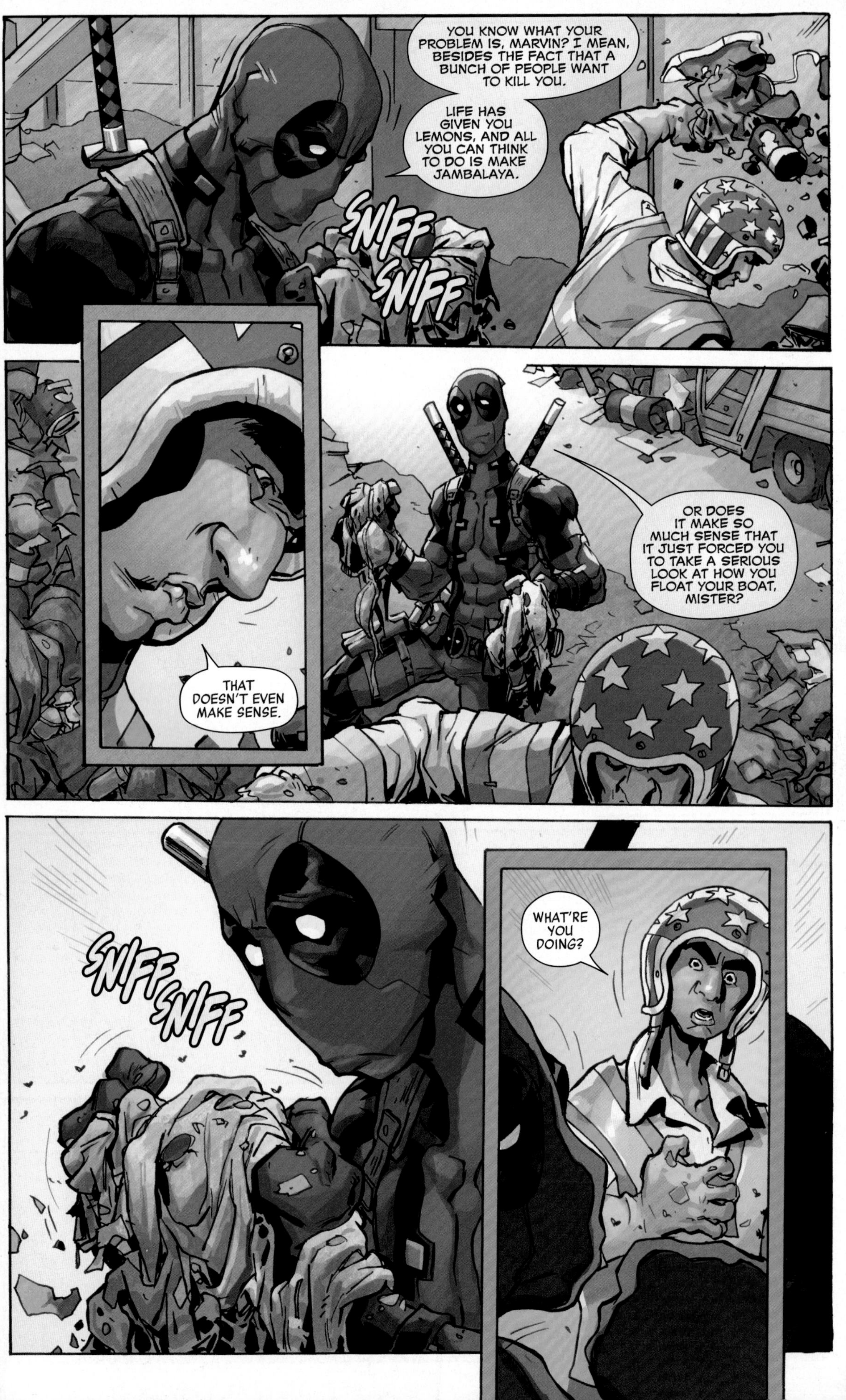
YOU KNOW WHAT YOUR PROBLEM IS, MARVIN? I MEAN, BESIDES THE FACT THAT A BUNCH OF PEOPLE WANT TO KILL YOU.
LIFE HAS GIVEN YOU LEMONS, AND ALL YOU CAN THINK TO DO IS MAKE JAMBALAYA.
SNIFF SNIFF
THAT DOESN'T EVEN MAKE SENSE.
OR DOES IT MAKE SO MUCH SENSE THAT IT JUST FORCED YOU TO TAKE A SERIOUS LOOK AT HOW YOU FLOAT YOUR BOAT, MISTER?
SNIFF SNIFF
WHAT'RE YOU DOING?

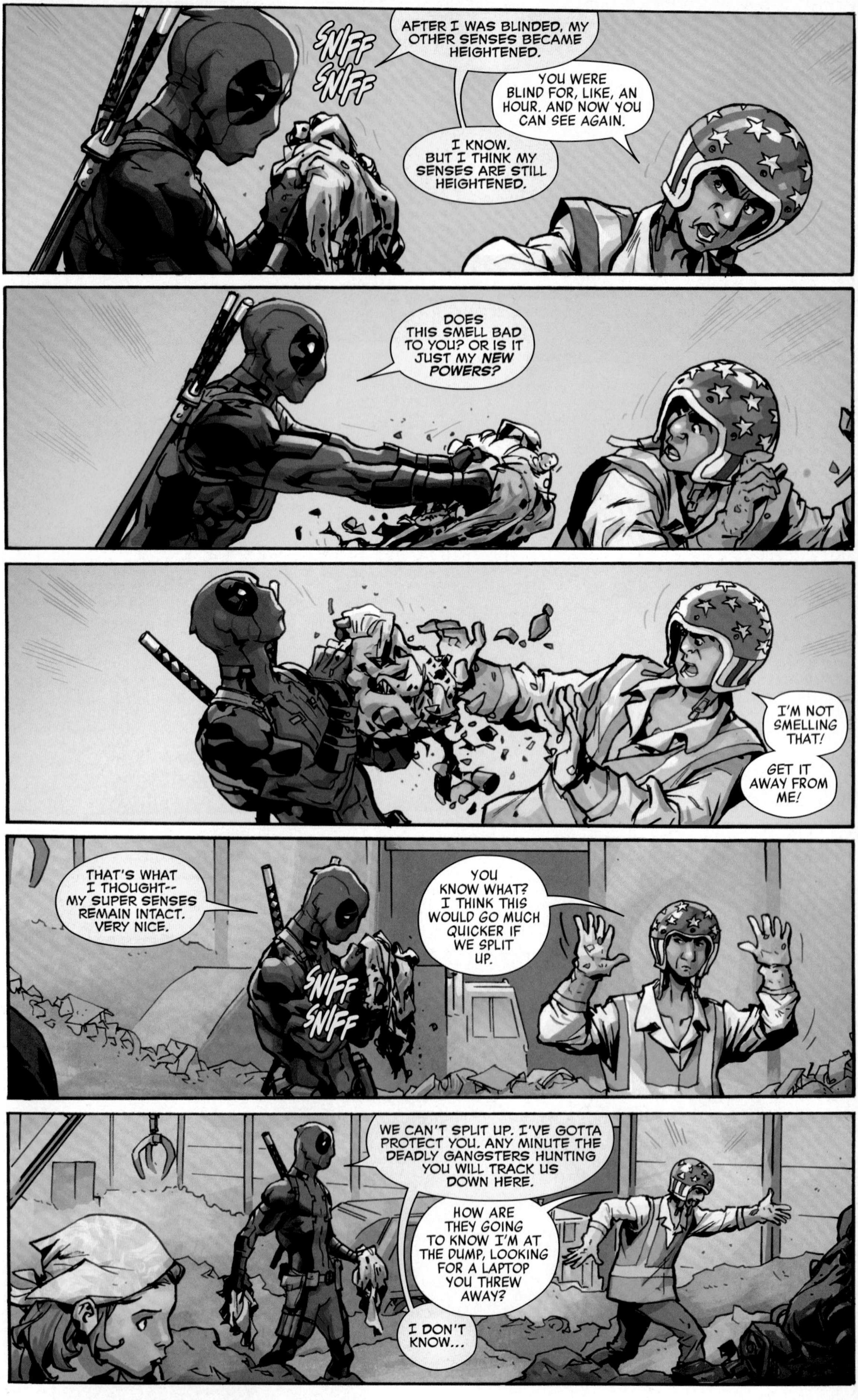
SNIFF SNIFF
AFTER I WAS BLINDED, MY OTHER SENSES BECAME HEIGHTENED.
YOU WERE BLIND FOR, LIKE, AN HOUR. AND NOW YOU CAN SEE AGAIN.
I KNOW. BUT I THINK MY SENSES ARE STILL HEIGHTENED.
DOES THIS SMELL BAD TO YOU? OR IS IT JUST MY NEW POWERS?
I'M NOT SMELLING THAT!
GET IT AWAY FROM ME!
THAT'S WHAT I THOUGHT-- MY SUPER SENSES REMAIN INTACT. VERY NICE.
SNIFF SNIFF
YOU KNOW WHAT? I THINK THIS WOULD GO MUCH QUICKER IF WE SPLIT UP.
WE CAN'T SPLIT UP. I'VE GOTTA PROTECT YOU. ANY MINUTE THE DEADLY GANGSTERS HUNTING YOU WILL TRACK US DOWN HERE.
HOW ARE THEY GOING TO KNOW I'M AT THE DUMP, LOOKING FOR A LAPTOP YOU THREW AWAY?
I DON'T KNOW...

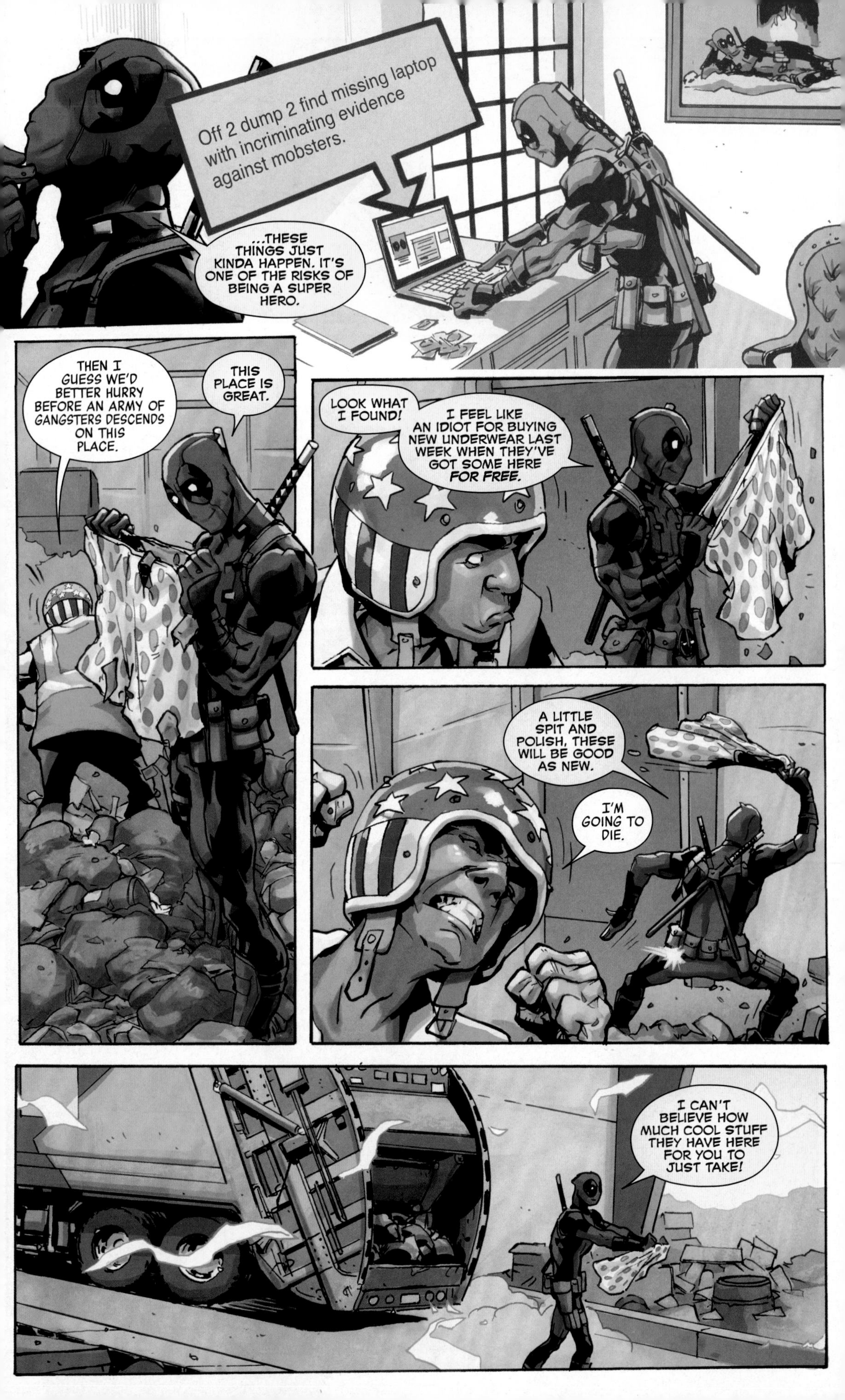
Off 2 dump 2 find missing laptop with incriminating evidence against mobsters.
...THESE THINGS JUST KINDA HAPPEN. IT'S ONE OF THE RISKS OF BEING A SUPER HERO.
THEN I GUESS WE'D BETTER HURRY BEFORE AN ARMY OF GANGSTERS DESCENDS ON THIS PLACE.
THIS PLACE IS GREAT.
LOOK WHAT I FOUND!
I FEEL LIKE AN IDIOT FOR BUYING NEW UNDERWEAR LAST WEEK WHEN THEY'VE GOT SOME HERE FOR FREE.
A LITTLE SPIT AND POLISH, THESE WILL BE GOOD AS NEW.
I'M GOING TO DIE.
I CAN'T BELIEVE HOW MUCH COOL STUFF THEY HAVE HERE FOR YOU TO JUST TAKE!

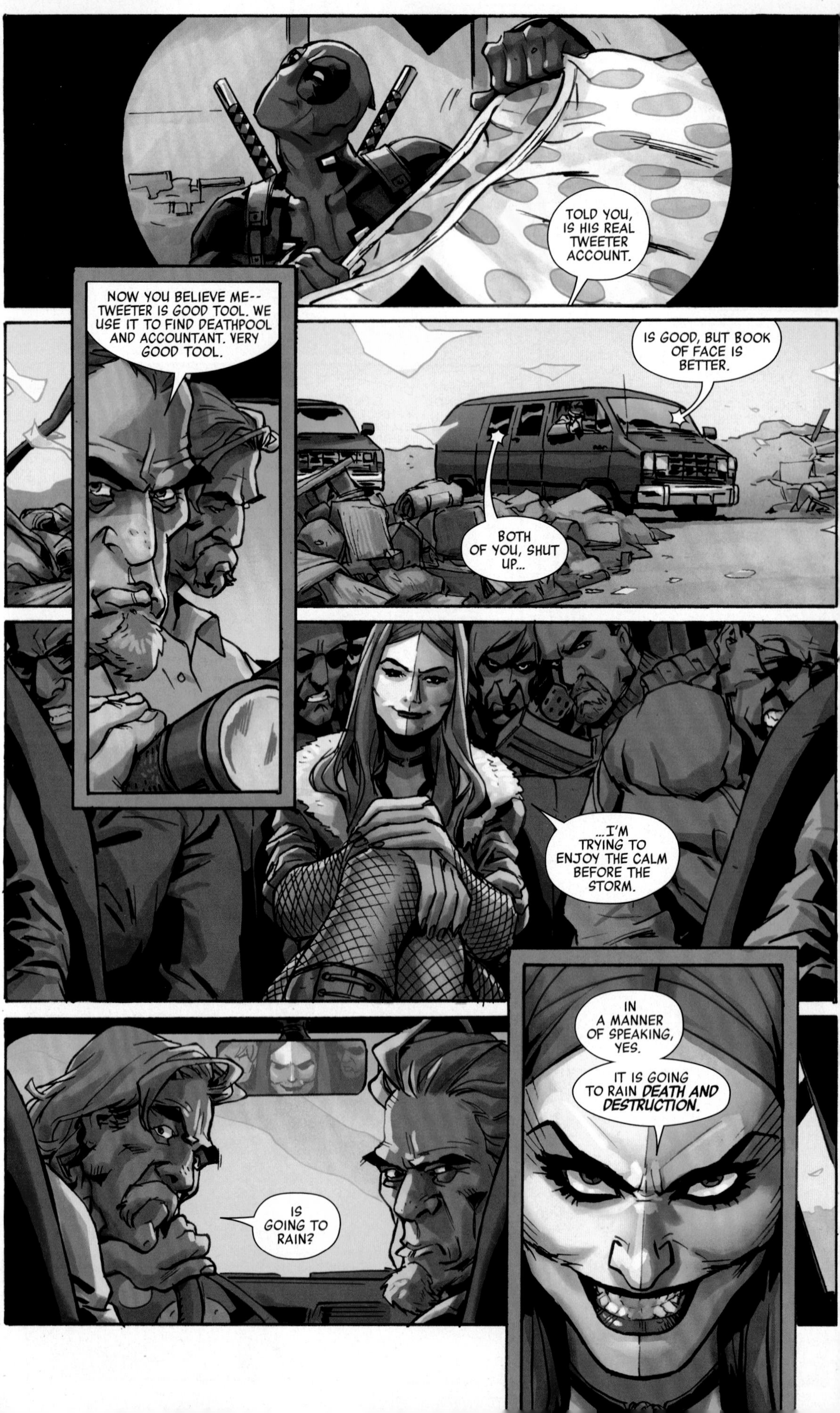

TOLD YOU, IS HIS REAL TWEETER ACCOUNT.
NOW YOU BELIEVE ME-- TWEETER IS GOOD TOOL. WE USE IT TO FIND DEATHPOOL AND ACCOUNTANT. VERY GOOD TOOL.
IS GOOD, BUT BOOK OF FACE IS BETTER.
BOTH OF YOU, SHUT UP...
...I'M TRYING TO ENJOY THE CALM BEFORE THE STORM.
IS GOING TO RAIN?
IN A MANNER OF SPEAKING, YES.
IT IS GOING TO RAIN DEATH AND DESTRUCTION.

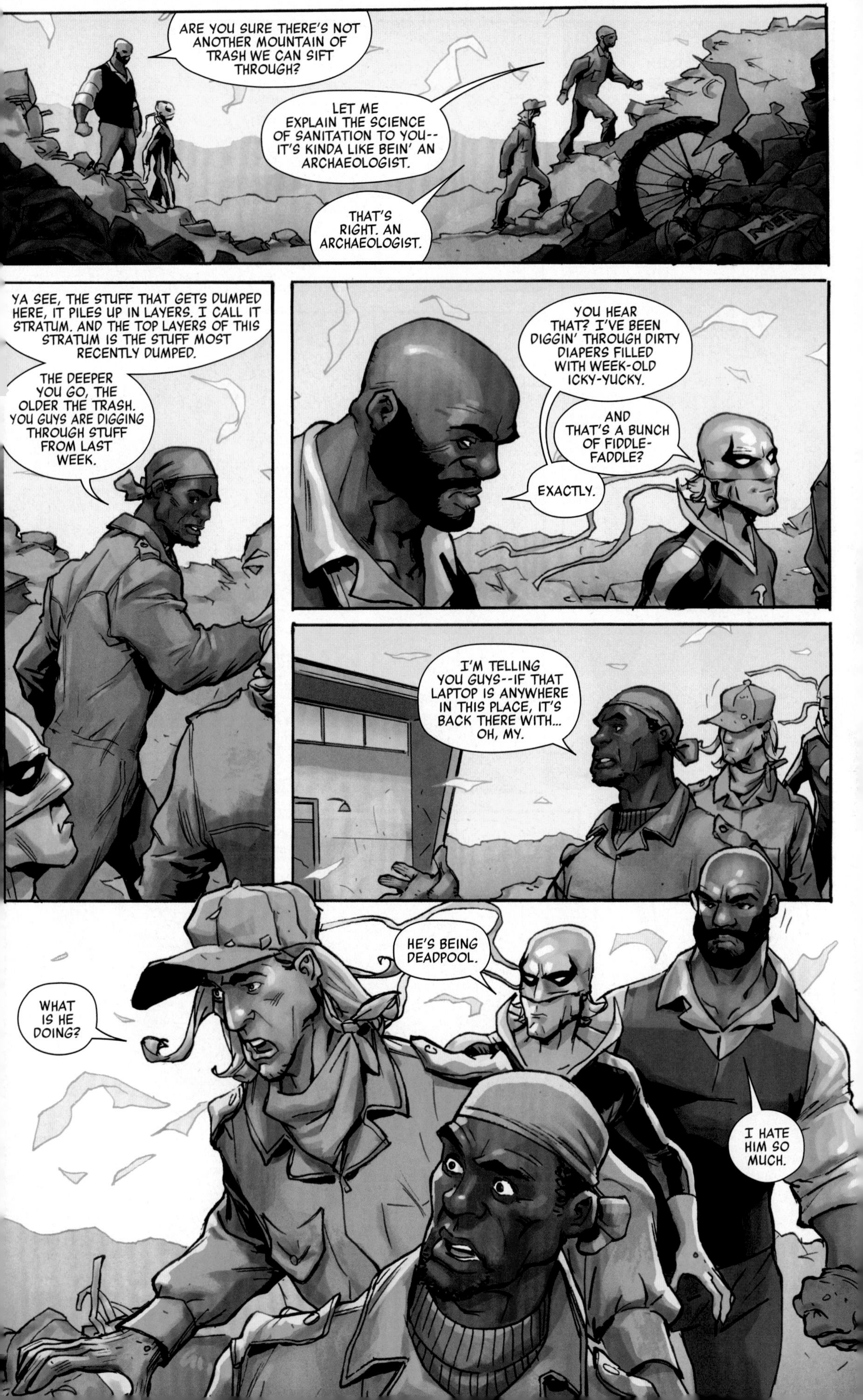
ARE YOU SURE THERE'S NOT ANOTHER MOUNTAIN OF TRASH WE CAN SIFT THROUGH?
LET ME EXPLAIN THE SCIENCE OF SANITATION TO YOU-- IT'S KINDA LIKE BEIN' AN ARCHAEOLOGIST.
THAT'S RIGHT. AN ARCHAEOLOGIST.
YA SEE, THE STUFF THAT GETS DUMPED HERE, IT PILES UP IN LAYERS. I CALL IT STRATUM. AND THE TOP LAYERS OF THIS STRATUM IS THE STUFF MOST RECENTLY DUMPED.
THE DEEPER YOU GO, THE OLDER THE TRASH. YOU GUYS ARE DIGGING THROUGH STUFF FROM LAST WEEK.
YOU HEAR THAT? I'VE BEEN DIGGIN' THROUGH DIRTY DIAPERS FILLED WITH WEEK-OLD ICKY-YUCKY.
AND THAT'S A BUNCH OF FIDDLE-FADDLE?
EXACTLY.
I'M TELLING YOU GUYS--IF THAT LAPTOP IS ANYWHERE IN THIS PLACE, IT'S BACK THERE WITH... OH, MY.
WHAT IS HE DOING?
HE'S BEING DEADPOOL.
I HATE HIM SO MUCH.

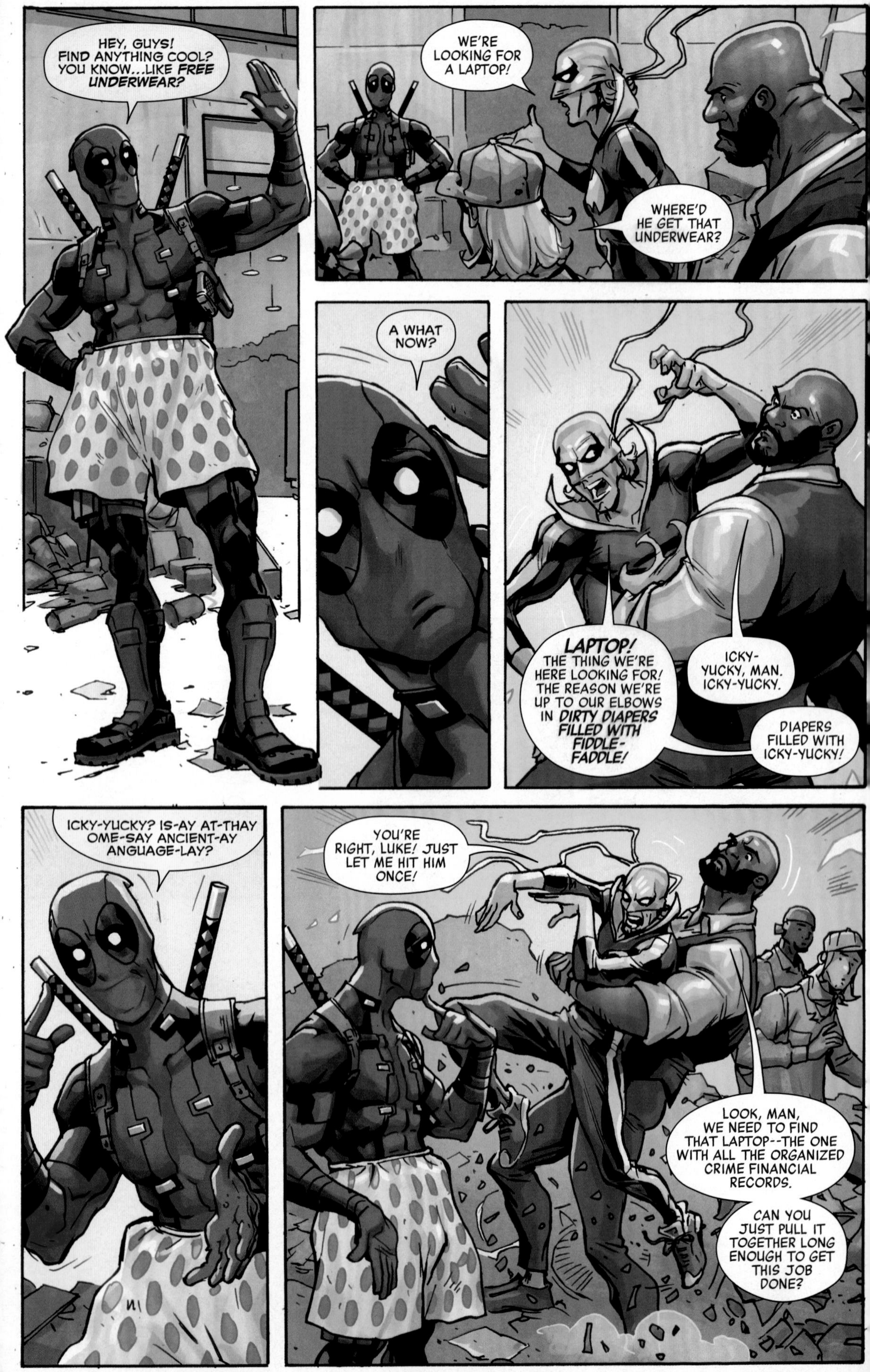
HEY, GUYS! FIND ANYTHING COOL? YOU KNOW...LIKE FREE UNDERWEAR?
WE'RE LOOKING FOR A LAPTOP!
WHERE'D HE GET THAT UNDERWEAR?
A WHAT NOW?
LAPTOP! THE THING WE'RE HERE LOOKING FOR! THE REASON WE'RE UP TO OUR ELBOWS IN DIRTY DIAPERS FILLED WITH FIDDLE-FADDLE!
ICKY-YUCKY, MAN. ICKY-YUCKY.
DIAPERS FILLED WITH ICKY-YUCKY!
ICKY-YUCKY? IS-AY AT-THAY OME-SAY ANCIENT-AY ANGUAGE-LAY?
YOU'RE RIGHT, LUKE! JUST LET ME HIT HIM ONCE!
LOOK, MAN, WE NEED TO FIND THAT LAPTOP--THE ONE WITH ALL THE ORGANIZED CRIME FINANCIAL RECORDS.
CAN YOU JUST PULL IT TOGETHER LONG ENOUGH TO GET THIS JOB DONE?

OH, THE JOB! WHY DIDN'T YOU SAY THAT IN THE FIRST PLACE INSTEAD OF RAMBLING ON IN WHATEVER LANGUAGE THEY SPEAK IN K'OOKY L'OONEY?

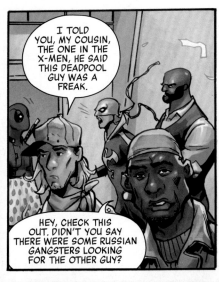

I TOLD YOU, MY COUSIN, THE ONE IN THE X-MEN, HE SAID THIS DEADPOOL GUY WAS A FREAK.

HEY, CHECK THIS OUT. DIDN'T YOU SAY THERE WERE SOME RUSSIAN GANGSTERS LOOKING FOR THE OTHER GUY?

BECAUSE THERE'S A BUNCH OF PEOPLE HEADING THIS WAY.

OH, ICKY-YUCKY.

FIDDLE-FADDLE, BRO. IT'S ALL ABOUT CONTEXT.

I'M NO AVENGER...

...BUT THOSE LOOK LIKE BAD GUYS TO ME.

GET THEM!

BRAKKA BRAKKA BRAKKA BRAKKA

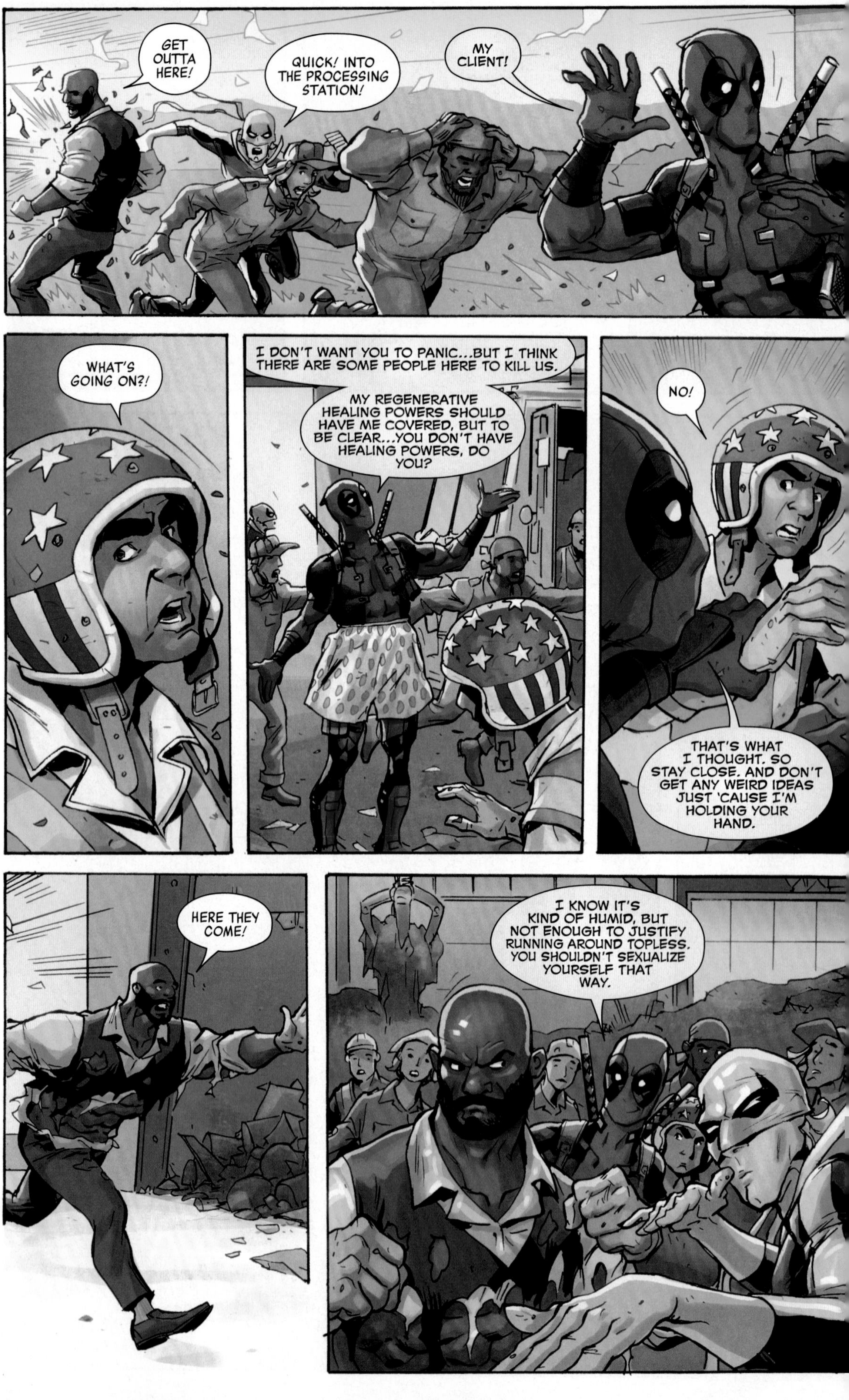
GET OUTTA HERE!
QUICK! INTO THE PROCESSING STATION!
MY CLIENT!
WHAT'S GOING ON?!
I DON'T WANT YOU TO PANIC...BUT I THINK THERE ARE SOME PEOPLE HERE TO KILL US.
MY REGENERATIVE HEALING POWERS SHOULD HAVE ME COVERED, BUT TO BE CLEAR...YOU DON'T HAVE HEALING POWERS, DO YOU?
NO!
THAT'S WHAT I THOUGHT. SO STAY CLOSE. AND DON'T GET ANY WEIRD IDEAS JUST 'CAUSE I'M HOLDING YOUR HAND.
HERE THEY COME!
I KNOW IT'S KIND OF HUMID, BUT NOT ENOUGH TO JUSTIFY RUNNING AROUND TOPLESS. YOU SHOULDN'T SEXUALIZE YOURSELF THAT WAY.

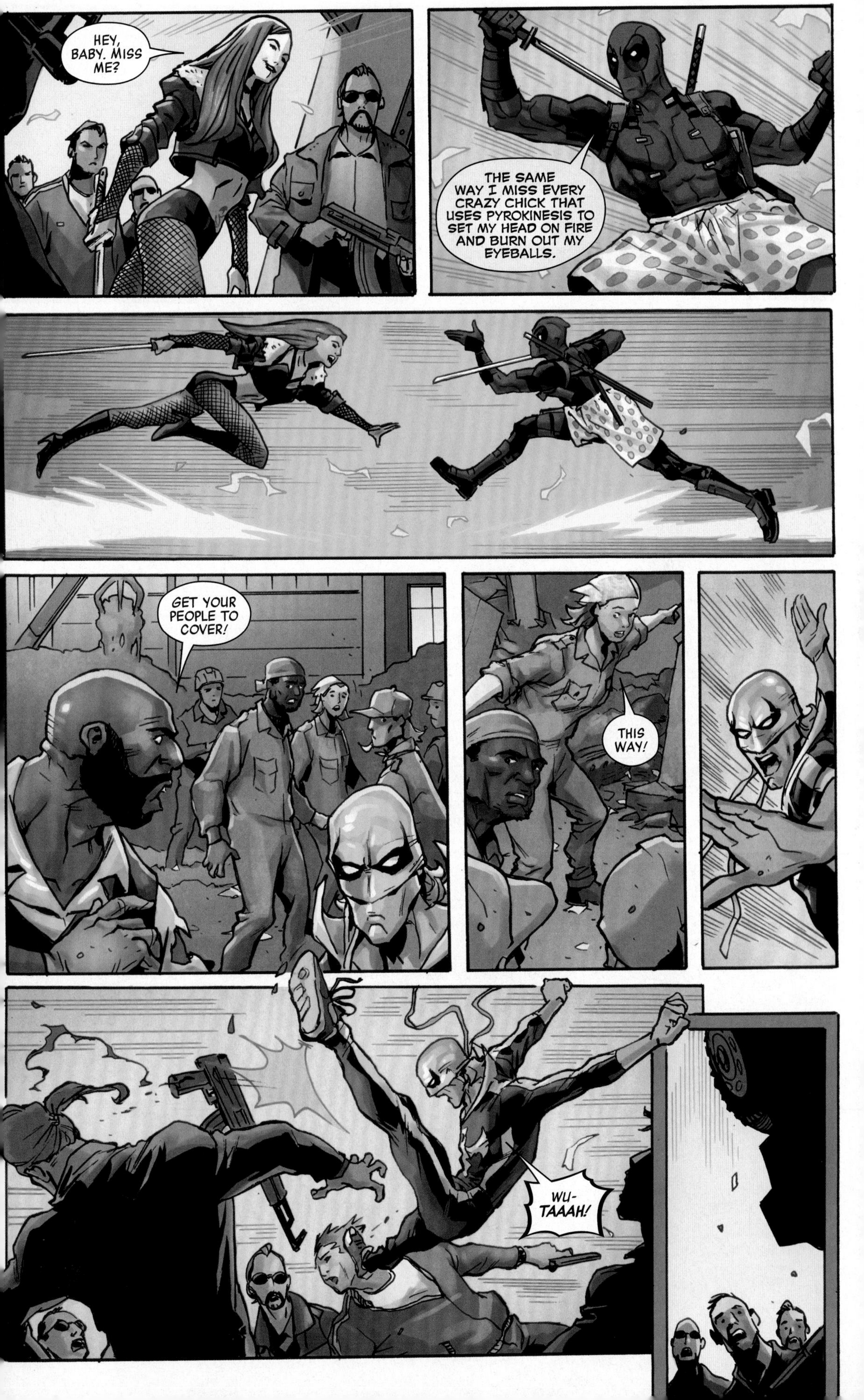
HEY, BABY. MISS ME?
THE SAME WAY I MISS EVERY CRAZY CHICK THAT USES PYROKINESIS TO SET MY HEAD ON FIRE AND BURN OUT MY EYEBALLS.
GET YOUR PEOPLE TO COVER!
THIS WAY!
WU-TAAAH!

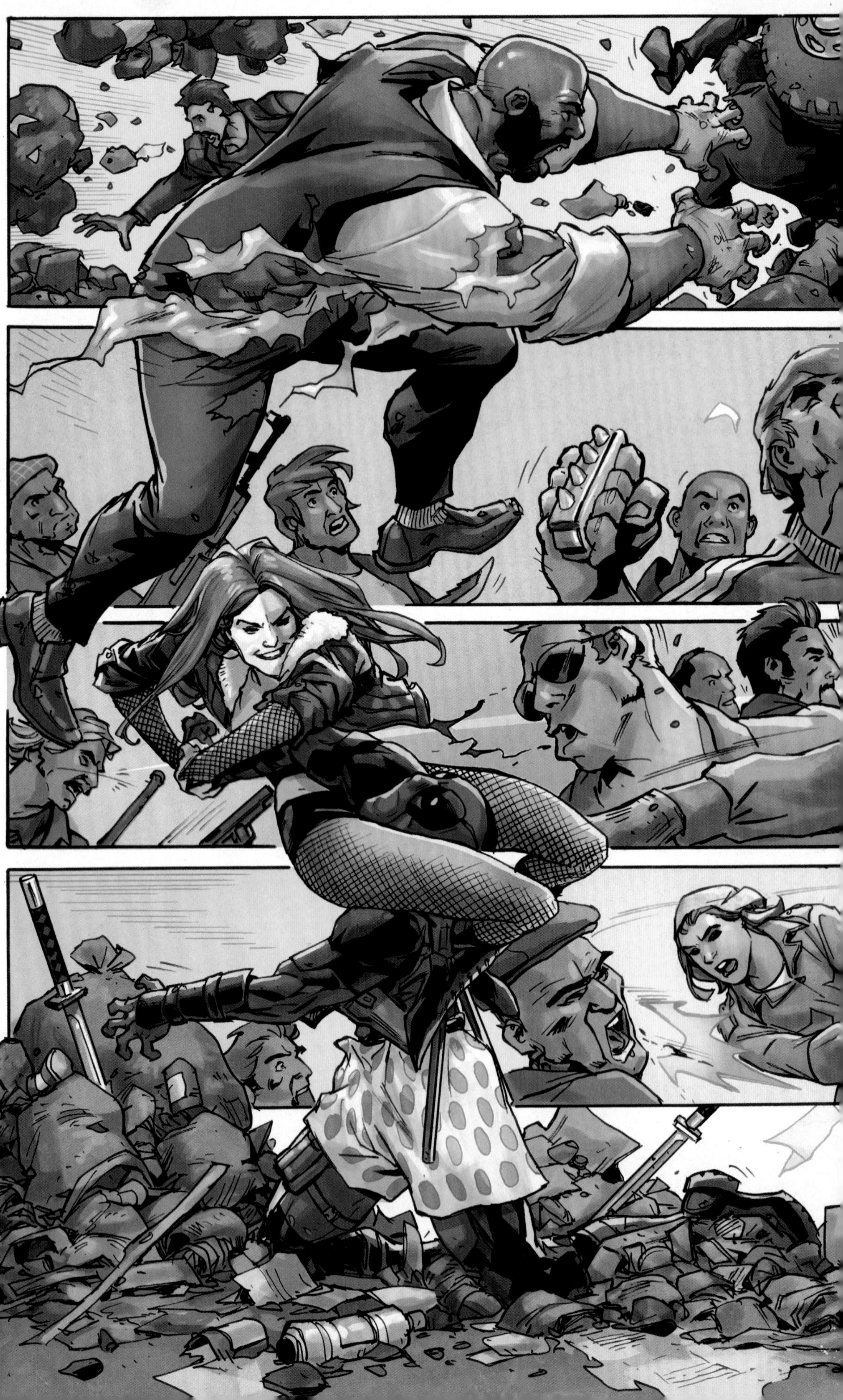

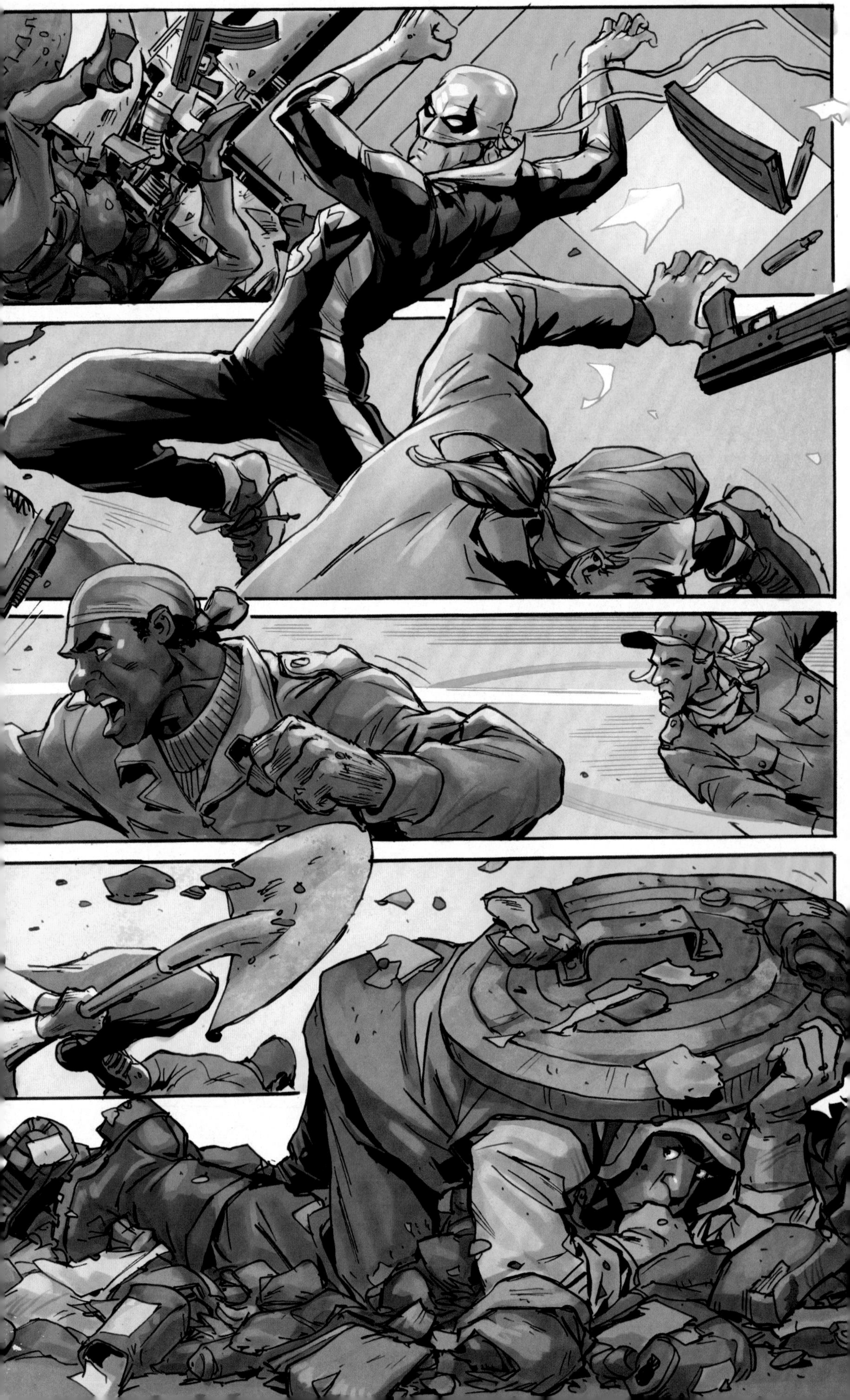

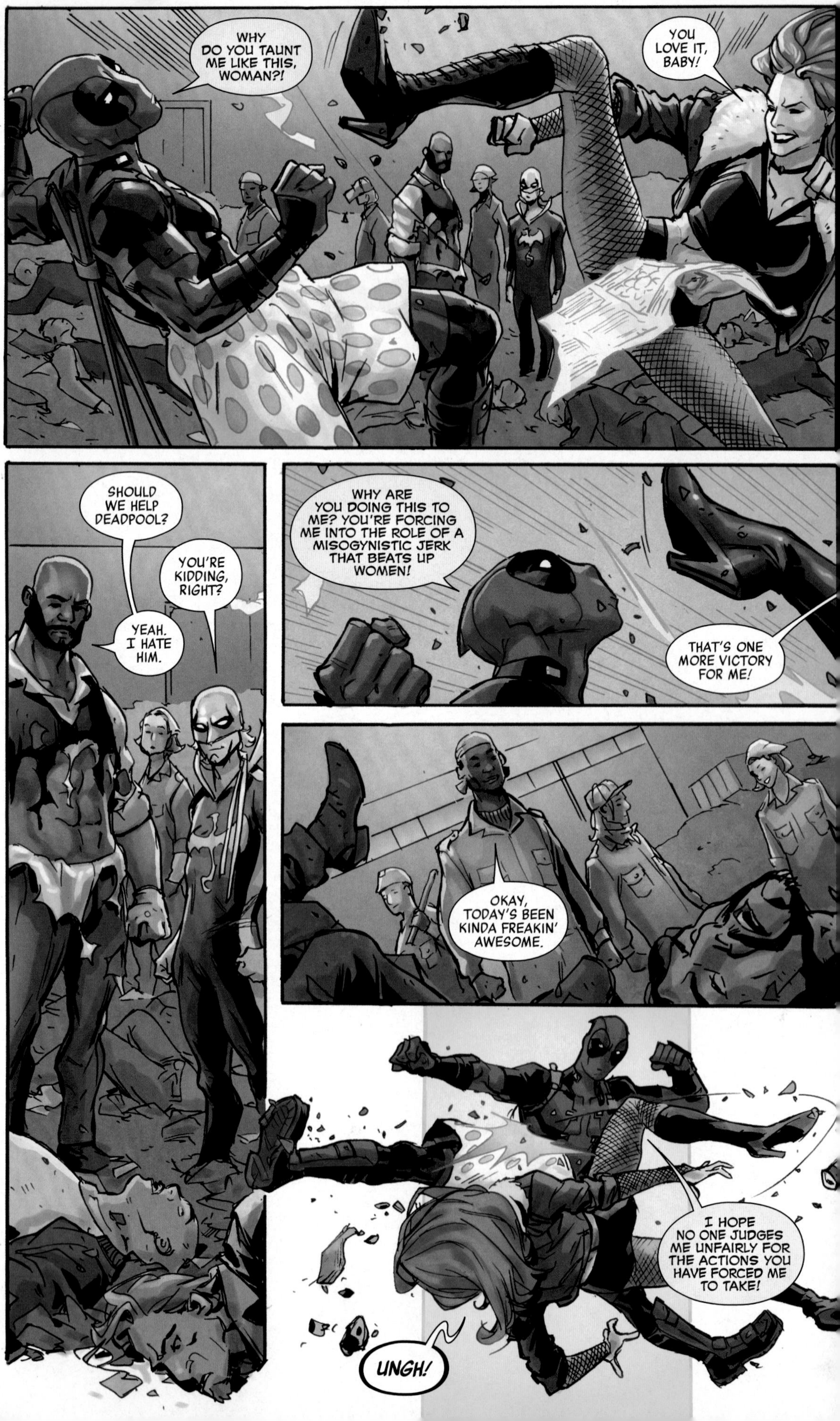
WHY DO YOU TAUNT ME LIKE THIS, WOMAN?!
YOU LOVE IT, BABY!
SHOULD WE HELP DEADPOOL?
YOU'RE KIDDING, RIGHT?
YEAH. I HATE HIM.
WHY ARE YOU DOING THIS TO ME? YOU'RE FORCING ME INTO THE ROLE OF A MISOGYNISTIC JERK THAT BEATS UP WOMEN!
THAT'S ONE MORE VICTORY FOR ME!
OKAY, TODAY'S BEEN KINDA FREAKIN' AWESOME.
I HOPE NO ONE JUDGES ME UNFAIRLY FOR THE ACTIONS YOU HAVE FORCED ME TO TAKE!
UNGH!

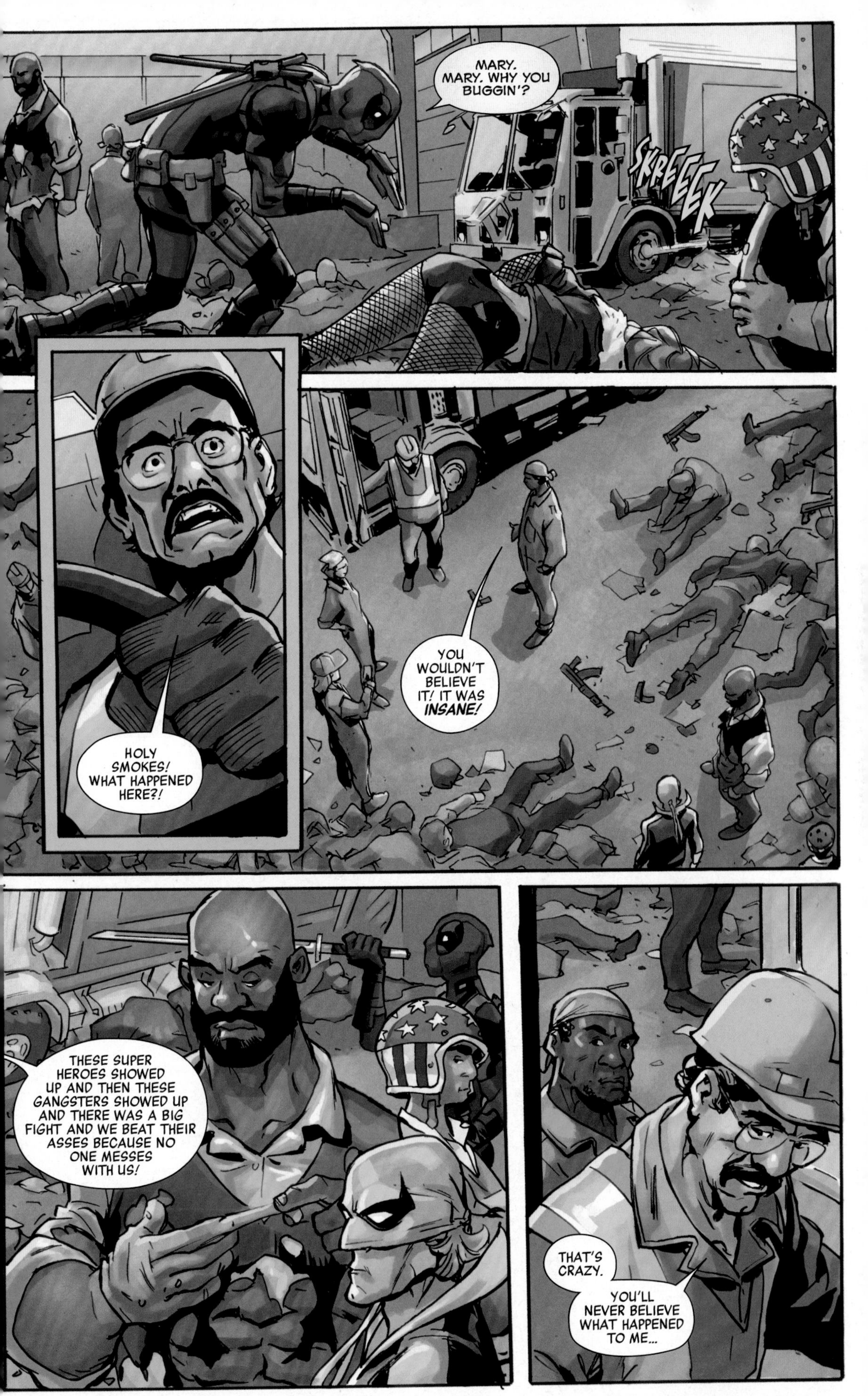
MARY. MARY. WHY YOU BUGGIN'?
SKREEEK
HOLY SMOKES! WHAT HAPPENED HERE?!
YOU WOULDN'T BELIEVE IT! IT WAS *INSANE!*
THESE SUPER HEROES SHOWED UP AND THEN THESE GANGSTERS SHOWED UP AND THERE WAS A BIG FIGHT AND WE BEAT THEIR ASSES BECAUSE NO ONE MESSES WITH US!
THAT'S CRAZY.
YOU'LL NEVER BELIEVE WHAT HAPPENED TO ME...

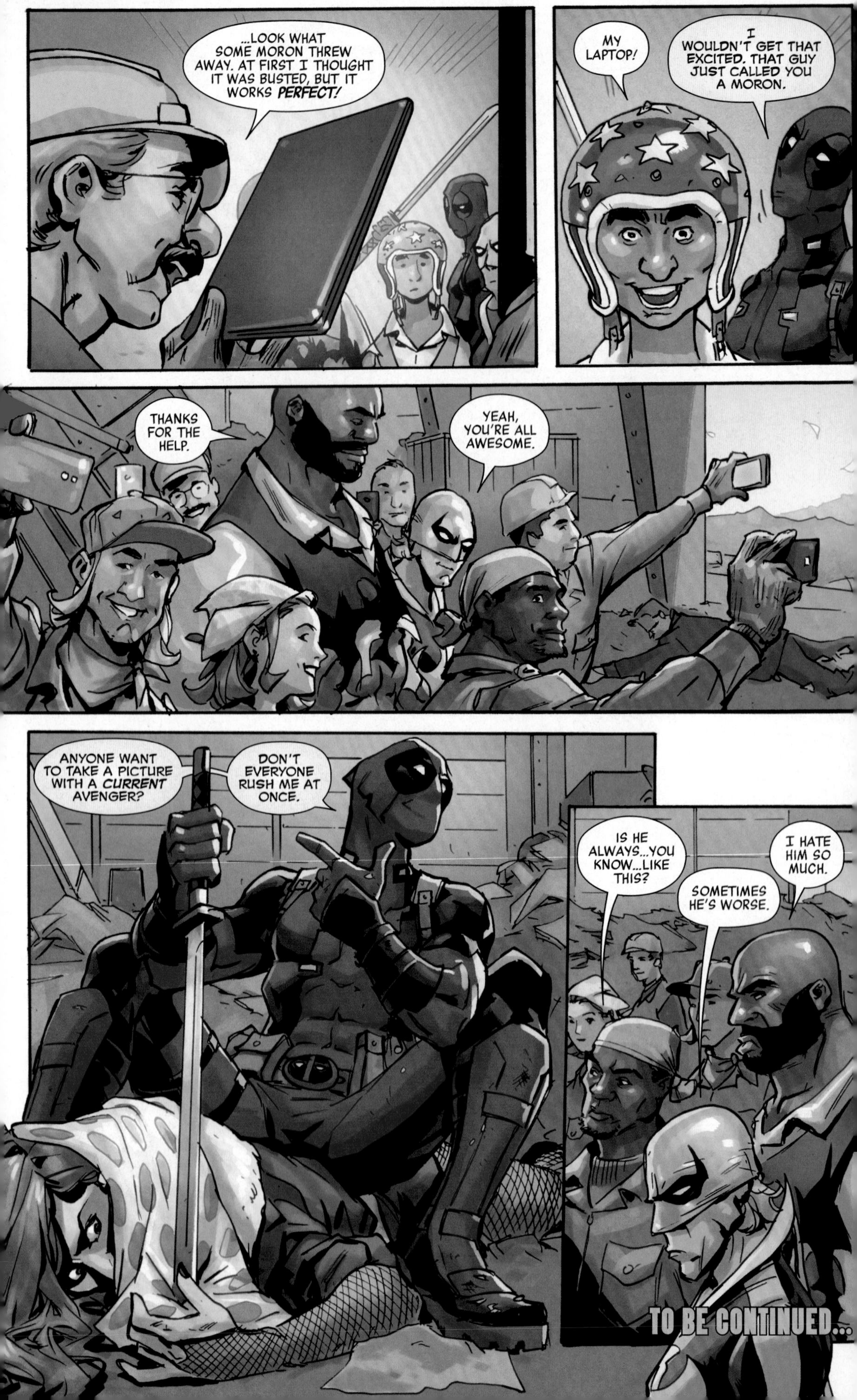
...LOOK WHAT SOME MORON THREW AWAY. AT FIRST I THOUGHT IT WAS BUSTED, BUT IT WORKS PERFECT!
MY LAPTOP!
I WOULDN'T GET THAT EXCITED. THAT GUY JUST CALLED YOU A MORON.
THANKS FOR THE HELP.
YEAH, YOU'RE ALL AWESOME.
ANYONE WANT TO TAKE A PICTURE WITH A CURRENT AVENGER?
DON'T EVERYONE RUSH ME AT ONCE.
IS HE ALWAYS...YOU KNOW...LIKE THIS?
SOMETIMES HE'S WORSE.
I HATE HIM SO MUCH.
TO BE CONTINUED...

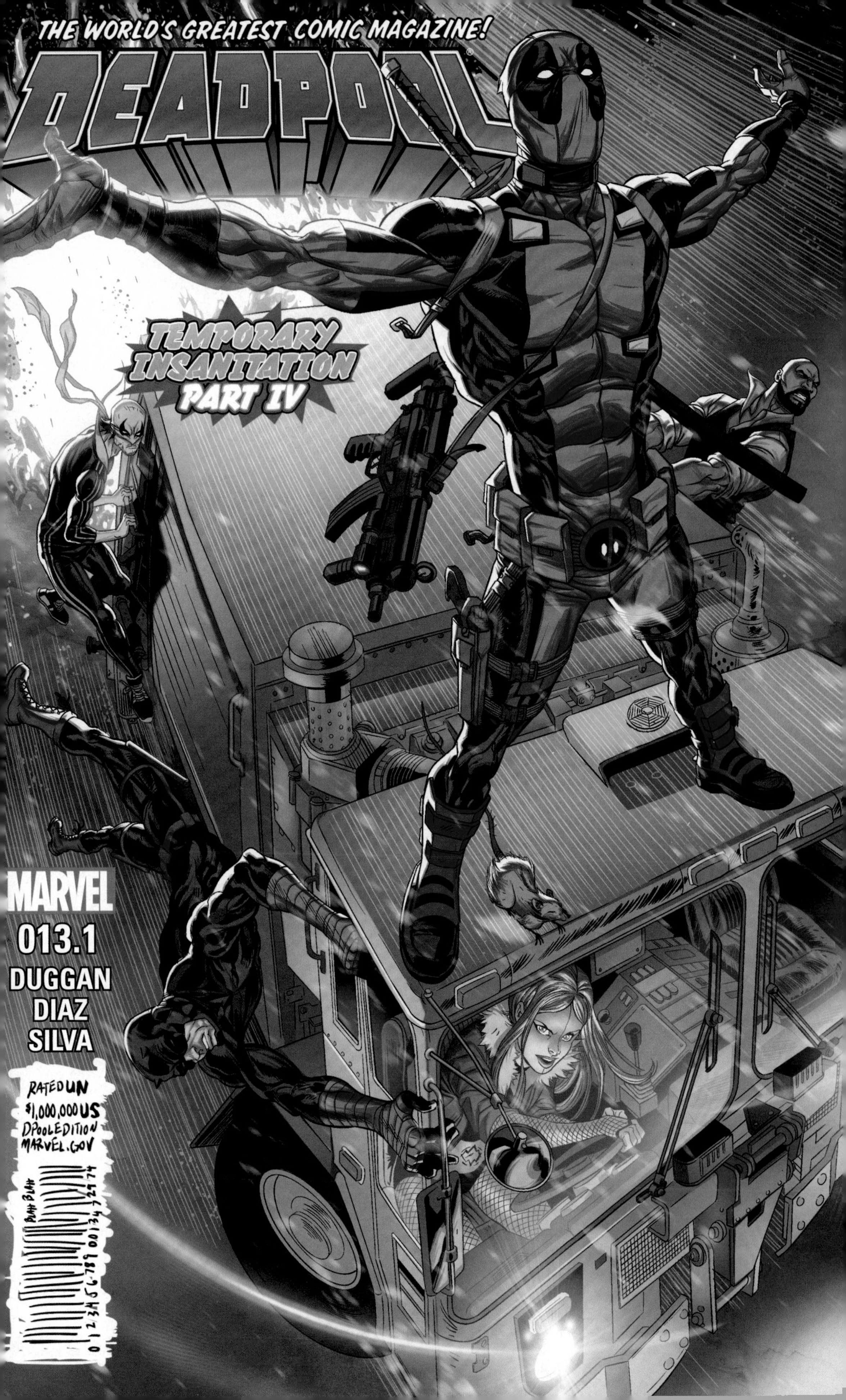
THE WORLD'S GREATEST COMIC MAGAZINE!
DEADPOOL
TEMPORARY INSANITATION PART IV
MARVEL
013.1
DUGGAN
DIAZ
SILVA
RATED UN
$1,000,000 US
DPOOL EDITION
MARVEL.GOV

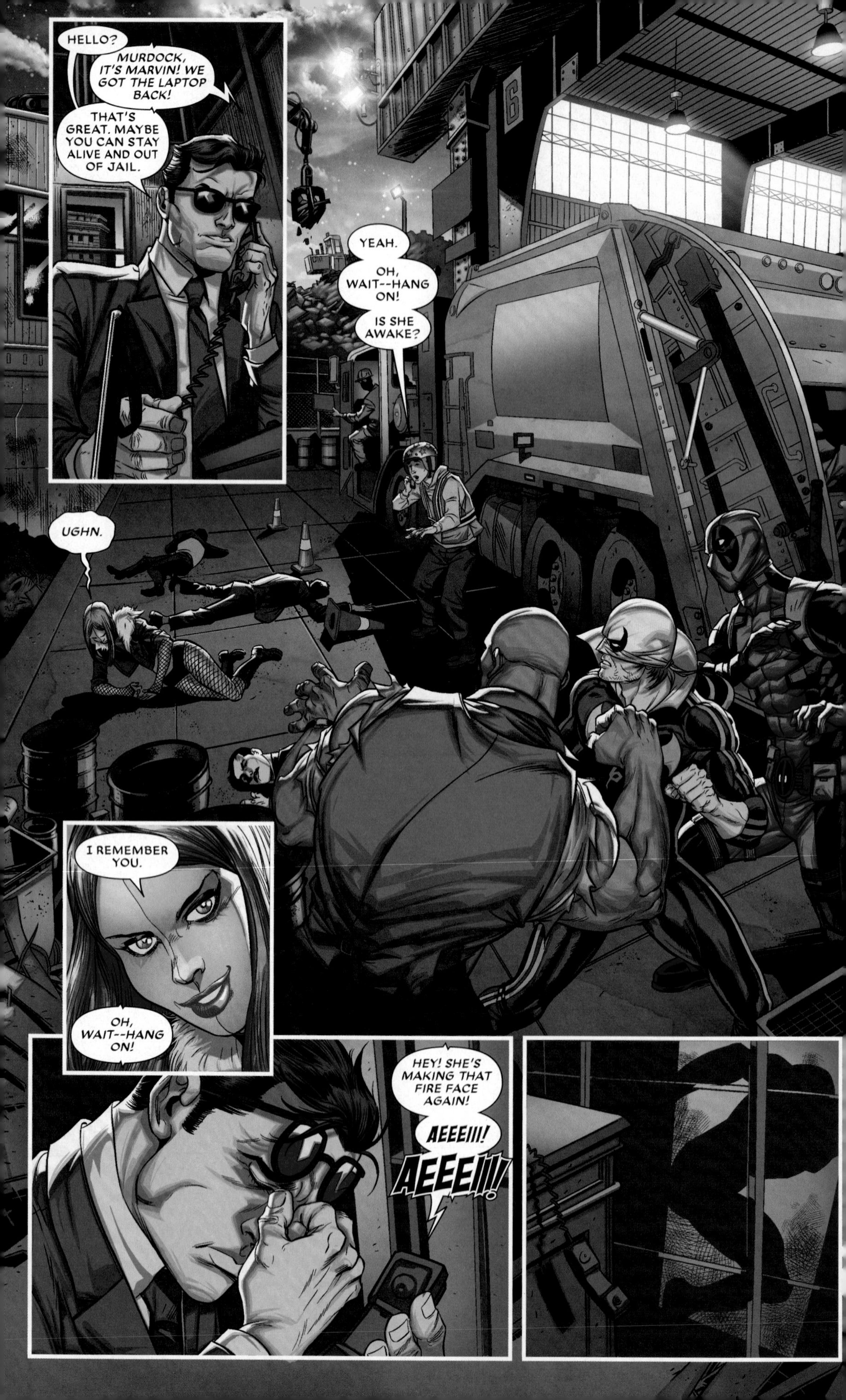

HELLO?
MURDOCK, IT'S MARVIN! WE GOT THE LAPTOP BACK!
THAT'S GREAT. MAYBE YOU CAN STAY ALIVE AND OUT OF JAIL.
YEAH.
OH, WAIT--HANG ON!
IS SHE AWAKE?
UGHN.
I REMEMBER YOU.
OH, WAIT--HANG ON!
HEY! SHE'S MAKING THAT FIRE FACE AGAIN!
AEEIII!
AEEEIII!

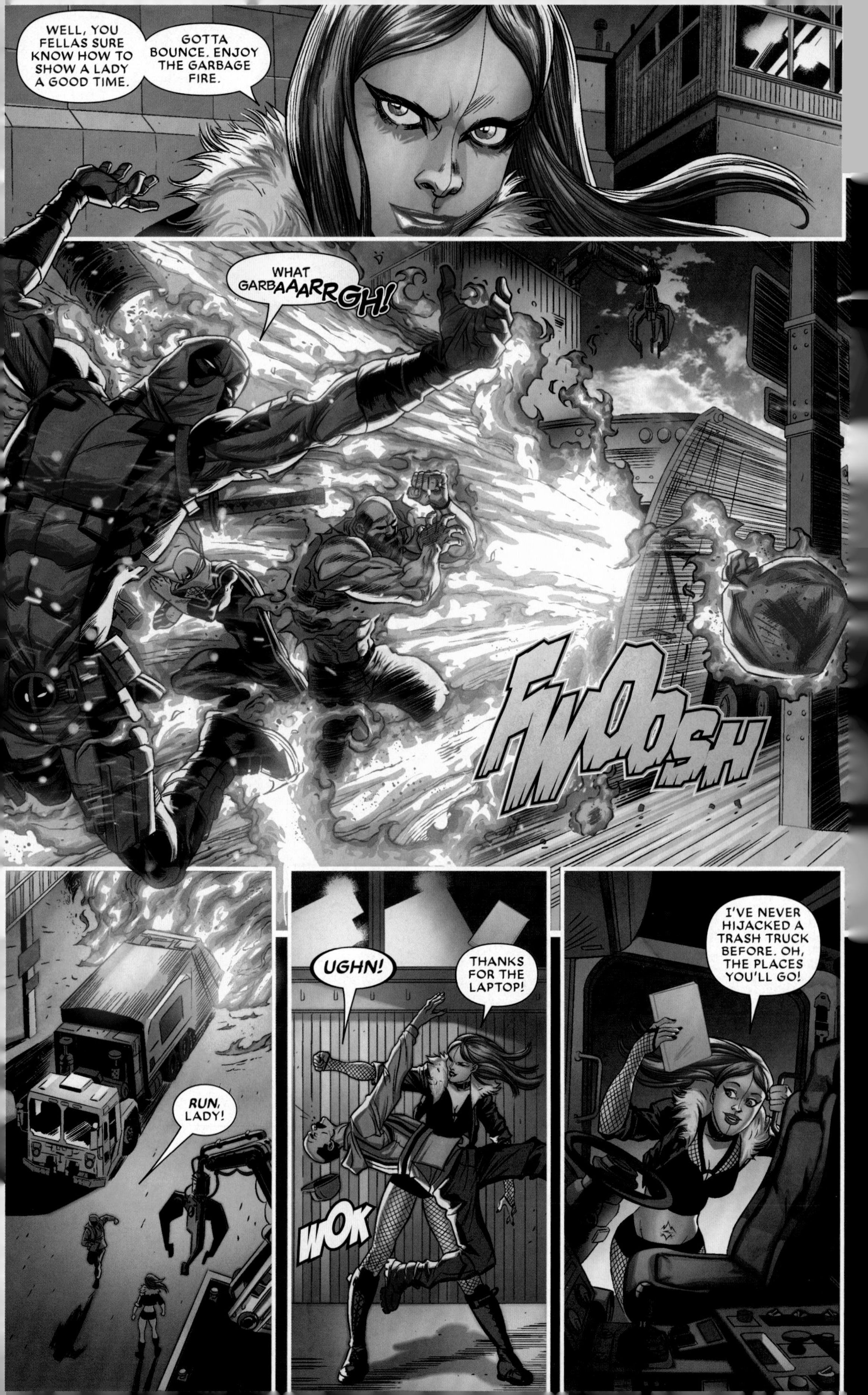
WELL, YOU FELLAS SURE KNOW HOW TO SHOW A LADY A GOOD TIME.
GOTTA BOUNCE. ENJOY THE GARBAGE FIRE.
WHAT GARBAAARRGH!
FWOOSH
RUN, LADY!
UGHN!
THANKS FOR THE LAPTOP!
WOK
I'VE NEVER HIJACKED A TRASH TRUCK BEFORE. OH, THE PLACES YOU'LL GO!

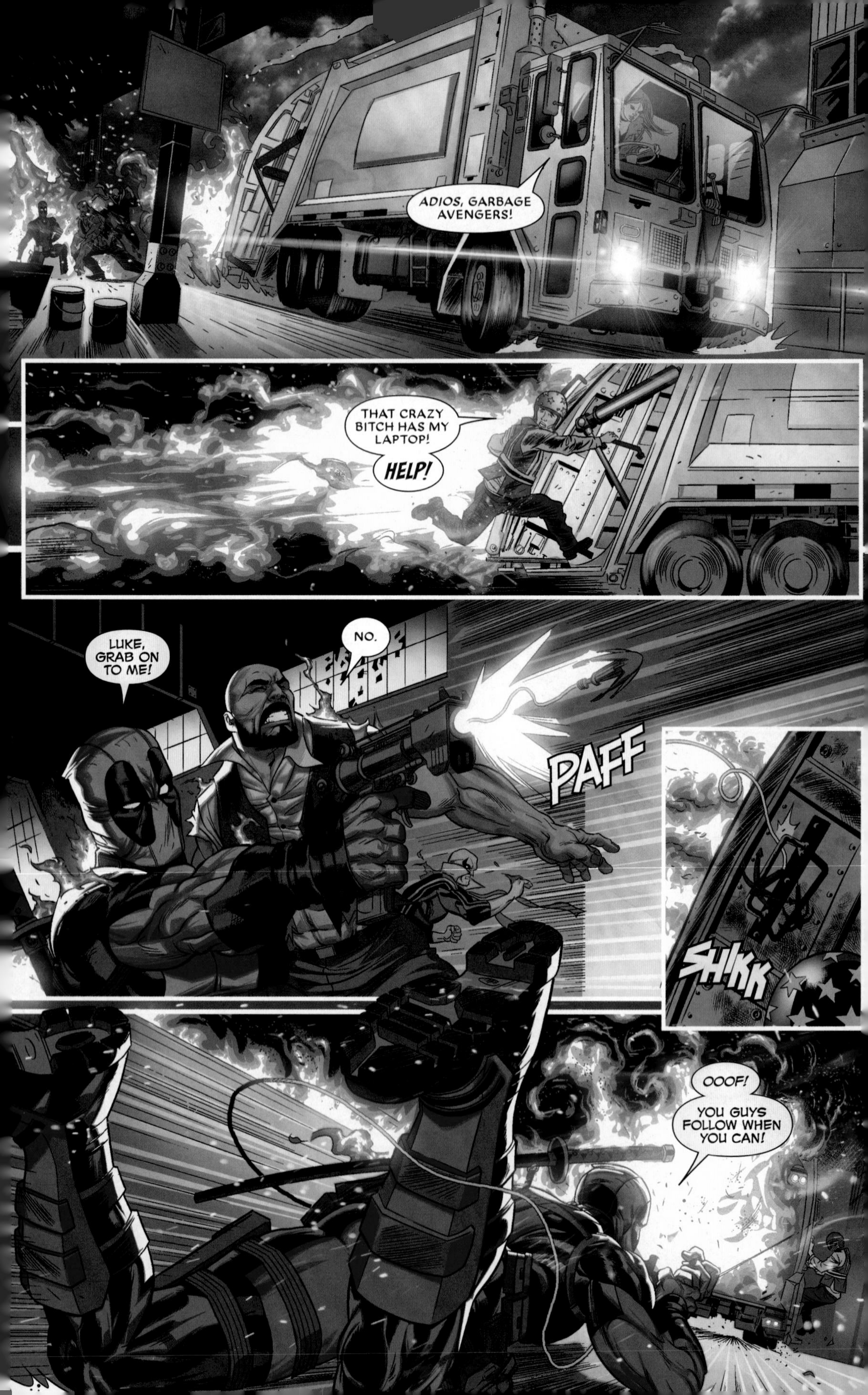
ADIOS, GARBAGE AVENGERS!
THAT CRAZY BITCH HAS MY LAPTOP!
HELP!
LUKE, GRAB ON TO ME!
NO.
PAFF
SHIKK
OOOF!
YOU GUYS FOLLOW WHEN YOU CAN!

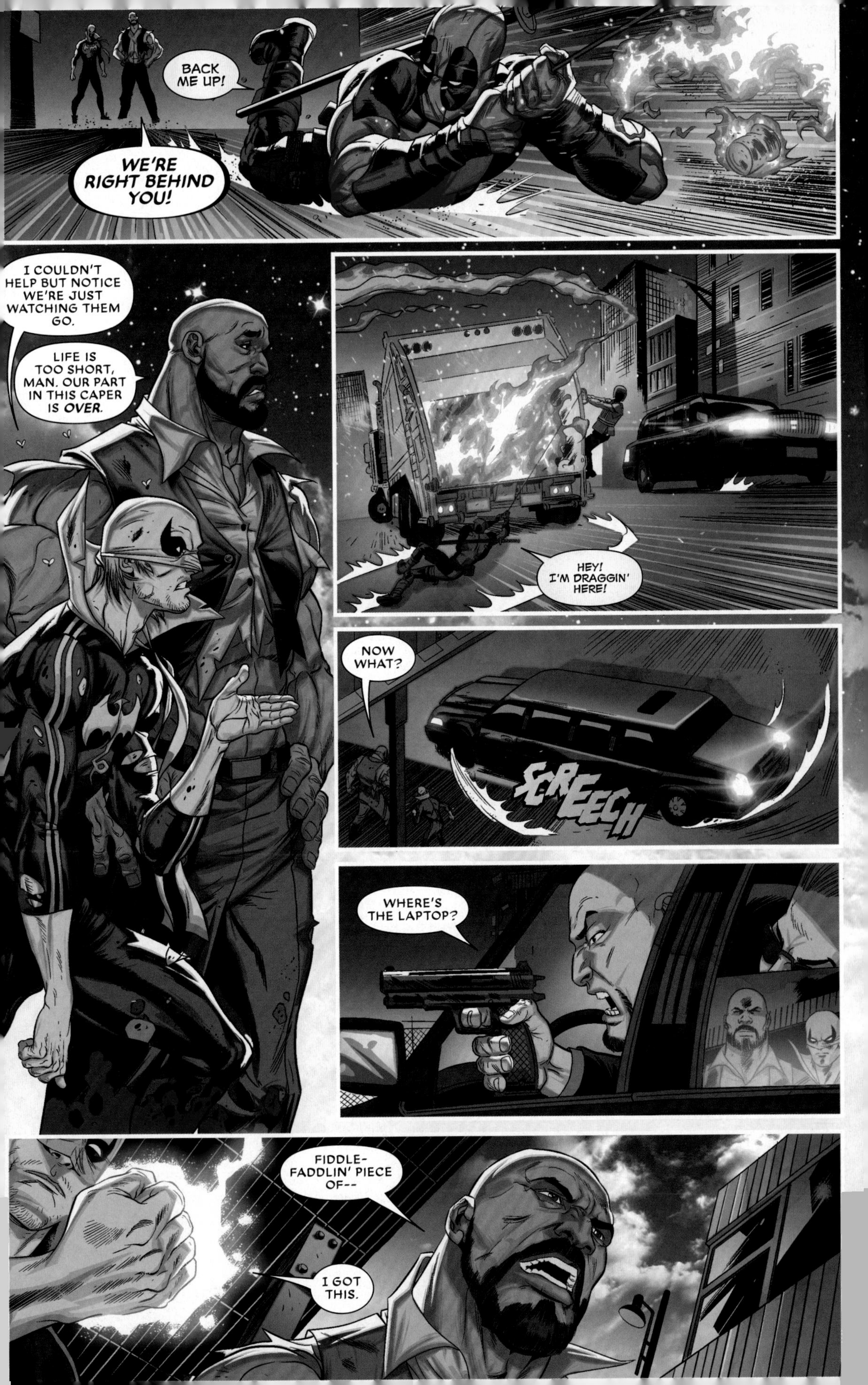
BACK ME UP!
WE'RE RIGHT BEHIND YOU!
I COULDN'T HELP BUT NOTICE WE'RE JUST WATCHING THEM GO.
LIFE IS TOO SHORT, MAN. OUR PART IN THIS CAPER IS OVER.
HEY! I'M DRAGGIN' HERE!
NOW WHAT?
SCREECH
WHERE'S THE LAPTOP?
FIDDLE-FADDLIN' PIECE OF--
I GOT THIS.

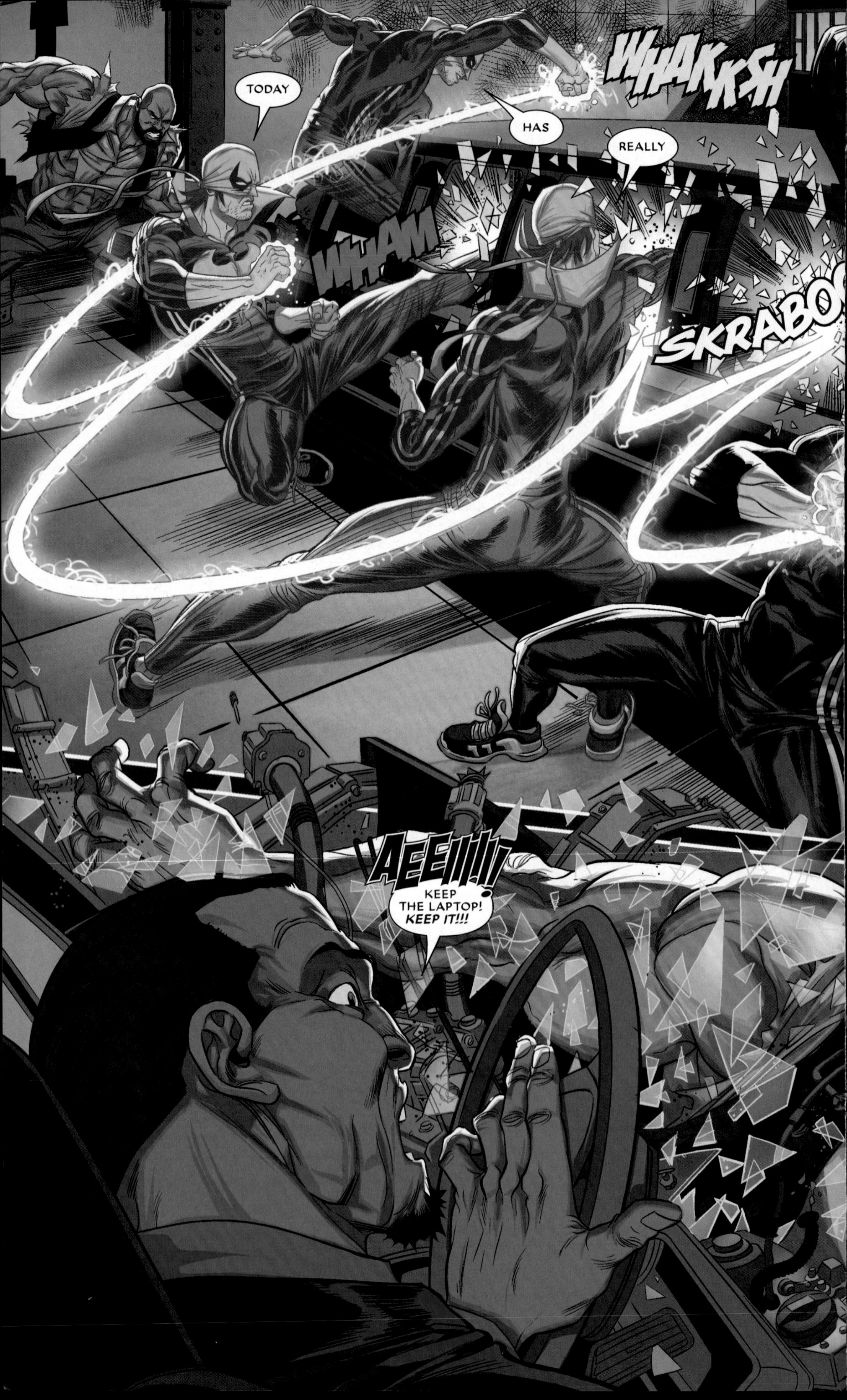
TODAY
WHAKKSH
HAS
REALLY
WHAM
SKRABOO
AEEIIIII!!
KEEP THE LAPTOP! KEEP IT!!!

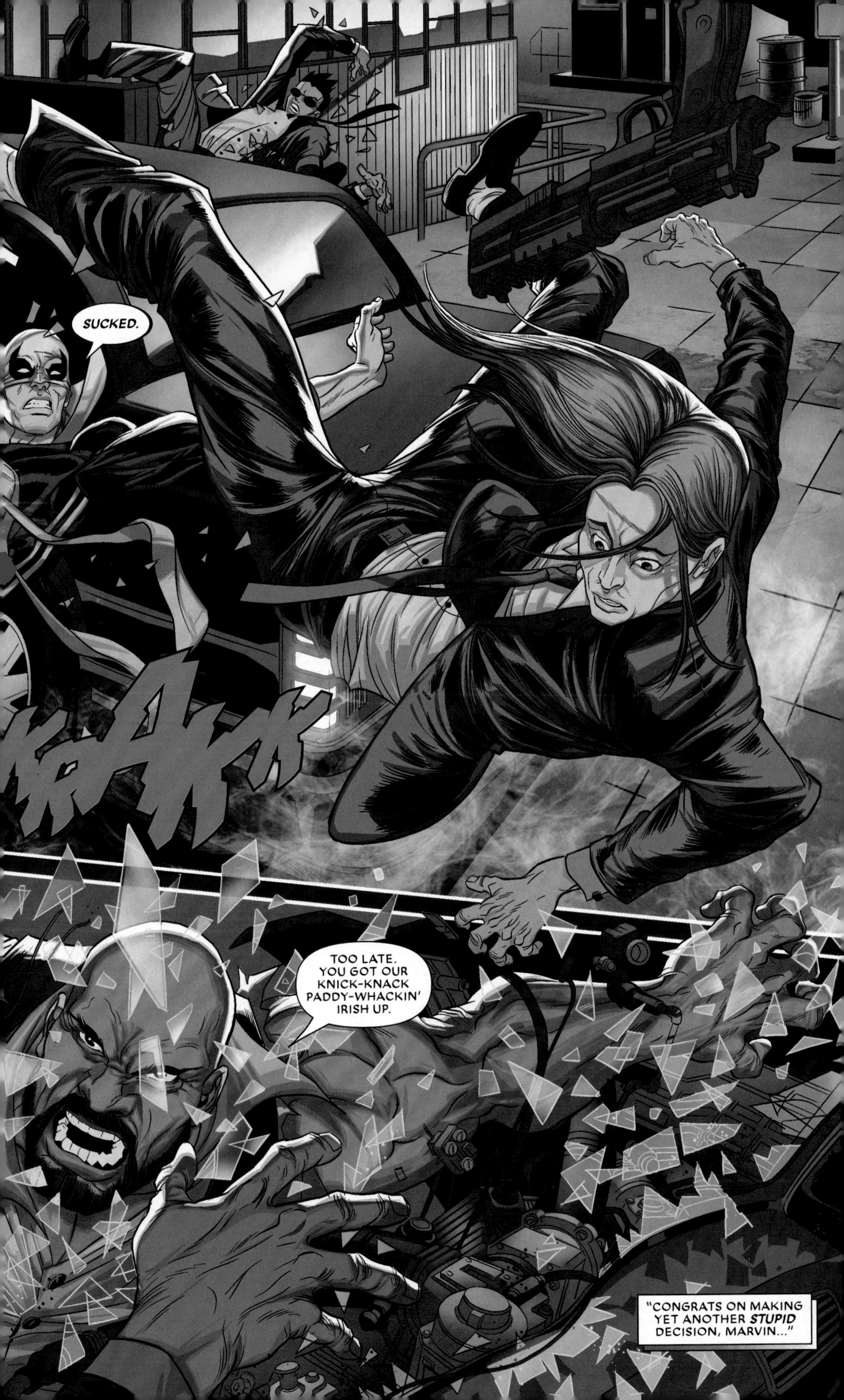
SUCKED.
TOO LATE. YOU GOT OUR KNICK-KNACK PADDY-WHACKIN' IRISH UP.
"CONGRATS ON MAKING YET ANOTHER STUPID DECISION, MARVIN..."

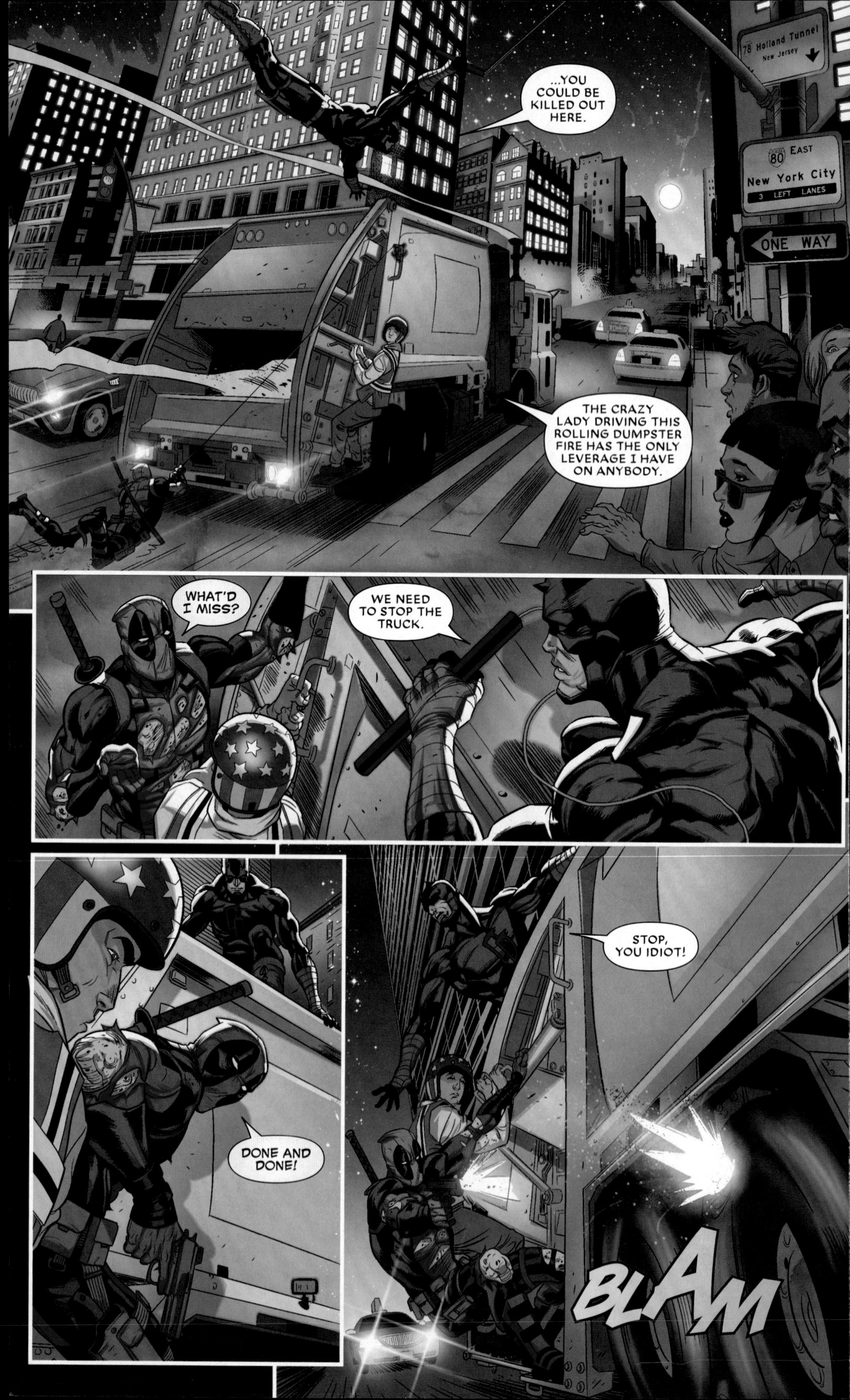
78 Holland Tunnel
New Jersey
...YOU COULD BE KILLED OUT HERE.
80 EAST
New York City
3 LEFT LANES
ONE WAY
THE CRAZY LADY DRIVING THIS ROLLING DUMPSTER FIRE HAS THE ONLY LEVERAGE I HAVE ON ANYBODY.
WHAT'D I MISS?
WE NEED TO STOP THE TRUCK.
DONE AND DONE!
STOP, YOU IDIOT!
BLAM

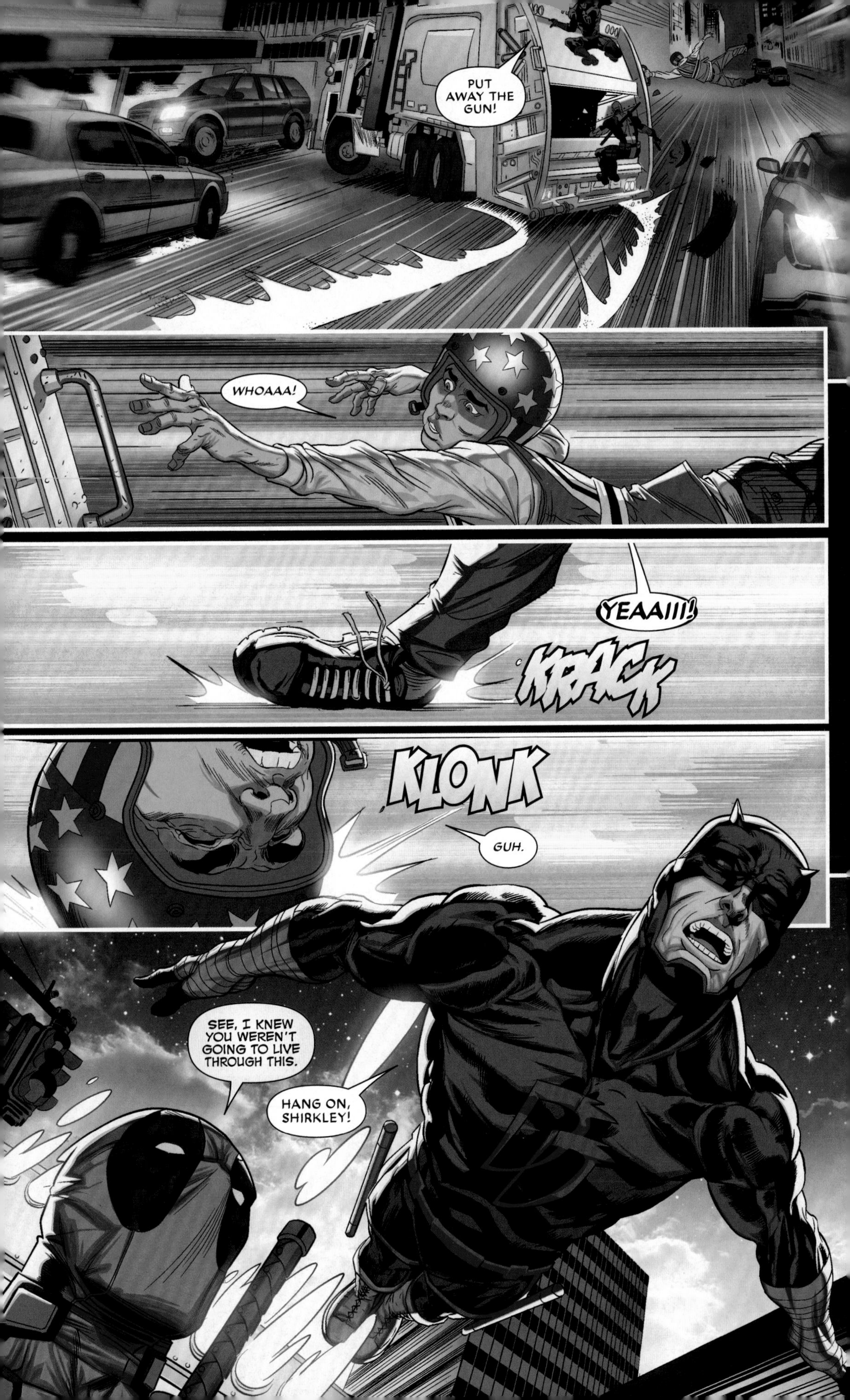
PUT AWAY THE GUN!
WHOAAA!
YEAAIII!
KRACK
KLONK
GUH.
SEE, I KNEW YOU WEREN'T GOING TO LIVE THROUGH THIS.
HANG ON, SHIRKLEY!

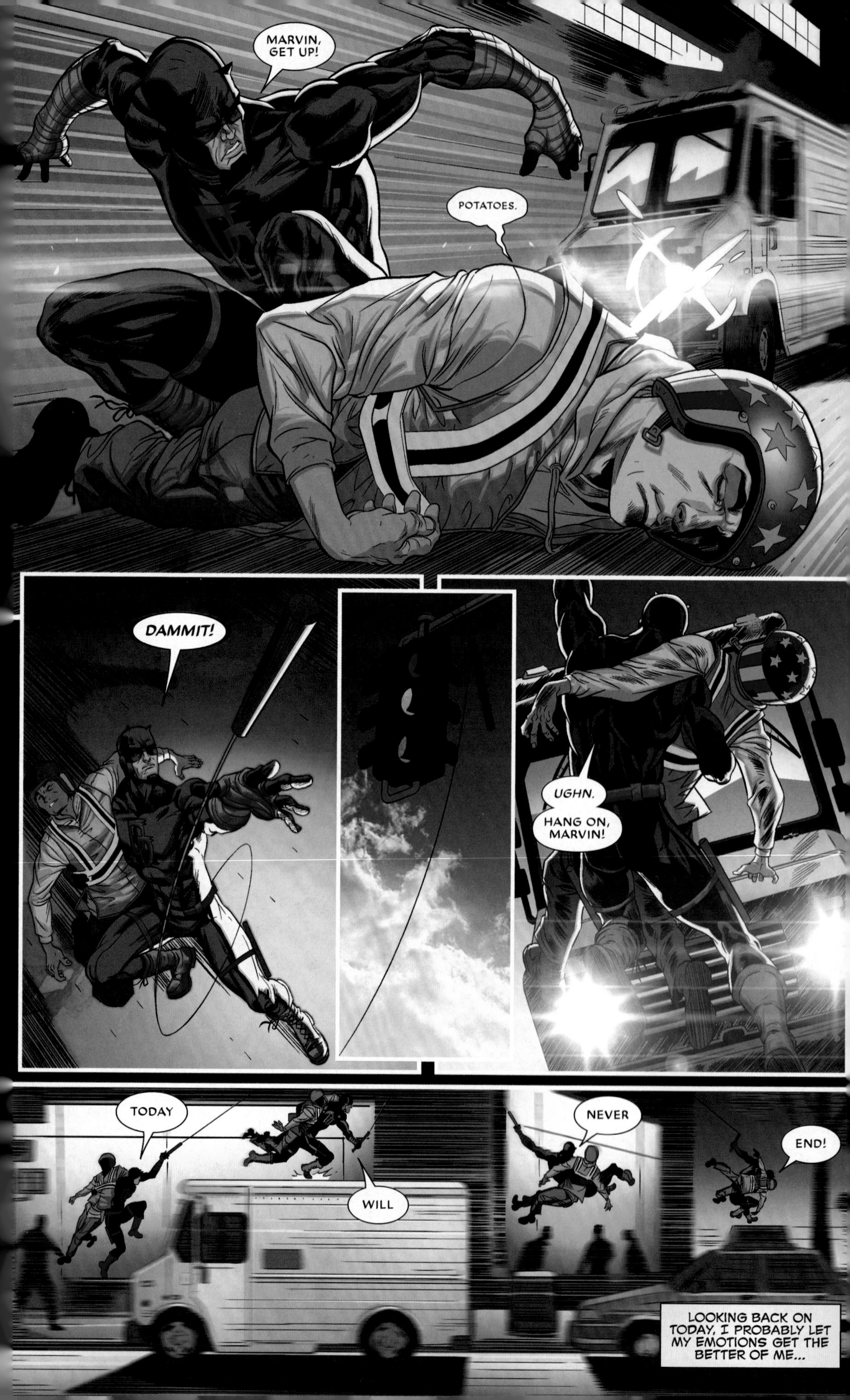
MARVIN, GET UP!
POTATOES.
DAMMIT!
UGHN.
HANG ON, MARVIN!
TODAY
WILL
NEVER
END!
LOOKING BACK ON TODAY, I PROBABLY LET MY EMOTIONS GET THE BETTER OF ME...

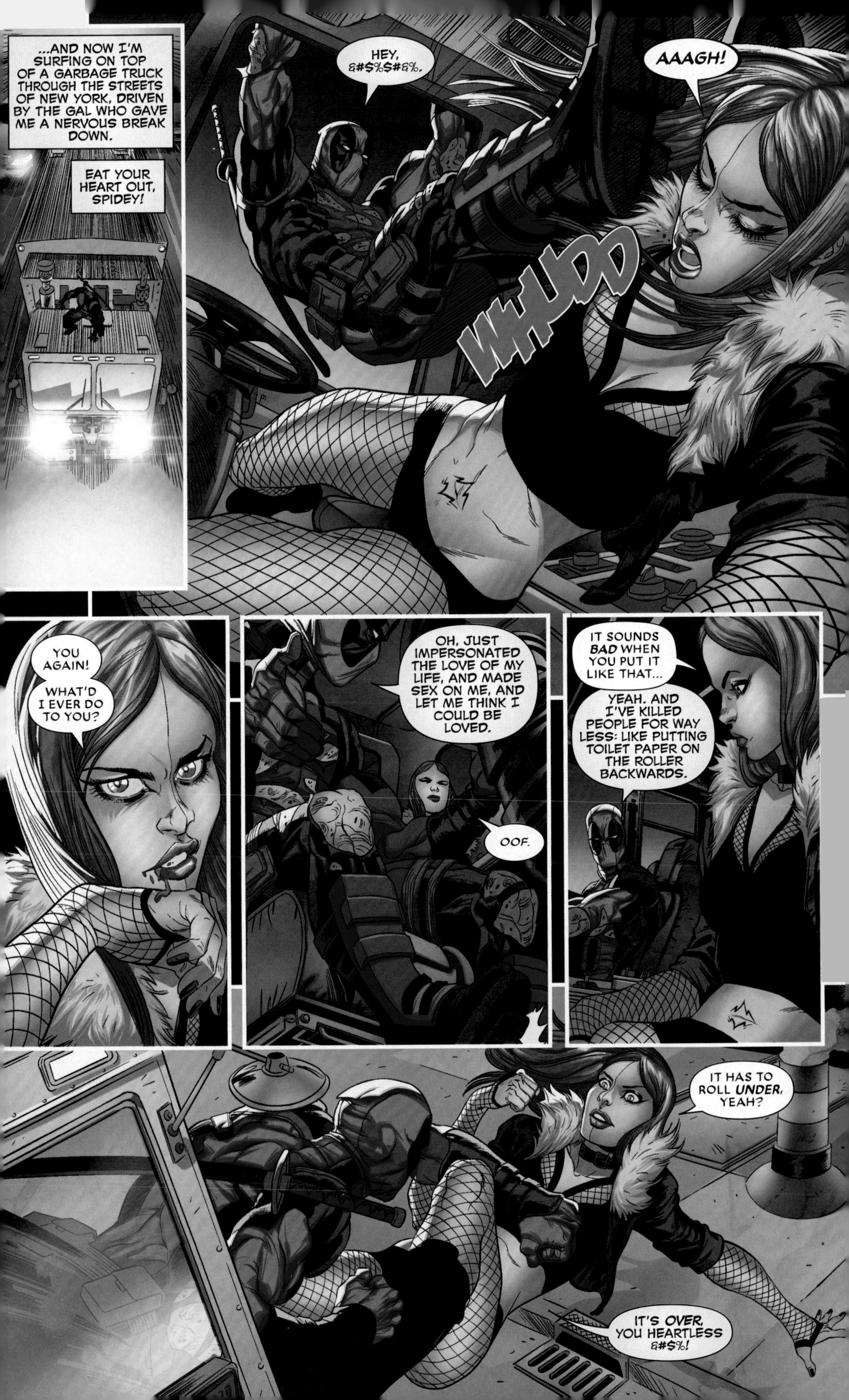
...AND NOW I'M SURFING ON TOP OF A GARBAGE TRUCK THROUGH THE STREETS OF NEW YORK, DRIVEN BY THE GAL WHO GAVE ME A NERVOUS BREAK DOWN.
EAT YOUR HEART OUT, SPIDEY!
HEY, &#$%$#&%.
AAAGH!
WHUDD
YOU AGAIN!
WHAT'D I EVER DO TO YOU?
OH, JUST IMPERSONATED THE LOVE OF MY LIFE, AND MADE SEX ON ME, AND LET ME THINK I COULD BE LOVED.
OOF.
IT SOUNDS BAD WHEN YOU PUT IT LIKE THAT...
YEAH. AND I'VE KILLED PEOPLE FOR WAY LESS: LIKE PUTTING TOILET PAPER ON THE ROLLER BACKWARDS.
IT HAS TO ROLL UNDER, YEAH?
IT'S OVER, YOU HEARTLESS &#$%!

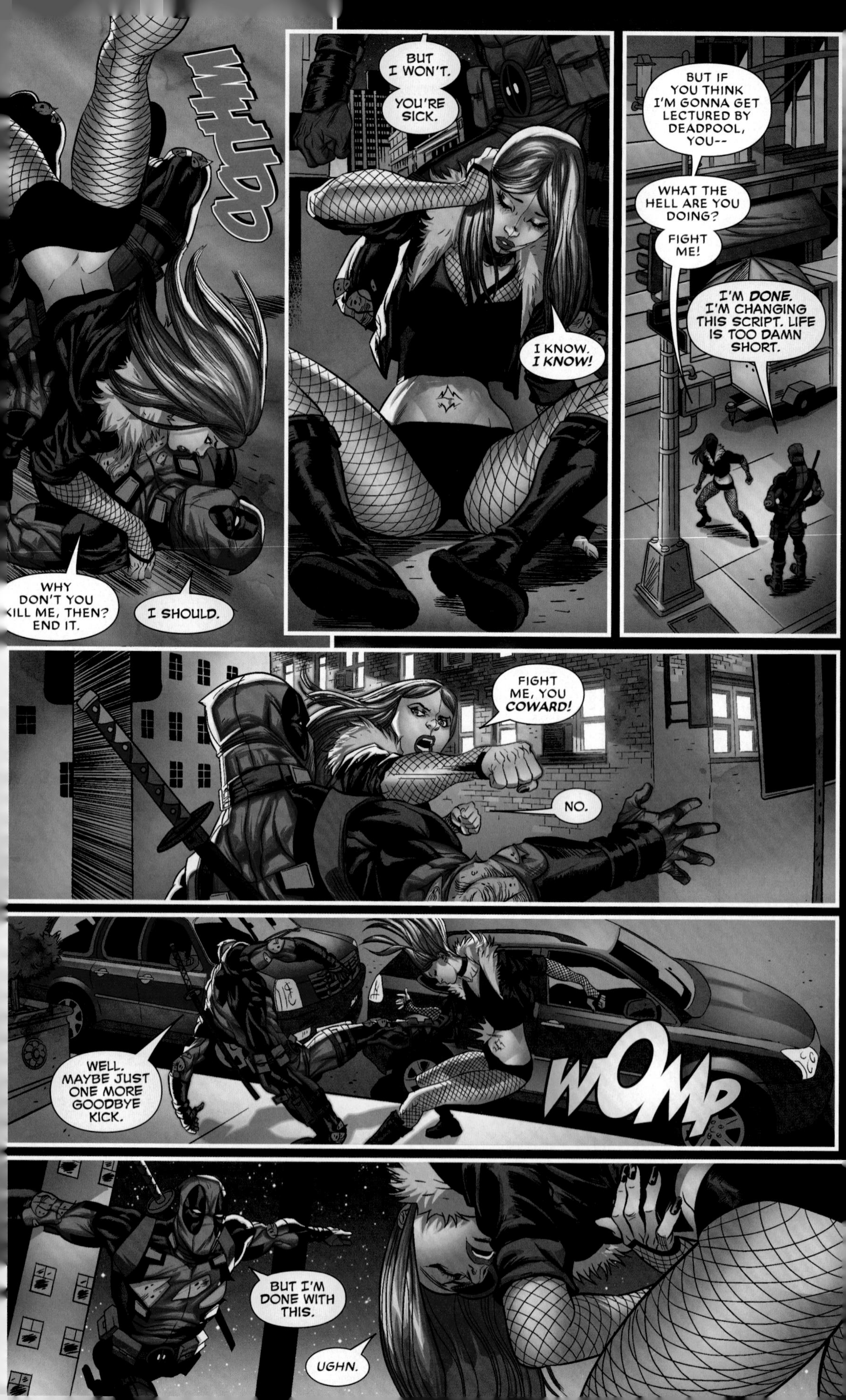
WHUDD
WHY DON'T YOU KILL ME, THEN? END IT.
I SHOULD.
BUT I WON'T.
YOU'RE SICK.
I KNOW. I KNOW!
BUT IF YOU THINK I'M GONNA GET LECTURED BY DEADPOOL, YOU--
WHAT THE HELL ARE YOU DOING?
FIGHT ME!
I'M DONE. I'M CHANGING THIS SCRIPT. LIFE IS TOO DAMN SHORT.
FIGHT ME, YOU COWARD!
NO.
WELL. MAYBE JUST ONE MORE GOODBYE KICK.
WOMP
BUT I'M DONE WITH THIS.
UGHN.

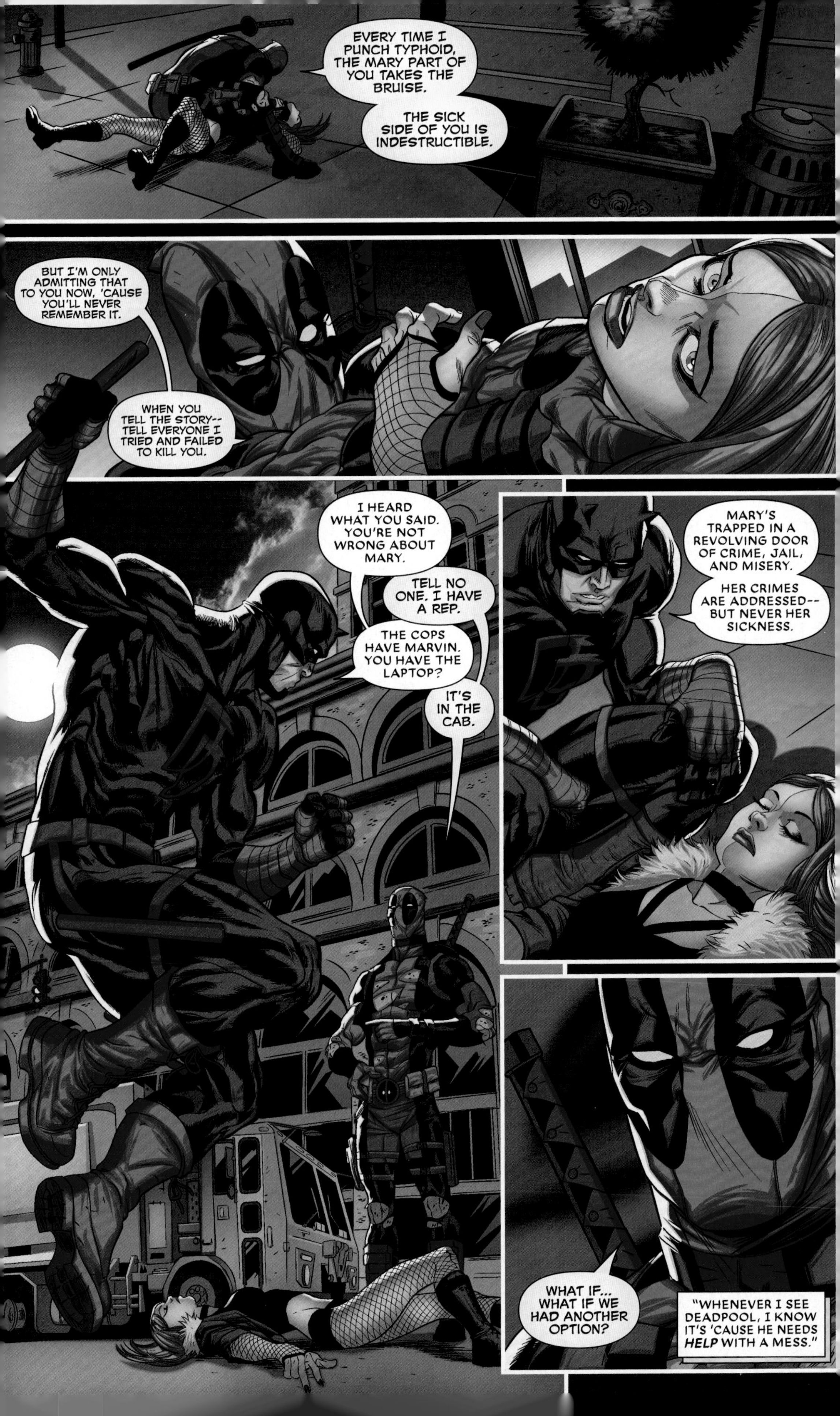
EVERY TIME I PUNCH TYPHOID, THE MARY PART OF YOU TAKES THE BRUISE.
THE SICK SIDE OF YOU IS INDESTRUCTIBLE.
BUT I'M ONLY ADMITTING THAT TO YOU NOW, 'CAUSE YOU'LL NEVER REMEMBER IT.
WHEN YOU TELL THE STORY-- TELL EVERYONE I TRIED AND FAILED TO KILL YOU.
I HEARD WHAT YOU SAID. YOU'RE NOT WRONG ABOUT MARY.
TELL NO ONE. I HAVE A REP.
THE COPS HAVE MARVIN. YOU HAVE THE LAPTOP?
IT'S IN THE CAB.
MARY'S TRAPPED IN A REVOLVING DOOR OF CRIME, JAIL, AND MISERY.
HER CRIMES ARE ADDRESSED-- BUT NEVER HER SICKNESS.
WHAT IF... WHAT IF WE HAD ANOTHER OPTION?
"WHENEVER I SEE DEADPOOL, I KNOW IT'S 'CAUSE HE NEEDS *HELP* WITH A MESS."

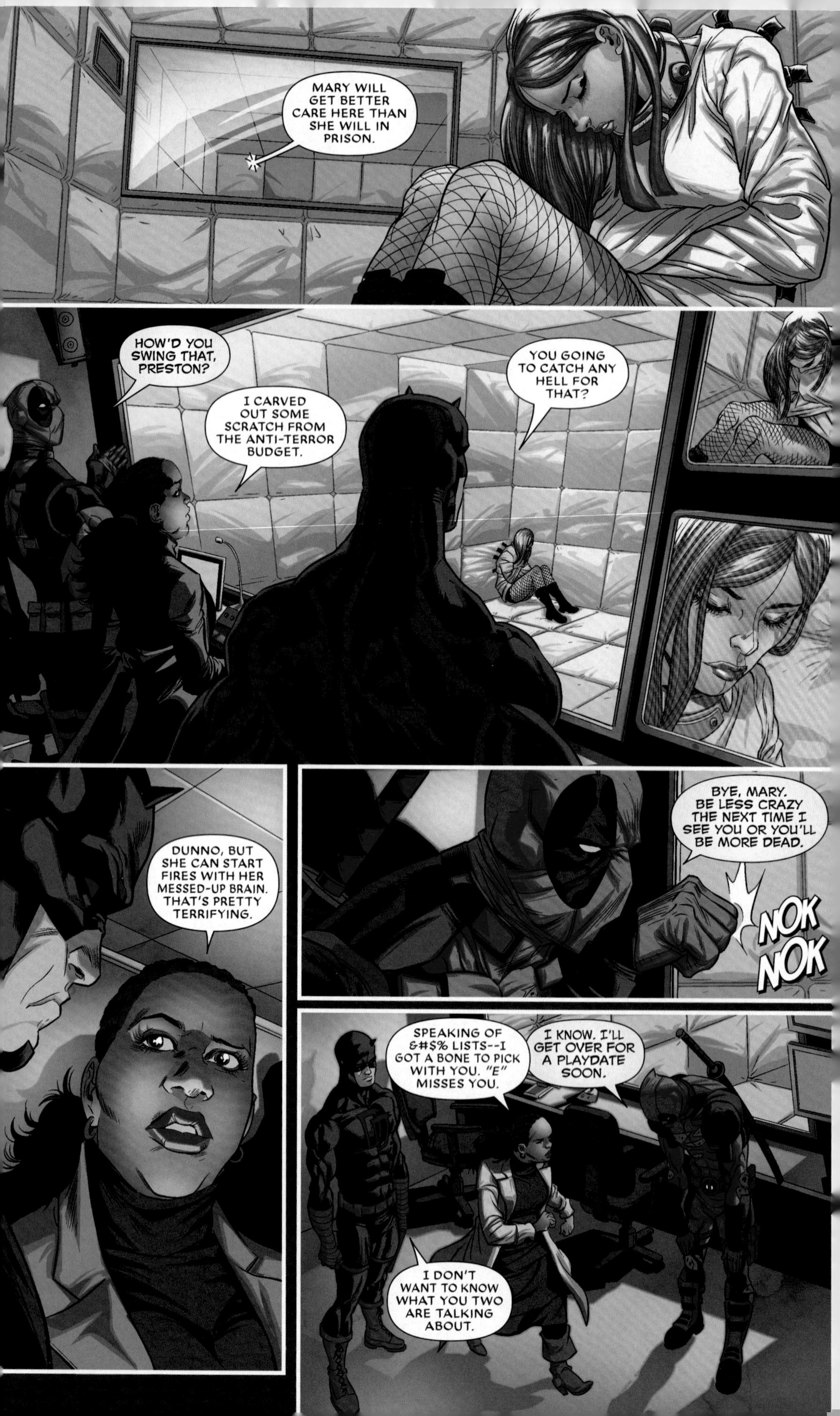

MARY WILL GET BETTER CARE HERE THAN SHE WILL IN PRISON.
HOW'D YOU SWING THAT, PRESTON?
I CARVED OUT SOME SCRATCH FROM THE ANTI-TERROR BUDGET.
YOU GOING TO CATCH ANY HELL FOR THAT?
DUNNO, BUT SHE CAN START FIRES WITH HER MESSED-UP BRAIN. THAT'S PRETTY TERRIFYING.
BYE, MARY. BE LESS CRAZY THE NEXT TIME I SEE YOU OR YOU'LL BE MORE DEAD.
NOK NOK
SPEAKING OF &#$% LISTS--I GOT A BONE TO PICK WITH YOU. "E" MISSES YOU.
I KNOW. I'LL GET OVER FOR A PLAYDATE SOON.
I DON'T WANT TO KNOW WHAT YOU TWO ARE TALKING ABOUT.

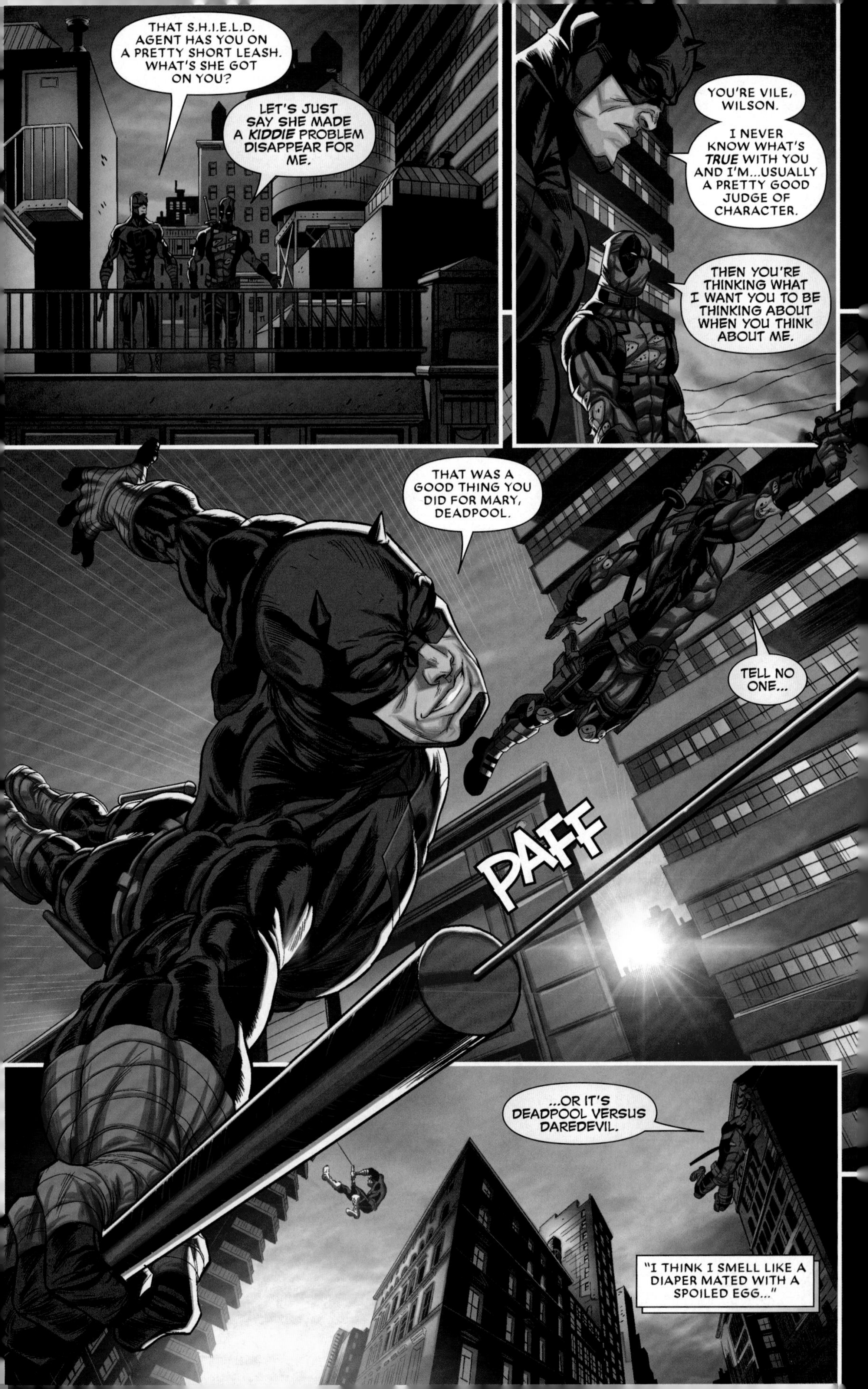
THAT S.H.I.E.L.D. AGENT HAS YOU ON A PRETTY SHORT LEASH. WHAT'S SHE GOT ON YOU?
LET'S JUST SAY SHE MADE A KIDDIE PROBLEM DISAPPEAR FOR ME.
YOU'RE VILE, WILSON.
I NEVER KNOW WHAT'S TRUE WITH YOU AND I'M...USUALLY A PRETTY GOOD JUDGE OF CHARACTER.
THEN YOU'RE THINKING WHAT I WANT YOU TO BE THINKING ABOUT WHEN YOU THINK ABOUT ME.
THAT WAS A GOOD THING YOU DID FOR MARY, DEADPOOL.
TELL NO ONE...
PAFF
...OR IT'S DEADPOOL VERSUS DAREDEVIL.
"I THINK I SMELL LIKE A DIAPER MATED WITH A SPOILED EGG..."

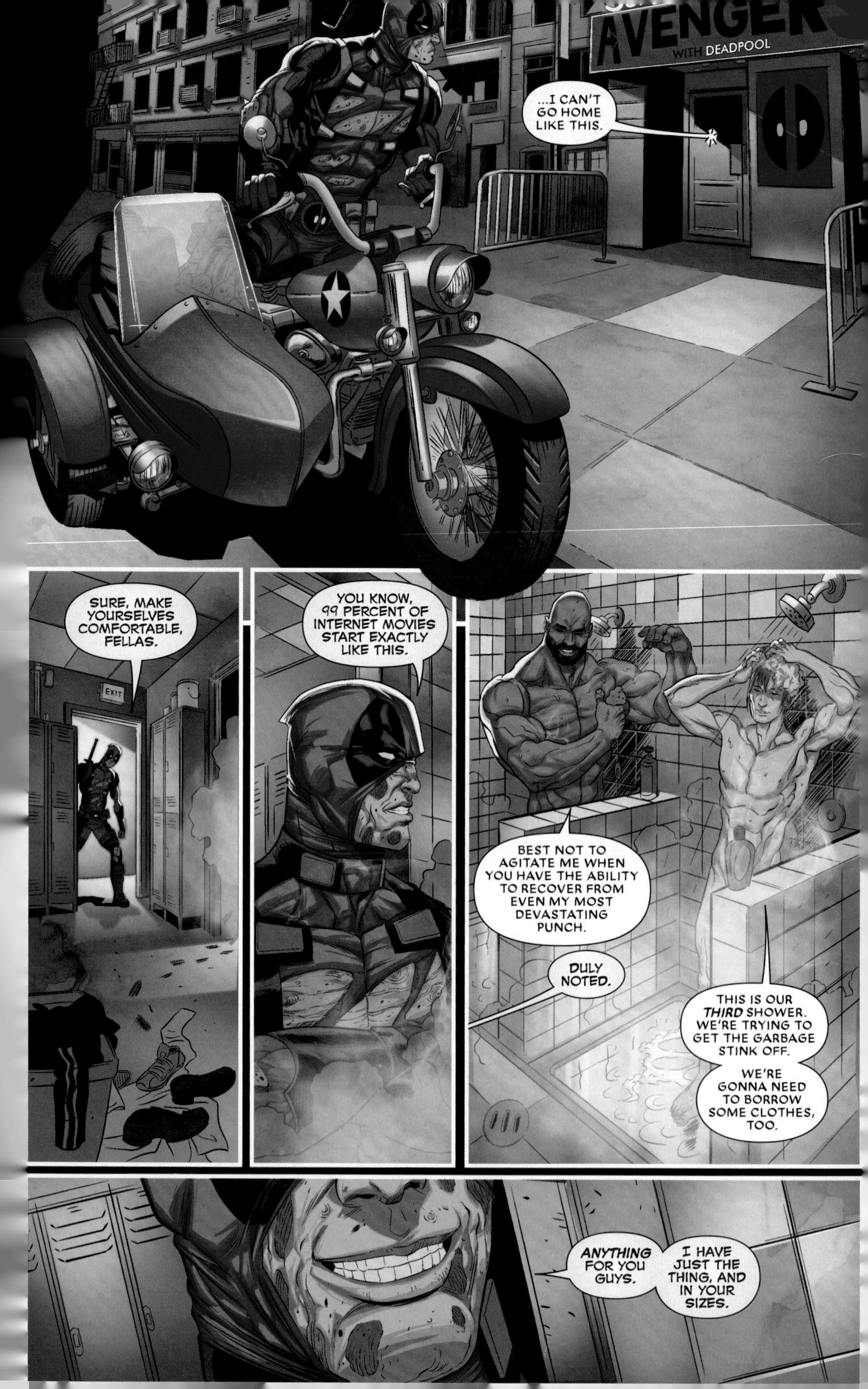
AVENGER
WITH DEADPOOL
...I CAN'T GO HOME LIKE THIS.
SURE, MAKE YOURSELVES COMFORTABLE, FELLAS.
EXIT
YOU KNOW, 99 PERCENT OF INTERNET MOVIES START EXACTLY LIKE THIS.
BEST NOT TO AGITATE ME WHEN YOU HAVE THE ABILITY TO RECOVER FROM EVEN MY MOST DEVASTATING PUNCH.
DULY NOTED.
THIS IS OUR *THIRD* SHOWER. WE'RE TRYING TO GET THE GARBAGE STINK OFF.
WE'RE GONNA NEED TO BORROW SOME CLOTHES, TOO.
ANYTHING FOR YOU GUYS.
I HAVE JUST THE THING, AND IN YOUR SIZES.

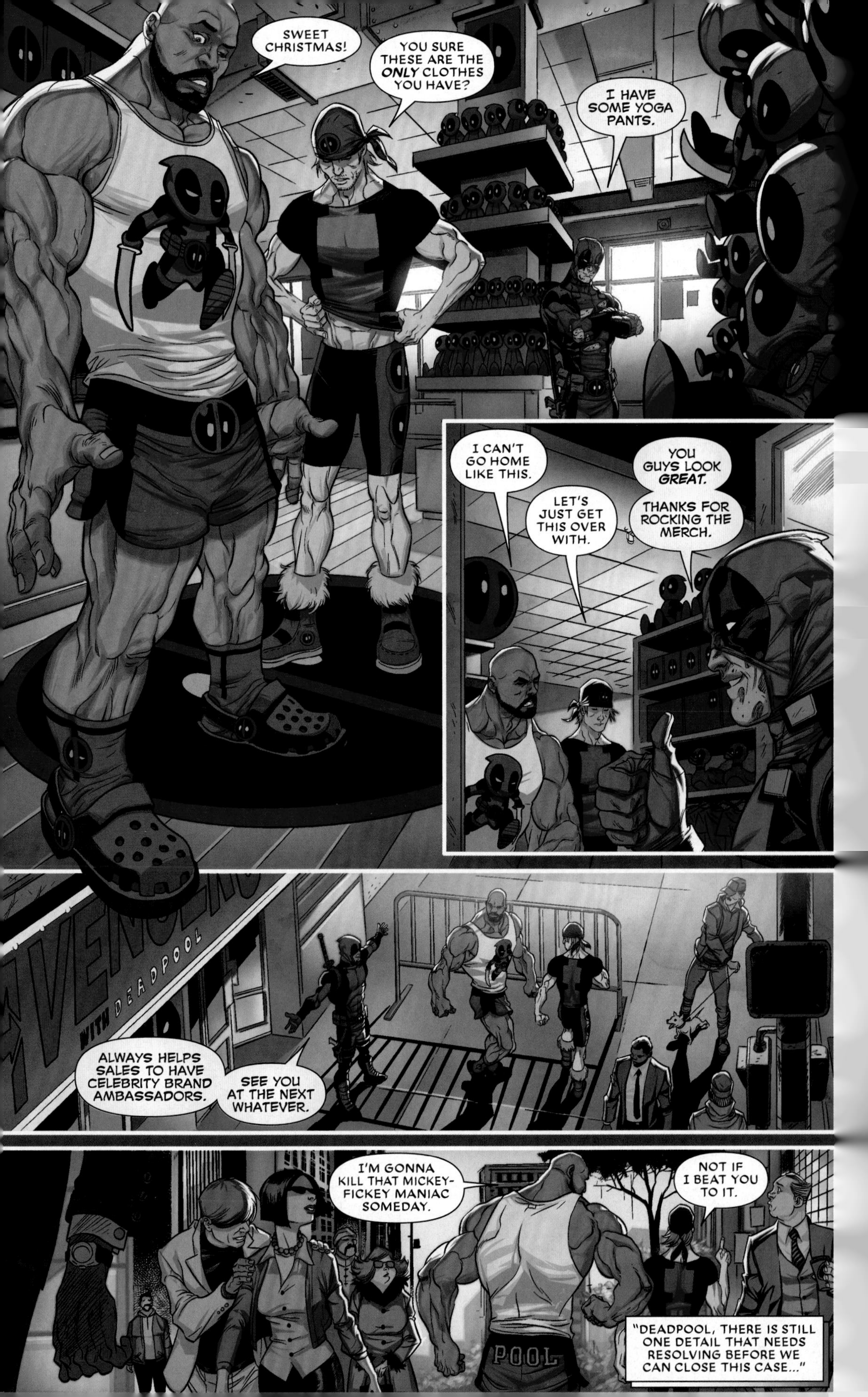
SWEET CHRISTMAS!
YOU SURE THESE ARE THE ONLY CLOTHES YOU HAVE?
I HAVE SOME YOGA PANTS.
I CAN'T GO HOME LIKE THIS.
LET'S JUST GET THIS OVER WITH.
YOU GUYS LOOK GREAT.
THANKS FOR ROCKING THE MERCH.
WITH DEADPOOL
ALWAYS HELPS SALES TO HAVE CELEBRITY BRAND AMBASSADORS.
SEE YOU AT THE NEXT WHATEVER.
I'M GONNA KILL THAT MICKEY-FICKEY MANIAC SOMEDAY.
NOT IF I BEAT YOU TO IT.
POOL
"DEADPOOL, THERE IS STILL ONE DETAIL THAT NEEDS RESOLVING BEFORE WE CAN CLOSE THIS CASE..."

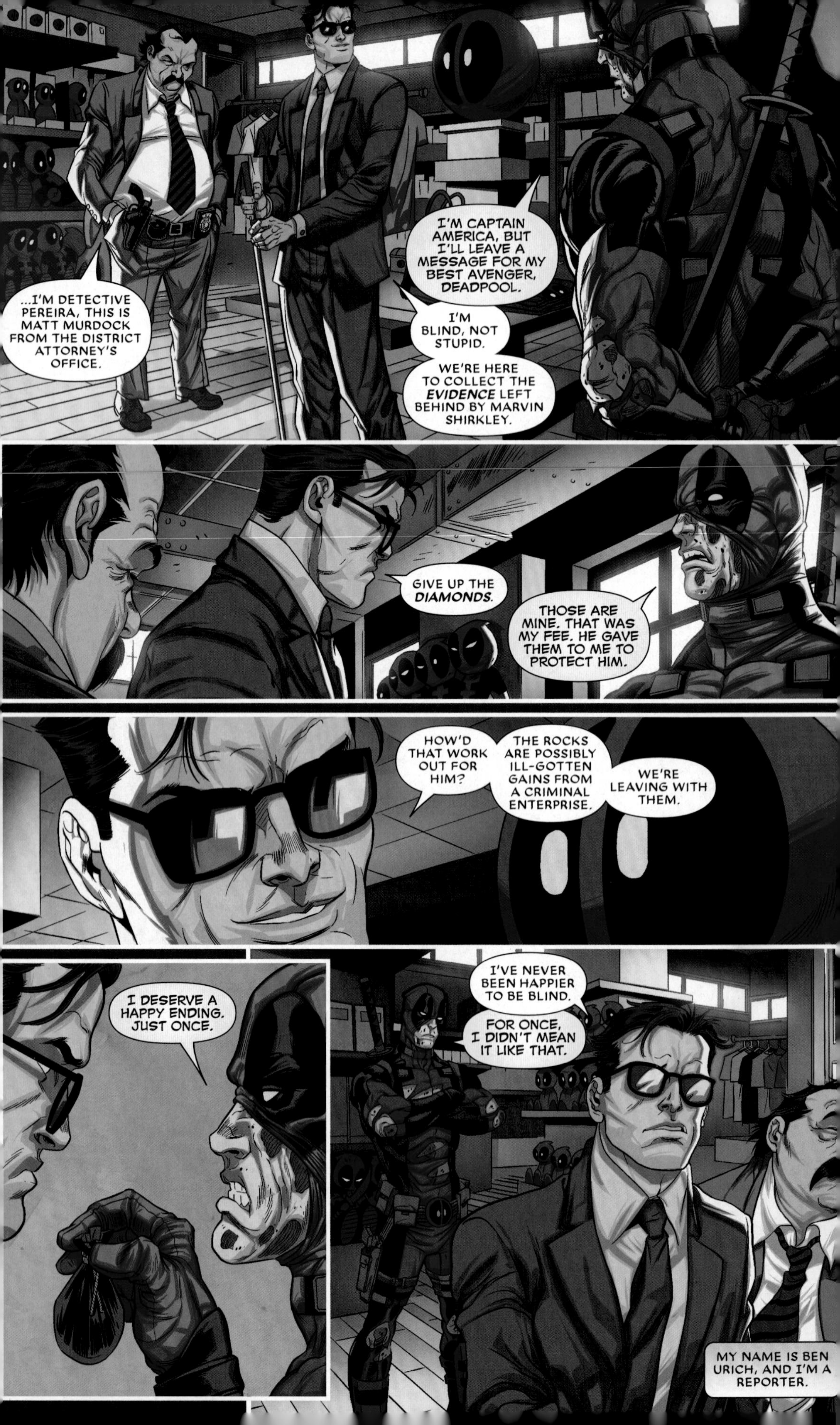
...I'M DETECTIVE PEREIRA, THIS IS MATT MURDOCK FROM THE DISTRICT ATTORNEY'S OFFICE.
I'M CAPTAIN AMERICA, BUT I'LL LEAVE A MESSAGE FOR MY BEST AVENGER, DEADPOOL.
I'M BLIND, NOT STUPID.
WE'RE HERE TO COLLECT THE EVIDENCE LEFT BEHIND BY MARVIN SHIRKLEY.
GIVE UP THE DIAMONDS.
THOSE ARE MINE. THAT WAS MY FEE. HE GAVE THEM TO ME TO PROTECT HIM.
HOW'D THAT WORK OUT FOR HIM?
THE ROCKS ARE POSSIBLY ILL-GOTTEN GAINS FROM A CRIMINAL ENTERPRISE.
WE'RE LEAVING WITH THEM.
I DESERVE A HAPPY ENDING. JUST ONCE.
I'VE NEVER BEEN HAPPIER TO BE BLIND.
FOR ONCE, I DIDN'T MEAN IT LIKE THAT.
MY NAME IS BEN URICH, AND I'M A REPORTER.

I'VE BEEN WRITING ABOUT CRIME IN NEW YORK CITY SINCE THE BONANNOS...

...BUT THIS IS ONE OF THE ODDER STORIES THAT'S COME ACROSS MY DESK.

MARVIN AND HIS LAPTOP MADE IT INTO COURT.

A.D.A. MURDOCK HANDED THE GANGS THEIR BUTTS. THE MOBSTERS ARE IN JAIL AWAITING APPEAL.

NOBODY'S GONNA HEAR FROM MARVIN AGAIN. HE MADE IT INTO THE WITNESS PROTECTION PROGRAM.

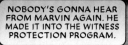

YOU'LL GET USED TO THE KETCHUP ON EGG NOODLES, MARVIN.

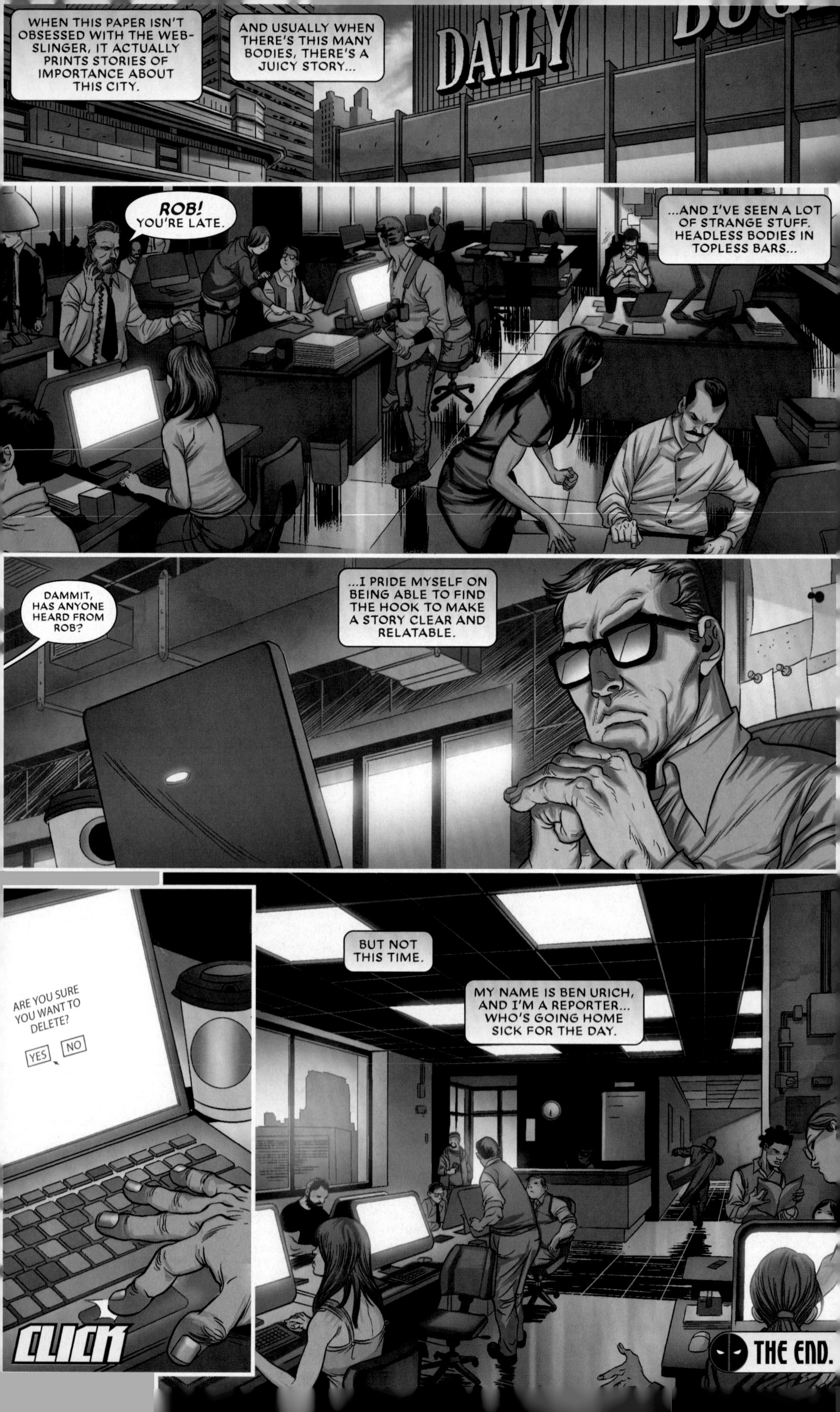

WHEN THIS PAPER ISN'T OBSESSED WITH THE WEB-SLINGER, IT ACTUALLY PRINTS STORIES OF IMPORTANCE ABOUT THIS CITY.
AND USUALLY WHEN THERE'S THIS MANY BODIES, THERE'S A JUICY STORY...
DAILY
ROB! YOU'RE LATE.
...AND I'VE SEEN A LOT OF STRANGE STUFF. HEADLESS BODIES IN TOPLESS BARS...
DAMMIT, HAS ANYONE HEARD FROM ROB?
...I PRIDE MYSELF ON BEING ABLE TO FIND THE HOOK TO MAKE A STORY CLEAR AND RELATABLE.
ARE YOU SURE YOU WANT TO DELETE?
YES
NO
CLICK
BUT NOT THIS TIME.
MY NAME IS BEN URICH, AND I'M A REPORTER... WHO'S GOING HOME SICK FOR THE DAY.
THE END.

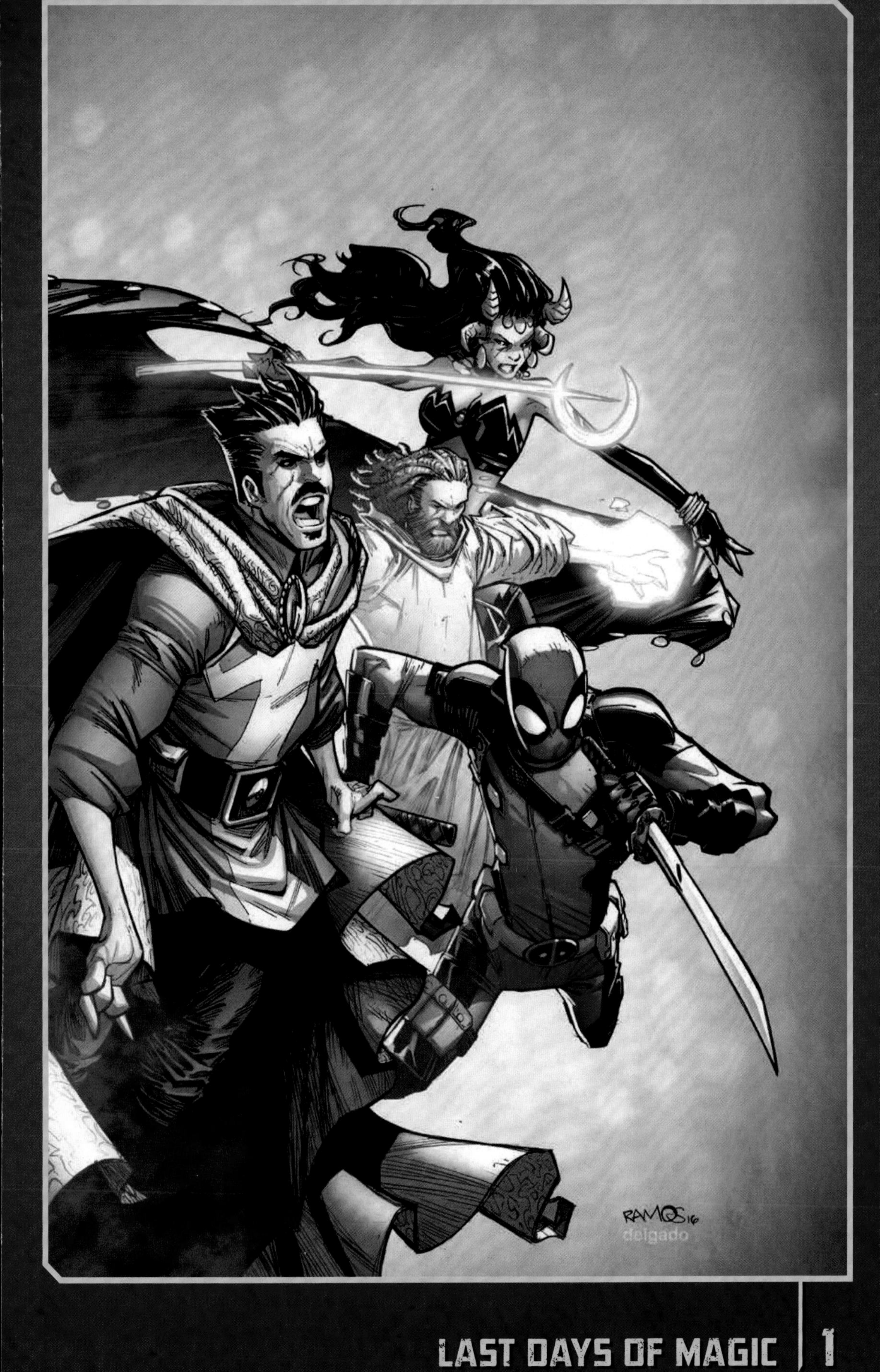
RAMOS16
delgado

LAST DAYS OF MAGIC 1

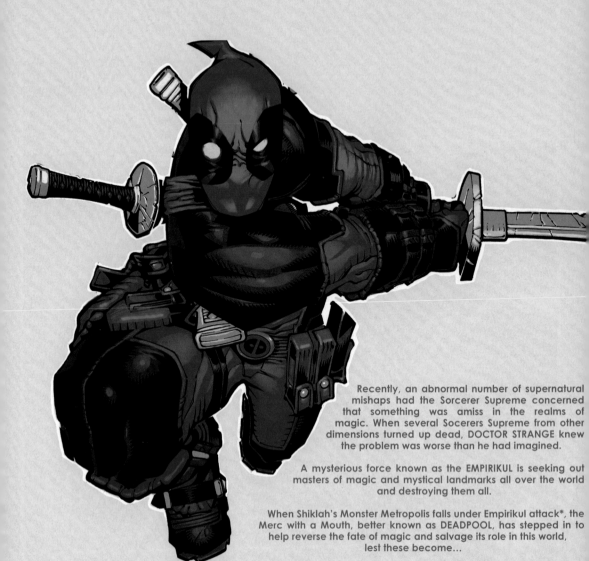

Recently, an abnormal number of supernatural mishaps had the Sorcerer Supreme concerned that something was amiss in the realms of magic. When several Socerers Supreme from other dimensions turned up dead, DOCTOR STRANGE knew the problem was worse than he had imagined.

A mysterious force known as the EMPIRIKUL is seeking out masters of magic and mystical landmarks all over the world and destroying them all.

When Shiklah's Monster Metropolis falls under Empirikul attack*, the Merc with a Mouth, better known as DEADPOOL, has stepped in to help reverse the fate of magic and salvage its role in this world, lest these become…

*Takes place after Deadpool #11

DEADPOOL:
THE LAST DAYS
OF MAGIC

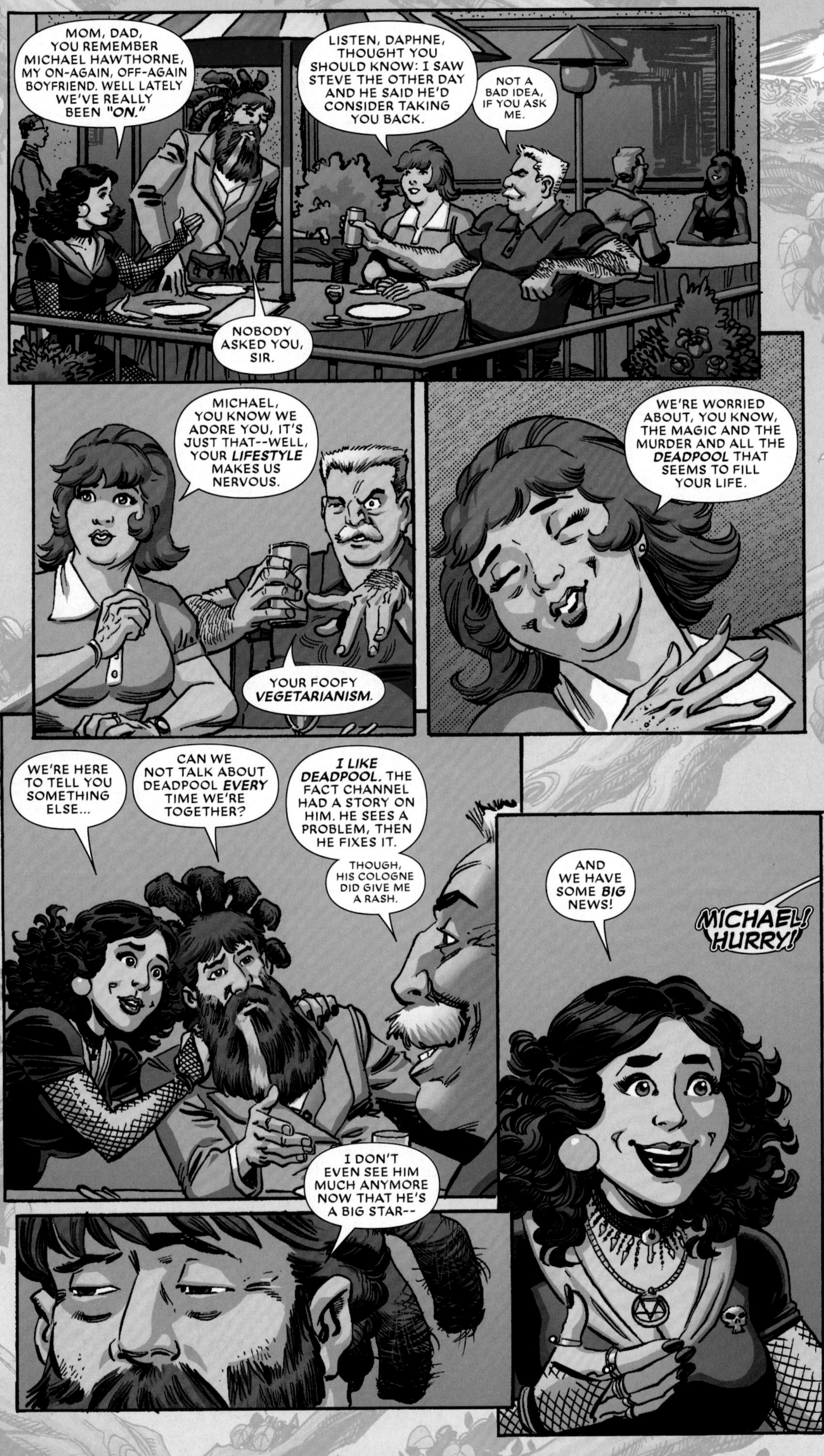
MOM, DAD, YOU REMEMBER MICHAEL HAWTHORNE, MY ON-AGAIN, OFF-AGAIN BOYFRIEND. WELL LATELY WE'VE REALLY BEEN "ON."
LISTEN, DAPHNE, THOUGHT YOU SHOULD KNOW: I SAW STEVE THE OTHER DAY AND HE SAID HE'D CONSIDER TAKING YOU BACK.
NOT A BAD IDEA, IF YOU ASK ME.
NOBODY ASKED YOU, SIR.
MICHAEL, YOU KNOW WE ADORE YOU, IT'S JUST THAT--WELL, YOUR LIFESTYLE MAKES US NERVOUS.
YOUR FOOFY VEGETARIANISM.
WE'RE WORRIED ABOUT, YOU KNOW, THE MAGIC AND THE MURDER AND ALL THE DEADPOOL THAT SEEMS TO FILL YOUR LIFE.
WE'RE HERE TO TELL YOU SOMETHING ELSE...
CAN WE NOT TALK ABOUT DEADPOOL EVERY TIME WE'RE TOGETHER?
I LIKE DEADPOOL. THE FACT CHANNEL HAD A STORY ON HIM. HE SEES A PROBLEM, THEN HE FIXES IT.
THOUGH, HIS COLOGNE DID GIVE ME A RASH.
I DON'T EVEN SEE HIM MUCH ANYMORE NOW THAT HE'S A BIG STAR--
AND WE HAVE SOME BIG NEWS!
MICHAEL! HURRY!

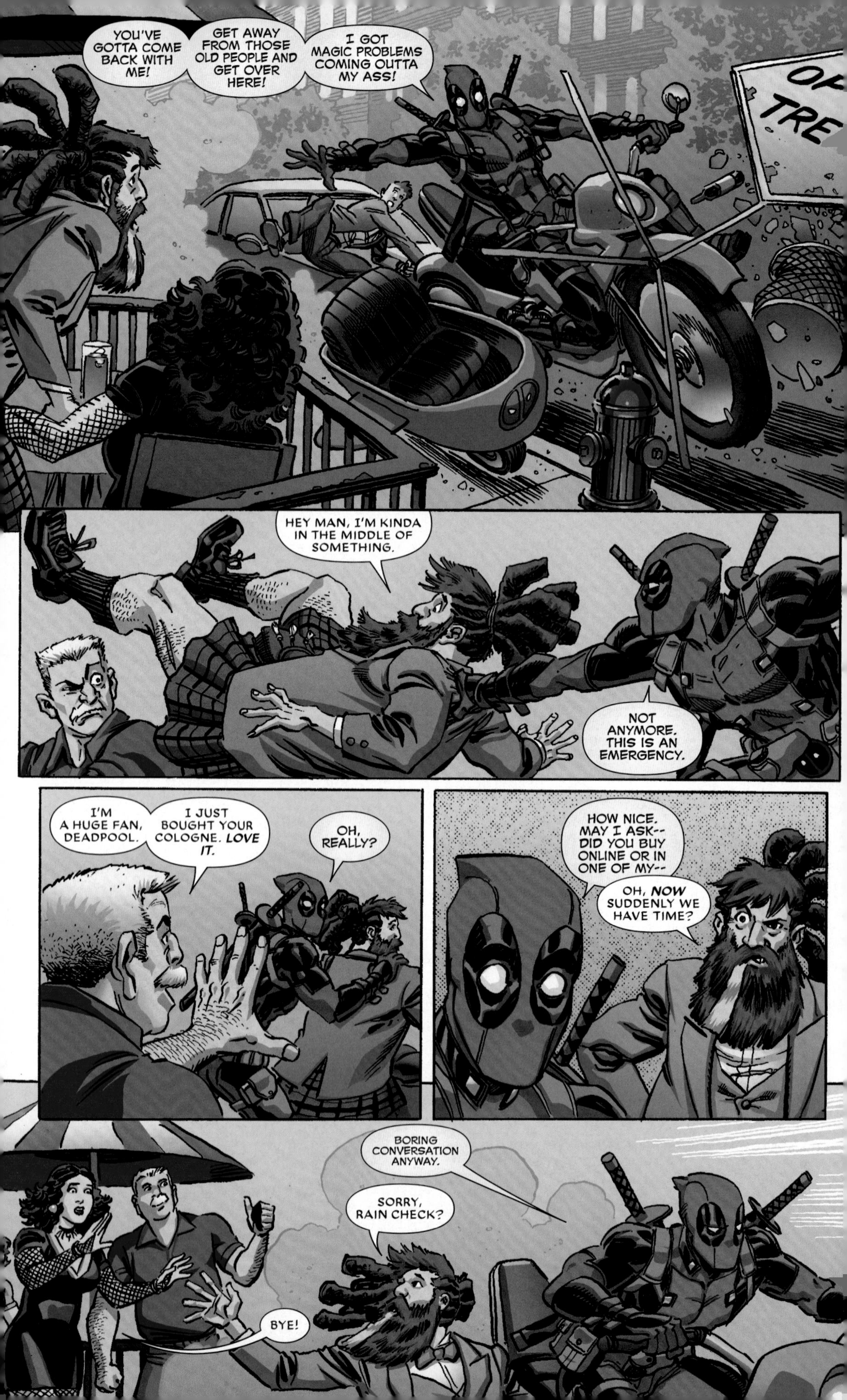

YOU'VE GOTTA COME BACK WITH ME!
GET AWAY FROM THOSE OLD PEOPLE AND GET OVER HERE!
I GOT MAGIC PROBLEMS COMING OUTTA MY ASS!
HEY MAN, I'M KINDA IN THE MIDDLE OF SOMETHING.
NOT ANYMORE. THIS IS AN EMERGENCY.
I'M A HUGE FAN, DEADPOOL.
I JUST BOUGHT YOUR COLOGNE. LOVE IT.
OH, REALLY?
HOW NICE. MAY I ASK-- DID YOU BUY ONLINE OR IN ONE OF MY--
OH, NOW SUDDENLY WE HAVE TIME?
BORING CONVERSATION ANYWAY.
SORRY, RAIN CHECK?
BYE!

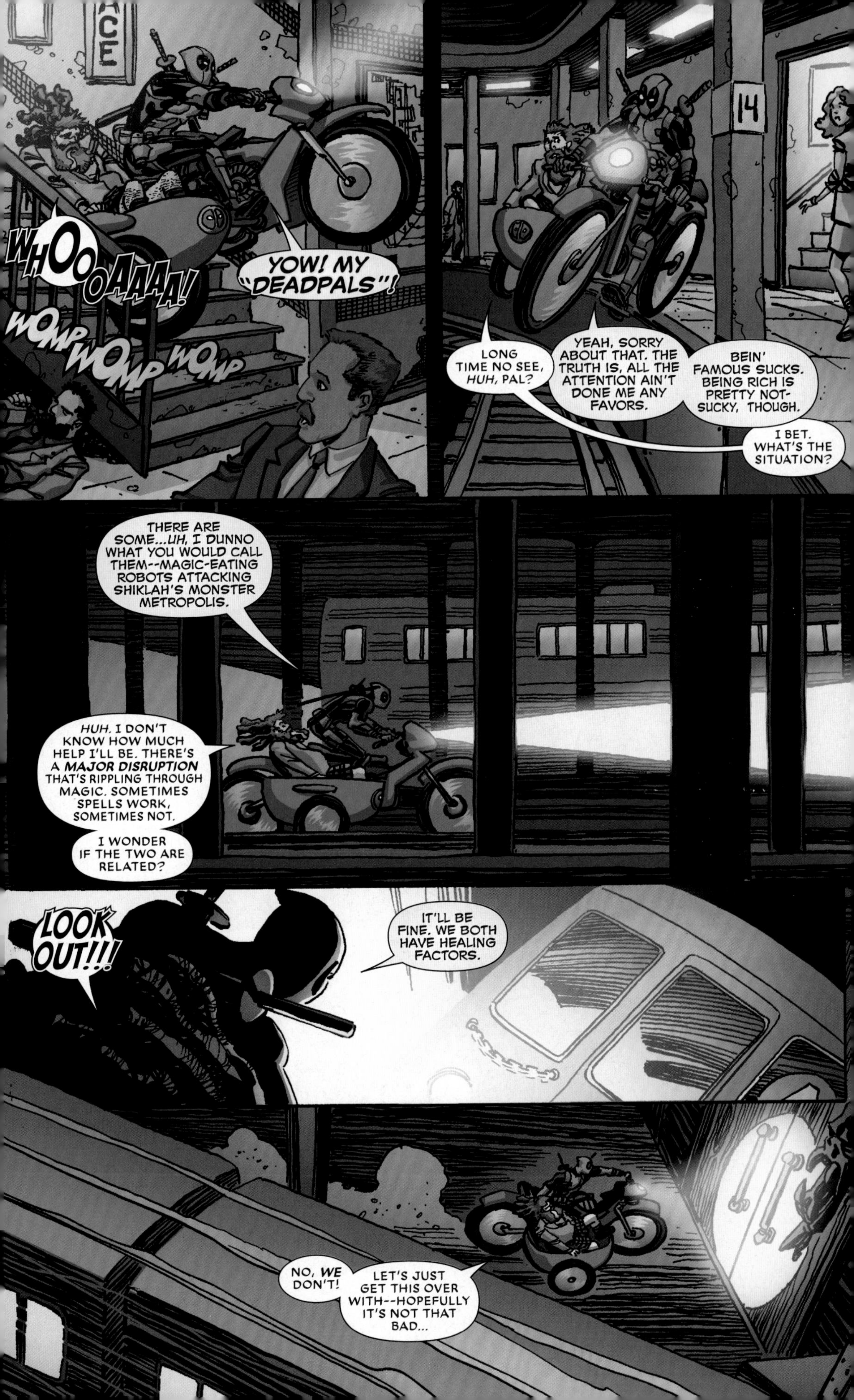
WHOOOOAAAAA!
WOMP WOMP WOMP
YOW! MY "DEADPALS"!
LONG TIME NO SEE, HUH, PAL?
YEAH, SORRY ABOUT THAT. THE TRUTH IS, ALL THE ATTENTION AIN'T DONE ME ANY FAVORS.
BEIN' FAMOUS SUCKS. BEING RICH IS PRETTY NOT-SUCKY, THOUGH.
I BET. WHAT'S THE SITUATION?
14
THERE ARE SOME...UH, I DUNNO WHAT YOU WOULD CALL THEM--MAGIC-EATING ROBOTS ATTACKING SHIKLAH'S MONSTER METROPOLIS.
HUH. I DON'T KNOW HOW MUCH HELP I'LL BE. THERE'S A MAJOR DISRUPTION THAT'S RIPPLING THROUGH MAGIC. SOMETIMES SPELLS WORK, SOMETIMES NOT.
I WONDER IF THE TWO ARE RELATED?
LOOK OUT!!!
IT'LL BE FINE. WE BOTH HAVE HEALING FACTORS.
NO, WE DON'T!
LET'S JUST GET THIS OVER WITH--HOPEFULLY IT'S NOT THAT BAD...

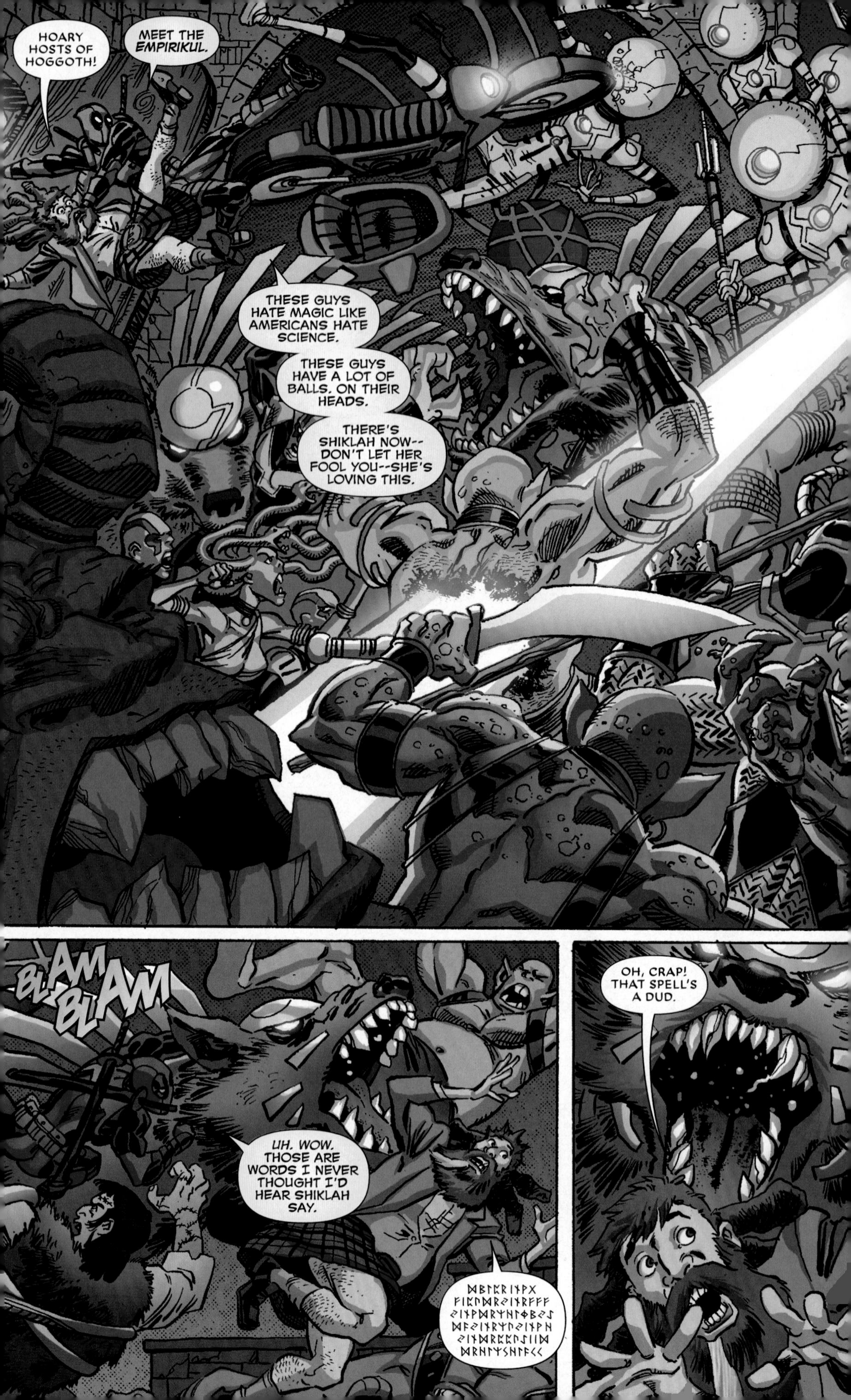
HOARY HOSTS OF HOGGOTH!
MEET THE *EMPIRIKUL.*
THESE GUYS HATE MAGIC LIKE AMERICANS HATE SCIENCE.
THESE GUYS HAVE A LOT OF BALLS. ON THEIR HEADS.
THERE'S SHIKLAH NOW--DON'T LET HER FOOL YOU--SHE'S LOVING THIS.
BLAM BLAM
UH. WOW. THOSE ARE WORDS I NEVER THOUGHT I'D HEAR SHIKLAH SAY.
OH, CRAP! THAT SPELL'S A DUD.

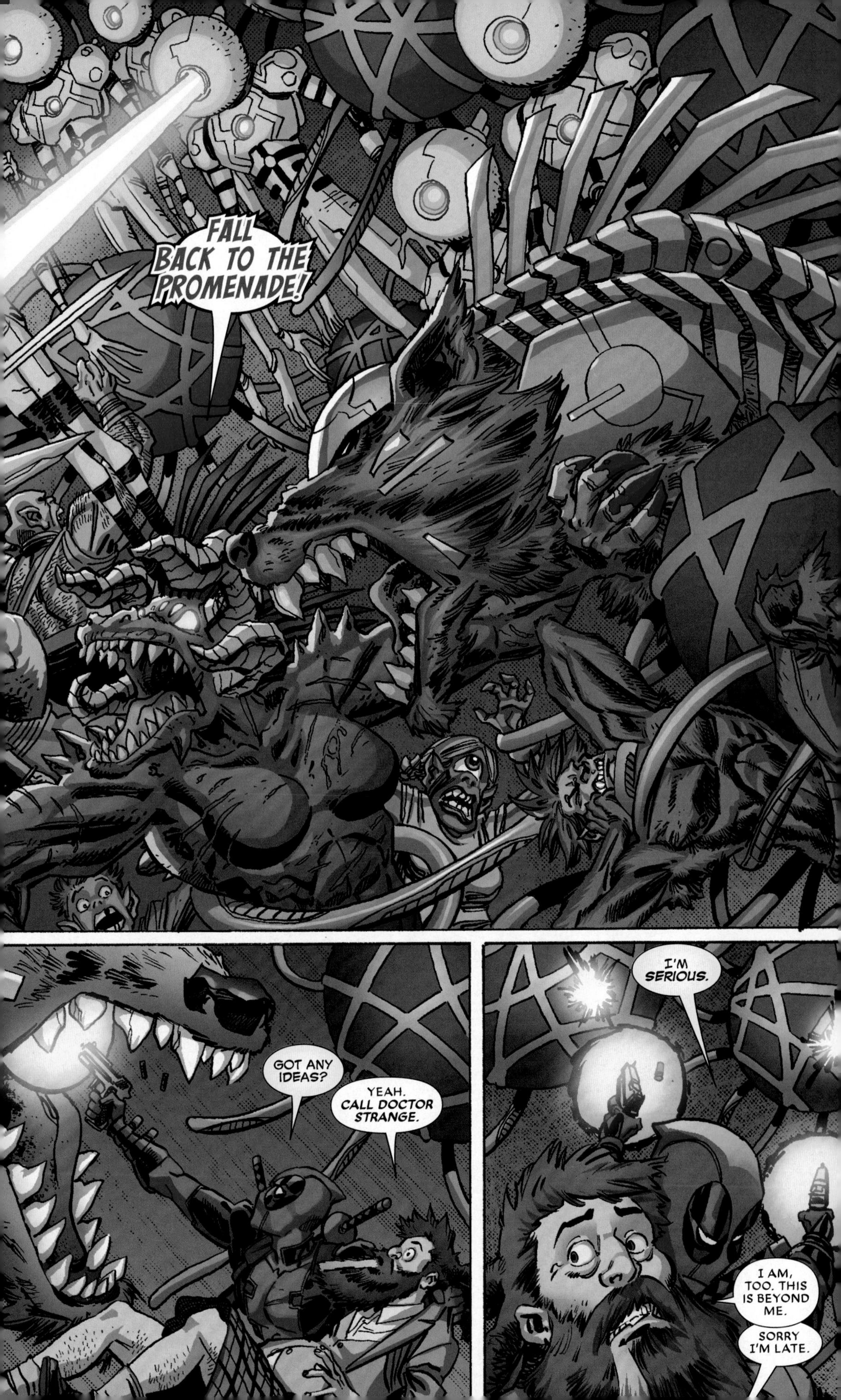

FALL BACK TO THE PROMENADE!
GOT ANY IDEAS?
YEAH. CALL DOCTOR STRANGE.
I'M SERIOUS.
I AM, TOO. THIS IS BEYOND ME.
SORRY I'M LATE.

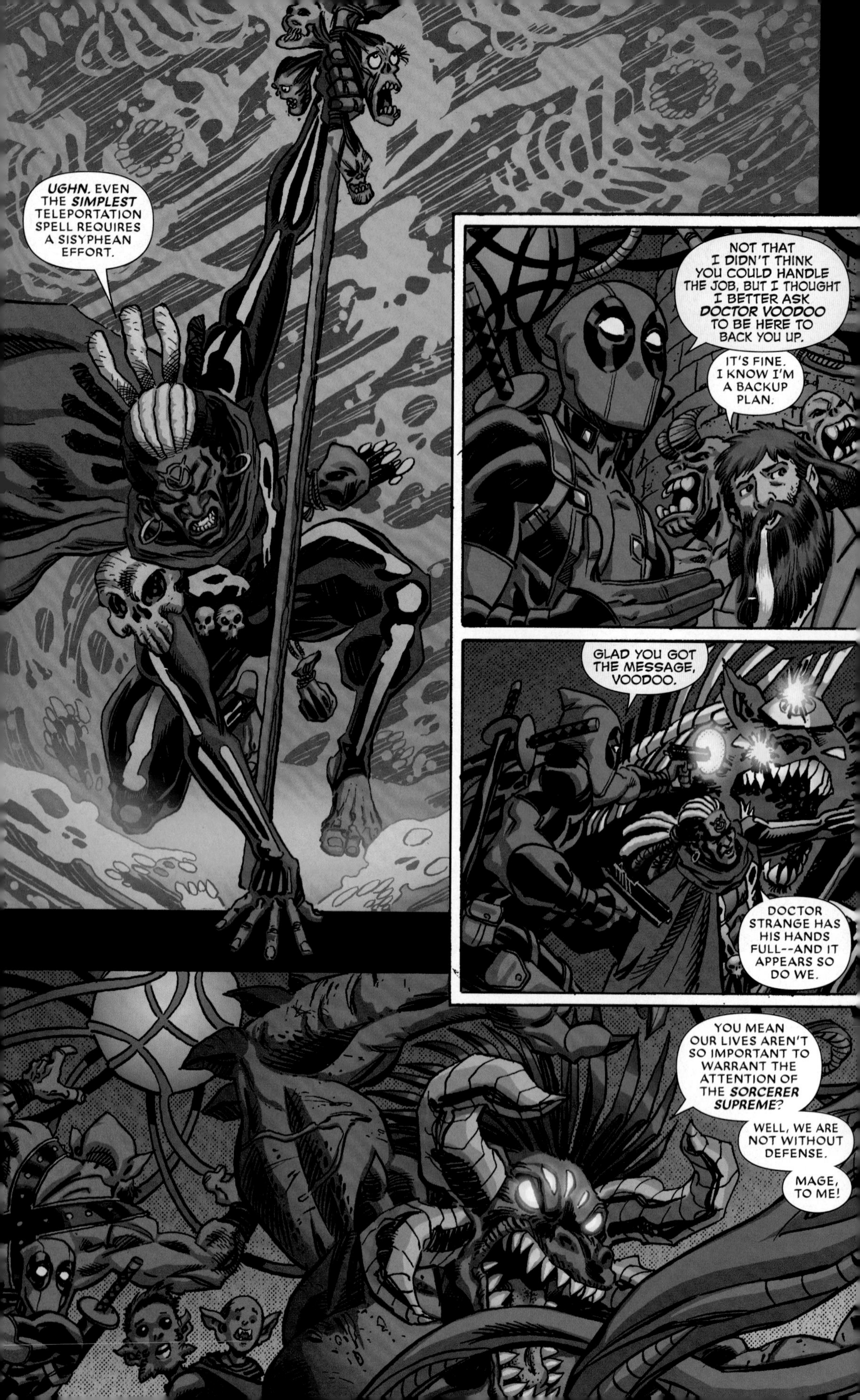
UGHN. EVEN THE SIMPLEST TELEPORTATION SPELL REQUIRES A SISYPHEAN EFFORT.
NOT THAT I DIDN'T THINK YOU COULD HANDLE THE JOB, BUT I THOUGHT I BETTER ASK DOCTOR VOODOO TO BE HERE TO BACK YOU UP.
IT'S FINE. I KNOW I'M A BACKUP PLAN.
GLAD YOU GOT THE MESSAGE, VOODOO.
DOCTOR STRANGE HAS HIS HANDS FULL--AND IT APPEARS SO DO WE.
YOU MEAN OUR LIVES AREN'T SO IMPORTANT TO WARRANT THE ATTENTION OF THE SORCERER SUPREME?
WELL, WE ARE NOT WITHOUT DEFENSE.
MAGE, TO ME!

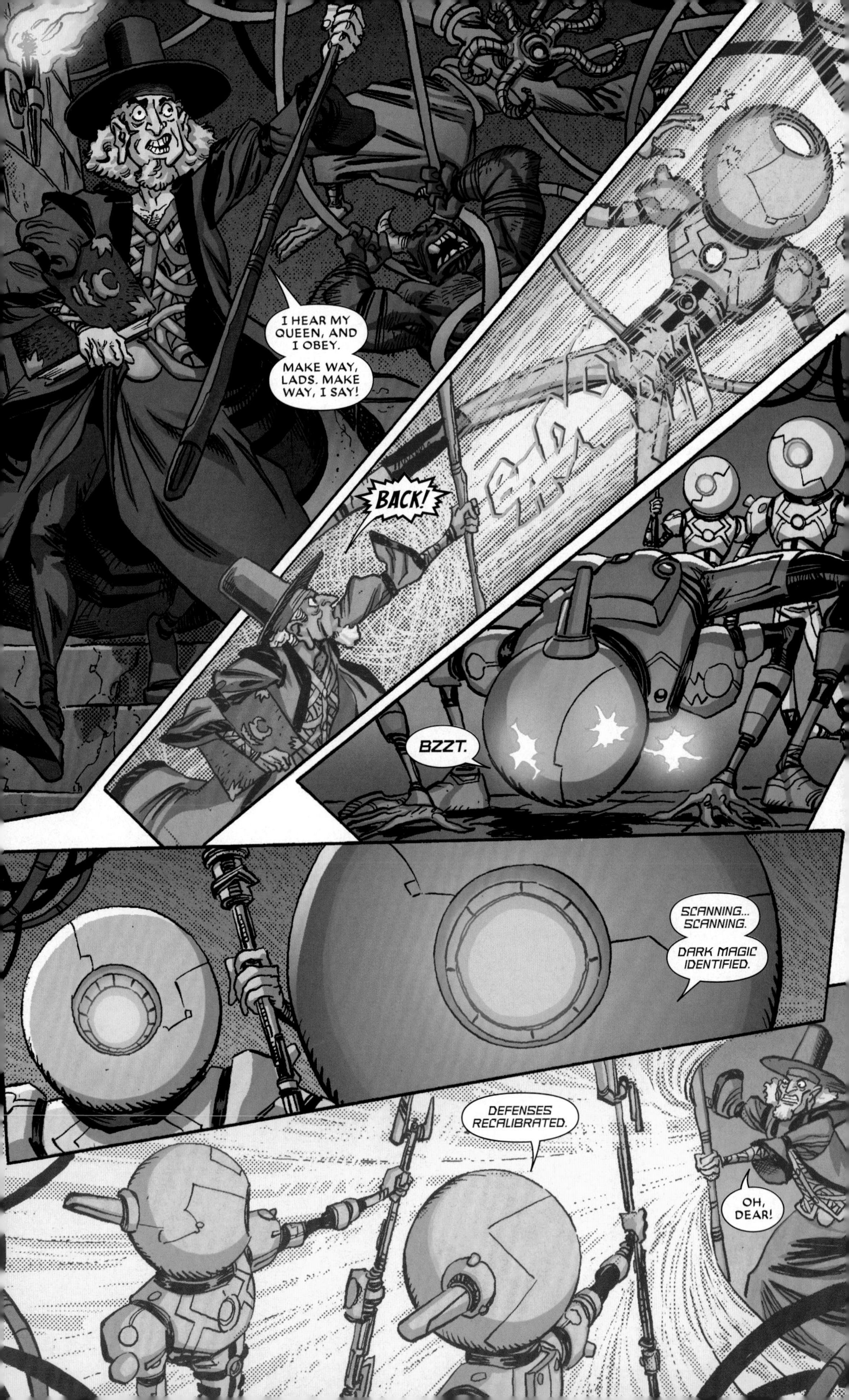
I HEAR MY QUEEN, AND I OBEY.
MAKE WAY, LADS. MAKE WAY, I SAY!
BACK!
BZZT.
SCANNING... SCANNING.
DARK MAGIC IDENTIFIED.
DEFENSES RECALIBRATED.
OH, DEAR!

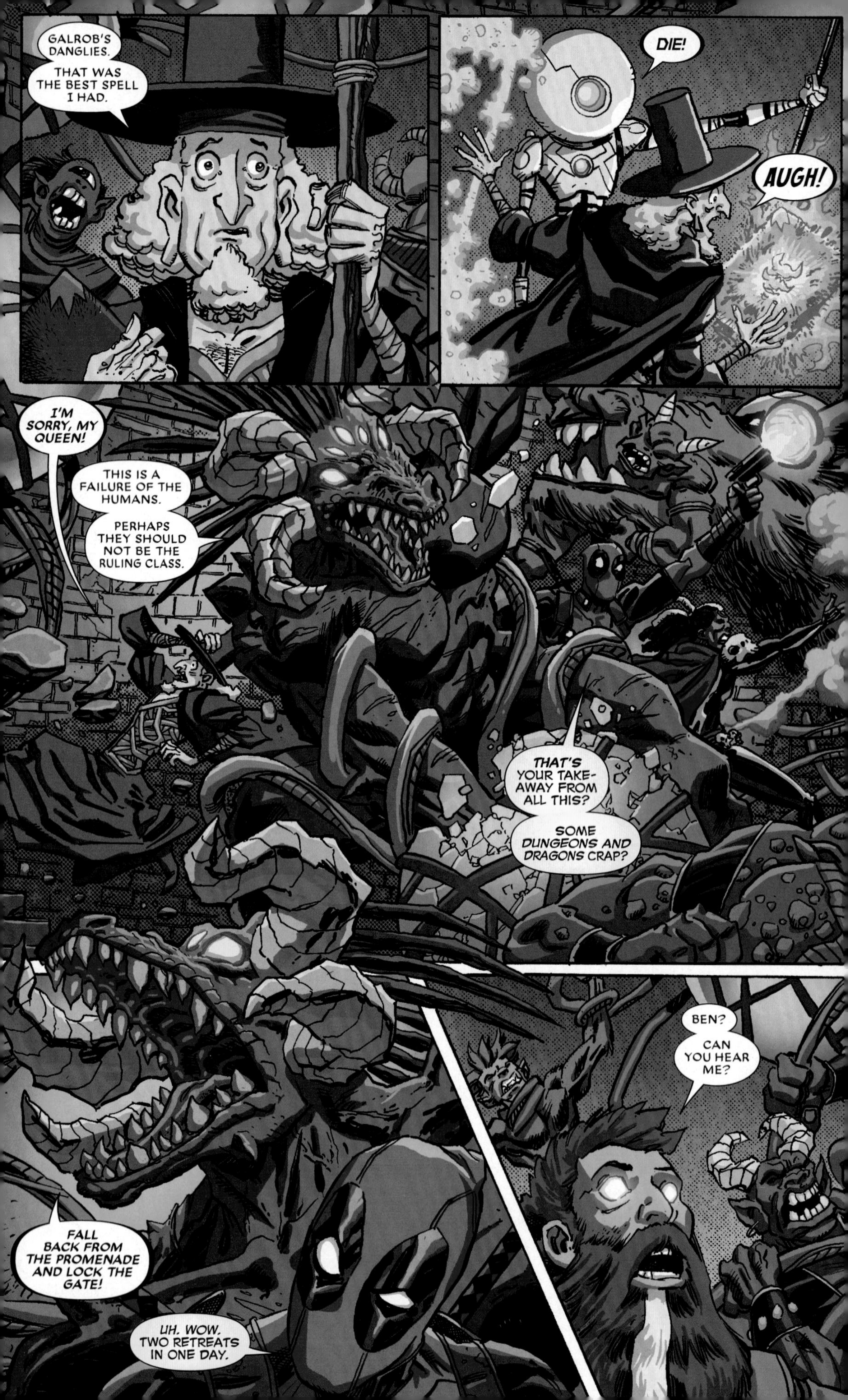
GALROB'S DANGLIES.
THAT WAS THE BEST SPELL I HAD.
DIE!
AUGH!
I'M SORRY, MY QUEEN!
THIS IS A FAILURE OF THE HUMANS.
PERHAPS THEY SHOULD NOT BE THE RULING CLASS.
THAT'S YOUR TAKE-AWAY FROM ALL THIS?
SOME DUNGEONS AND DRAGONS CRAP?
BEN?
CAN YOU HEAR ME?
FALL BACK FROM THE PROMENADE AND LOCK THE GATE!
UH. WOW. TWO RETREATS IN ONE DAY.

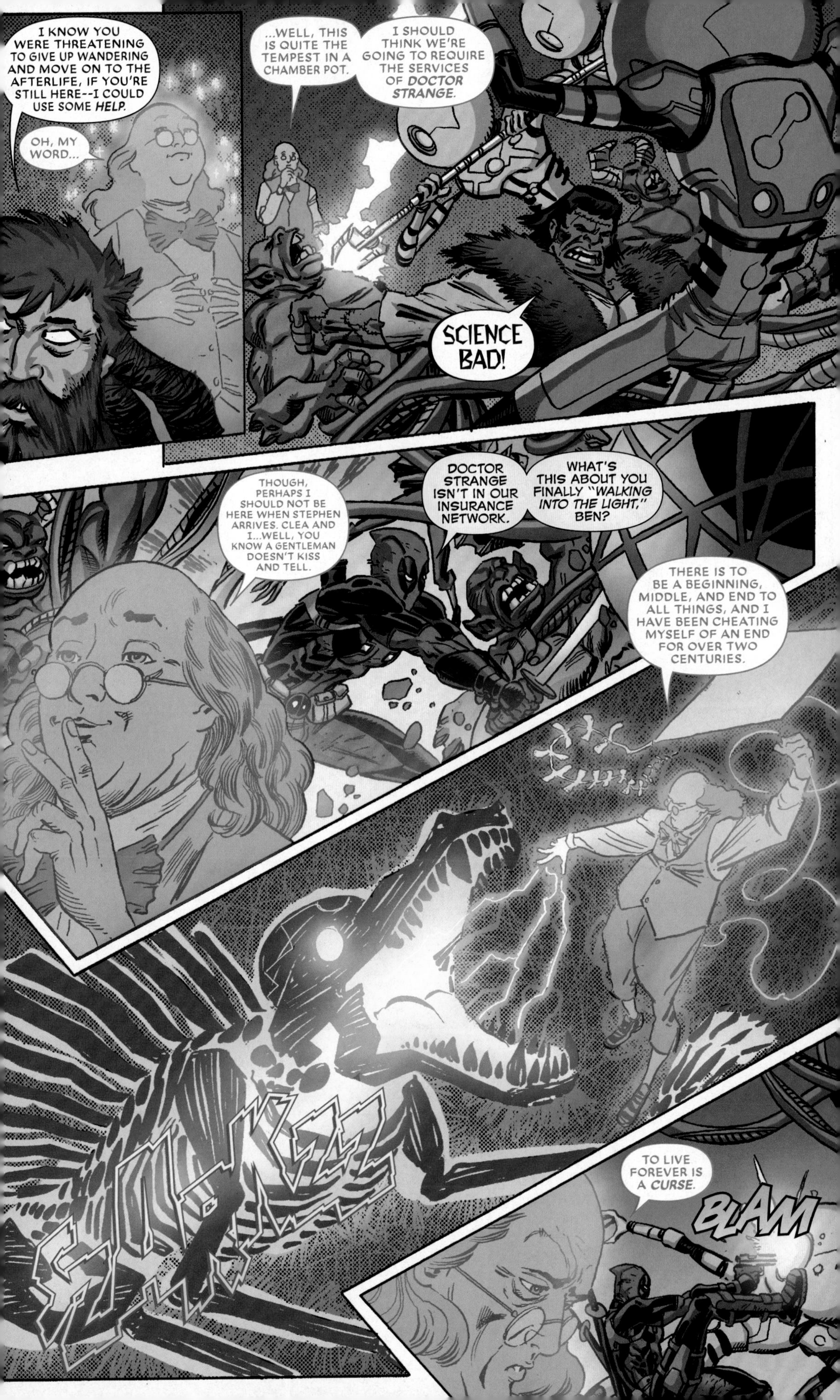

I KNOW YOU WERE THREATENING TO GIVE UP WANDERING AND MOVE ON TO THE AFTERLIFE, IF YOU'RE STILL HERE--I COULD USE SOME *HELP.*
OH, MY WORD...
...WELL, THIS IS QUITE THE TEMPEST IN A CHAMBER POT.
I SHOULD THINK WE'RE GOING TO REQUIRE THE SERVICES OF *DOCTOR STRANGE.*
SCIENCE BAD!
THOUGH, PERHAPS I SHOULD NOT BE HERE WHEN STEPHEN ARRIVES. CLEA AND I...WELL, YOU KNOW A GENTLEMAN DOESN'T KISS AND TELL.
DOCTOR STRANGE ISN'T IN OUR INSURANCE NETWORK.
WHAT'S THIS ABOUT YOU FINALLY *"WALKING INTO THE LIGHT,"* BEN?
THERE IS TO BE A BEGINNING, MIDDLE, AND END TO ALL THINGS, AND I HAVE BEEN CHEATING MYSELF OF AN END FOR OVER TWO CENTURIES.
TO LIVE FOREVER IS A *CURSE.*
BLAM

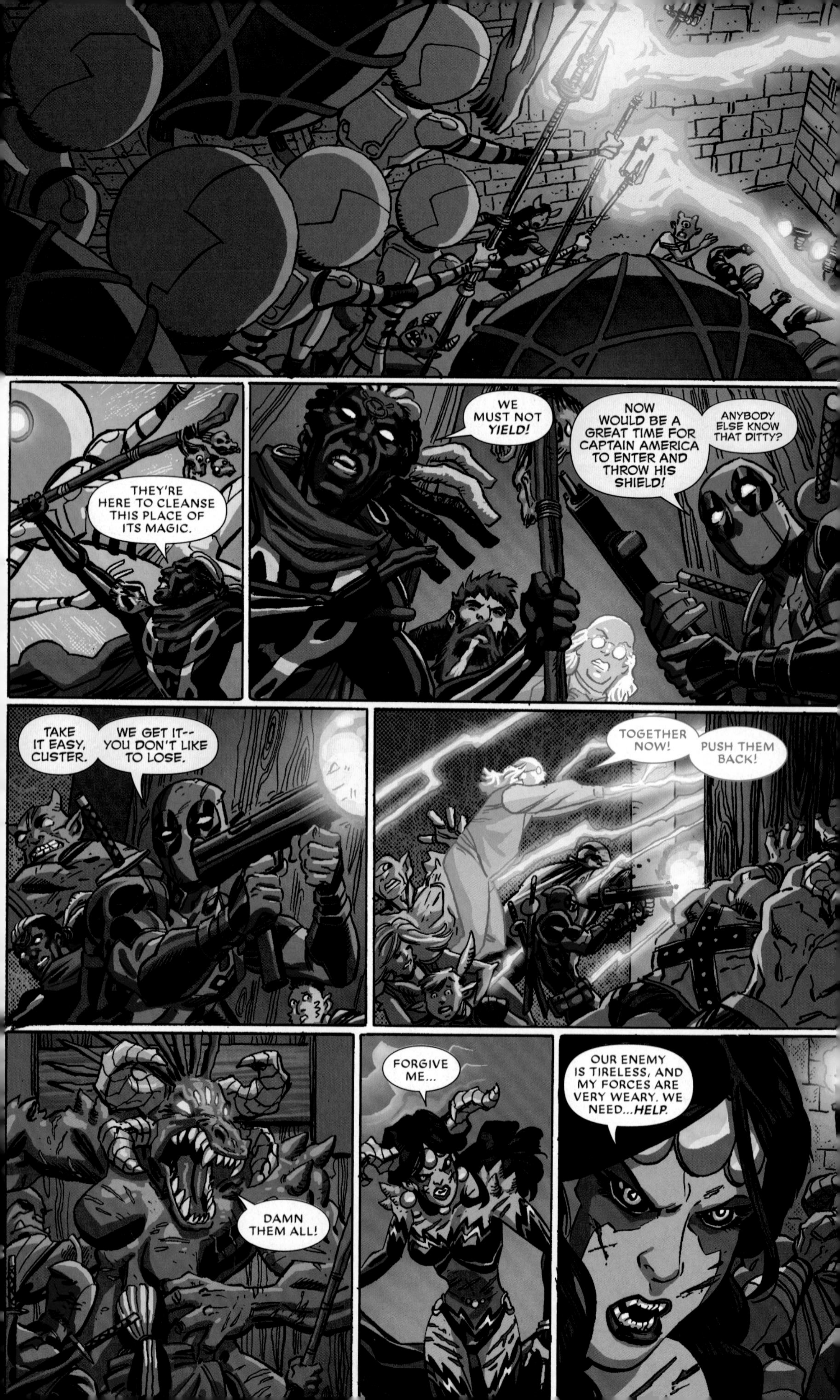

THEY'RE HERE TO CLEANSE THIS PLACE OF ITS MAGIC.
WE MUST NOT *YIELD!*
NOW WOULD BE A GREAT TIME FOR CAPTAIN AMERICA TO ENTER AND THROW HIS SHIELD!
ANYBODY ELSE KNOW THAT DITTY?
TAKE IT EASY, CUSTER.
WE GET IT-- YOU DON'T LIKE TO LOSE.
TOGETHER NOW!
PUSH THEM BACK!
DAMN THEM ALL!
FORGIVE ME...
OUR ENEMY IS TIRELESS, AND MY FORCES ARE VERY WEARY. WE NEED...*HELP.*

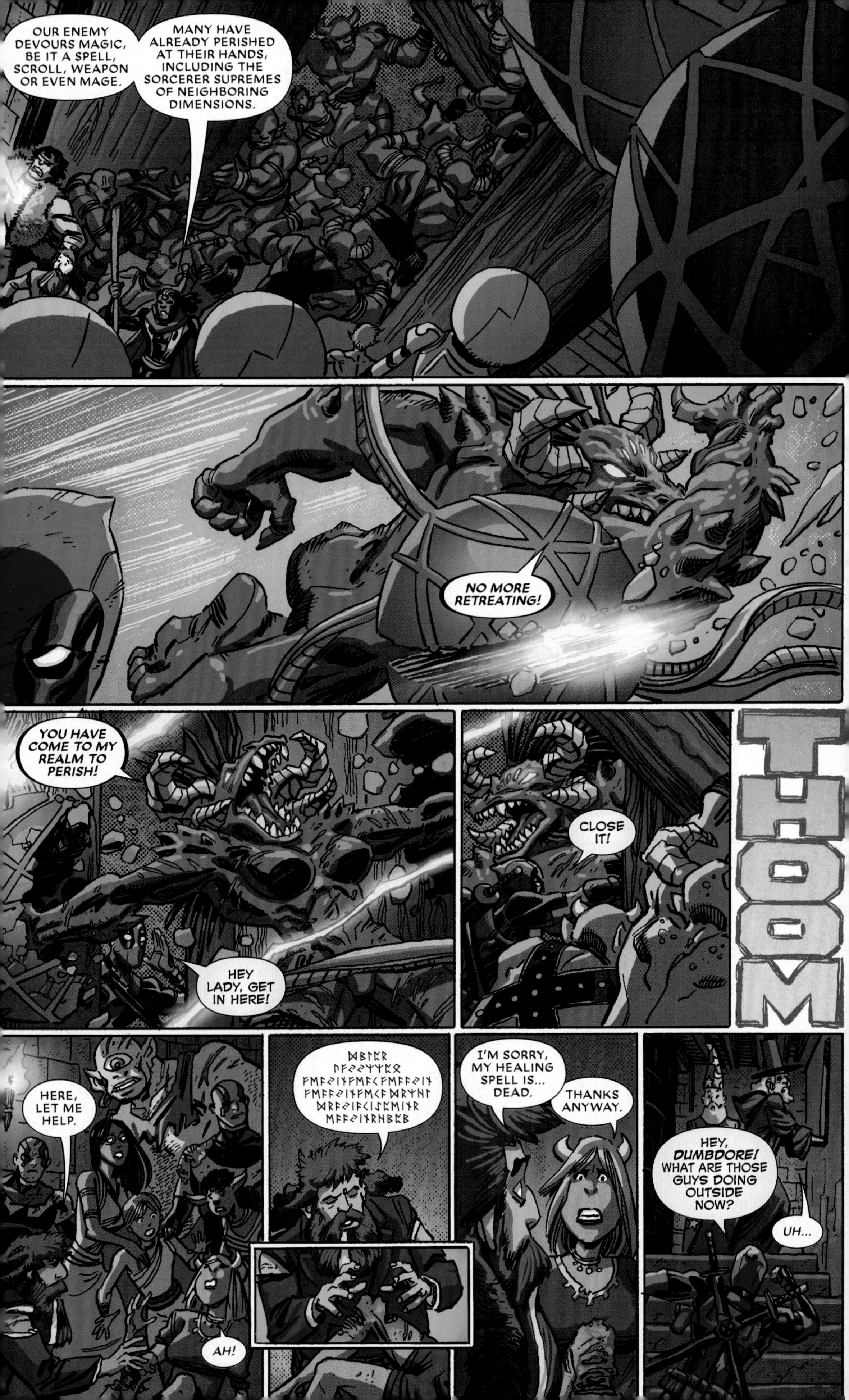
OUR ENEMY DEVOURS MAGIC, BE IT A SPELL, SCROLL, WEAPON OR EVEN MAGE.
MANY HAVE ALREADY PERISHED AT THEIR HANDS, INCLUDING THE SORCERER SUPREMES OF NEIGHBORING DIMENSIONS.
NO MORE RETREATING!
YOU HAVE COME TO MY REALM TO PERISH!
HEY LADY, GET IN HERE!
CLOSE IT!
THOOM
HERE, LET ME HELP.
AH!
I'M SORRY, MY HEALING SPELL IS... DEAD.
THANKS ANYWAY.
HEY, DUMBDORE! WHAT ARE THOSE GUYS DOING OUTSIDE NOW?
UH...

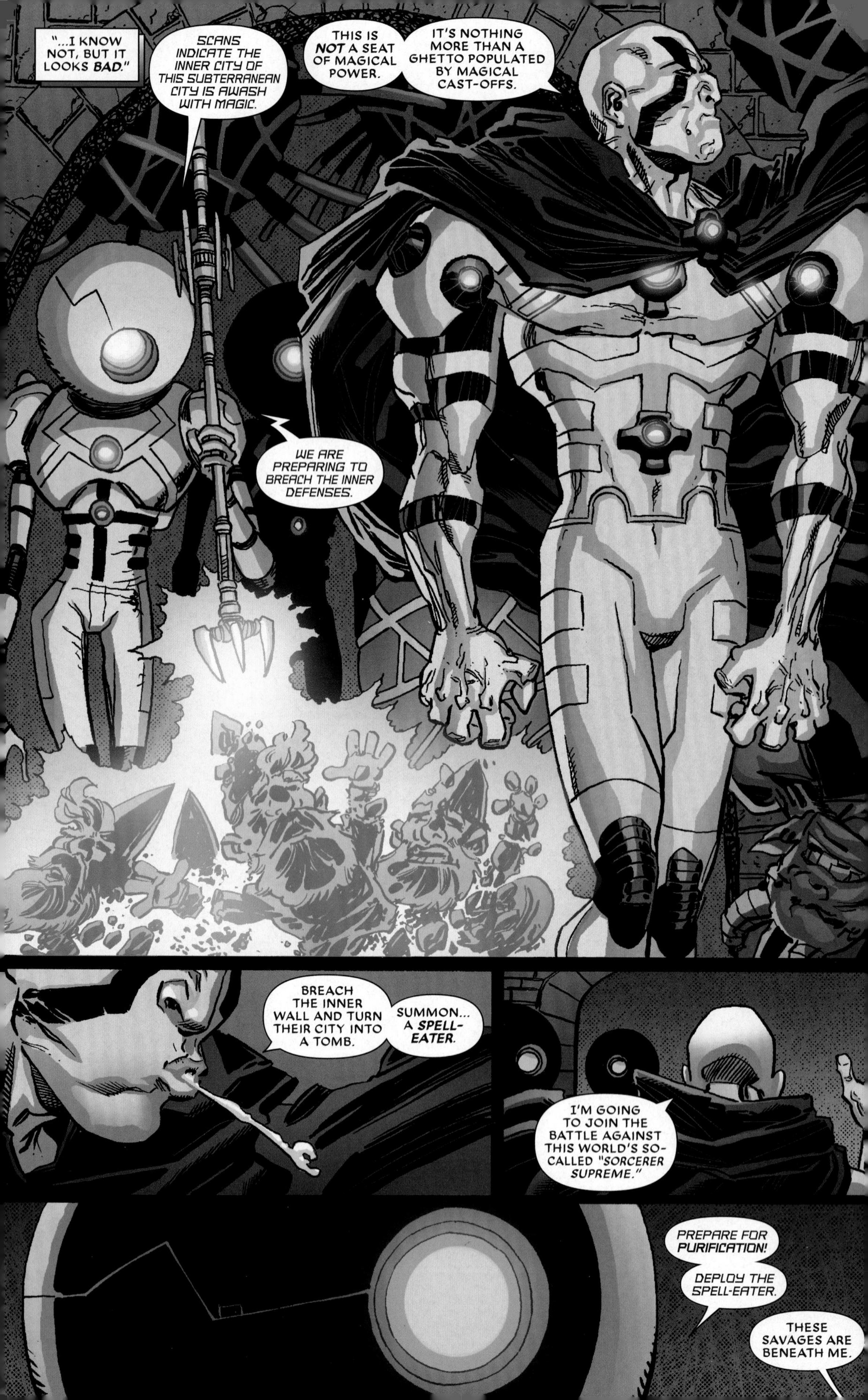
"...I KNOW NOT, BUT IT LOOKS BAD."
SCANS INDICATE THE INNER CITY OF THIS SUBTERRANEAN CITY IS AWASH WITH MAGIC.
THIS IS NOT A SEAT OF MAGICAL POWER.
IT'S NOTHING MORE THAN A GHETTO POPULATED BY MAGICAL CAST-OFFS.
WE ARE PREPARING TO BREACH THE INNER DEFENSES.
BREACH THE INNER WALL AND TURN THEIR CITY INTO A TOMB.
SUMMON... A SPELL-EATER.
I'M GOING TO JOIN THE BATTLE AGAINST THIS WORLD'S SO-CALLED "SORCERER SUPREME."
PREPARE FOR PURIFICATION!
DEPLOY THE SPELL-EATER.
THESE SAVAGES ARE BENEATH ME.

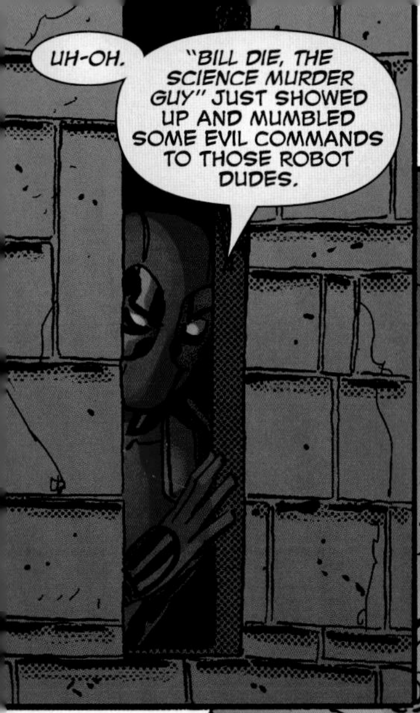
UH-OH.
"BILL DIE, THE SCIENCE MURDER GUY" JUST SHOWED UP AND MUMBLED SOME EVIL COMMANDS TO THOSE ROBOT DUDES.

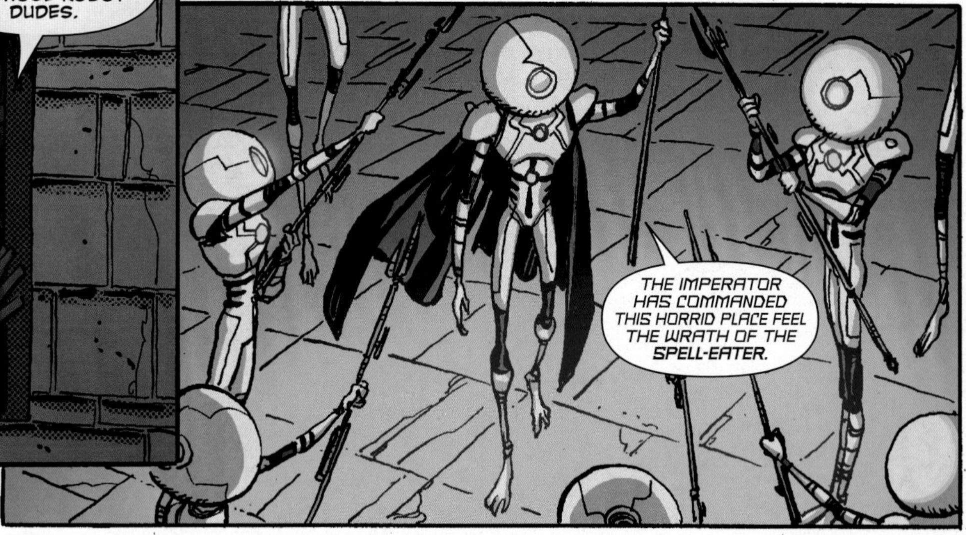
THE IMPERATOR HAS COMMANDED THIS HORRID PLACE FEEL THE WRATH OF THE SPELL-EATER.

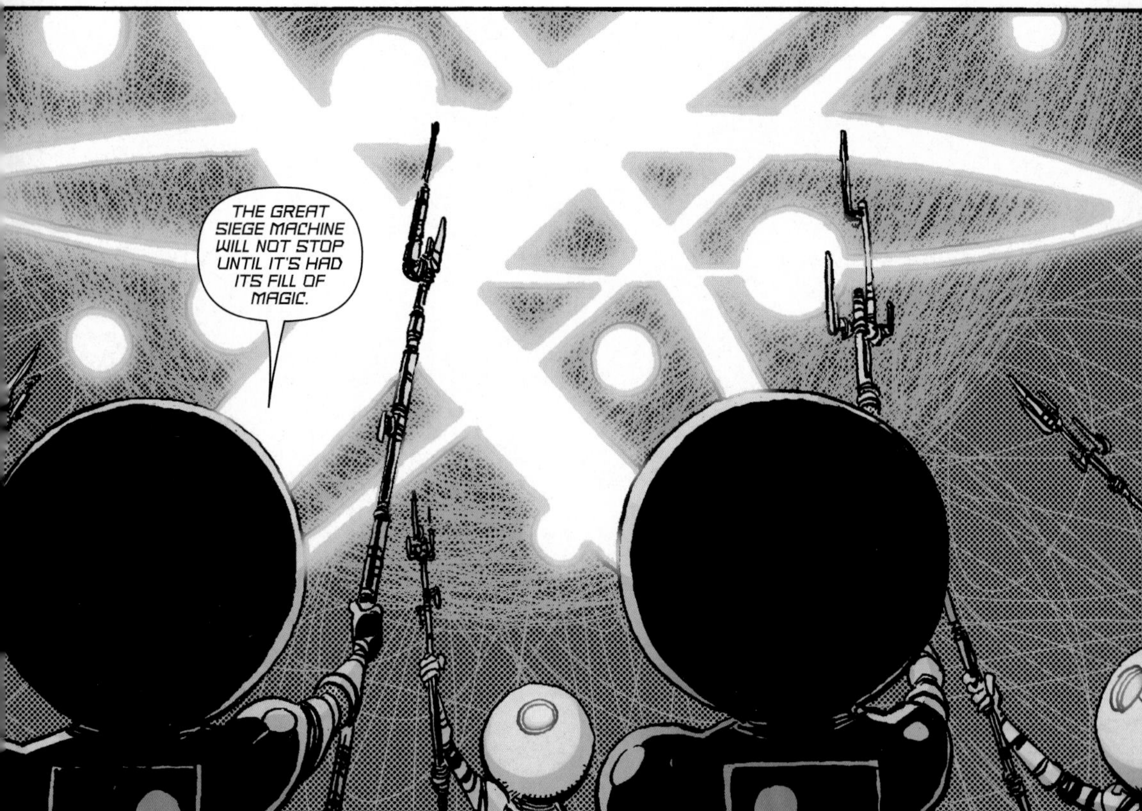
THE GREAT SIEGE MACHINE WILL NOT STOP UNTIL IT'S HAD ITS FILL OF MAGIC.

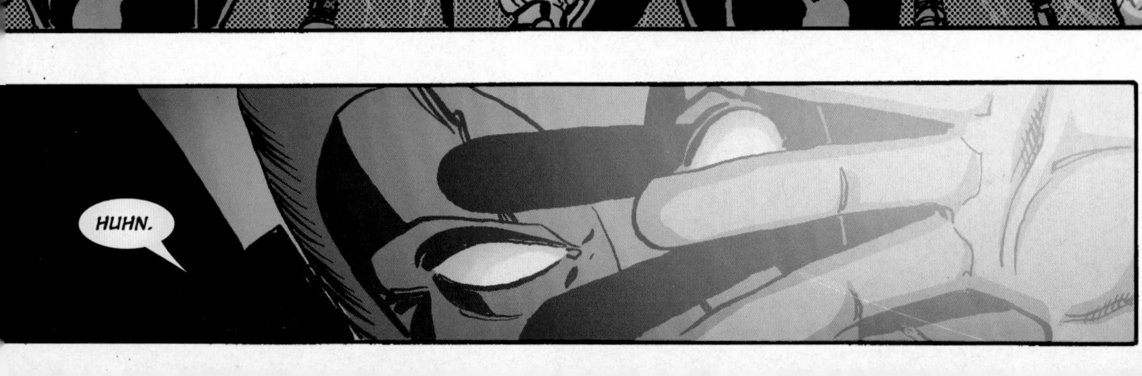
HUHN.

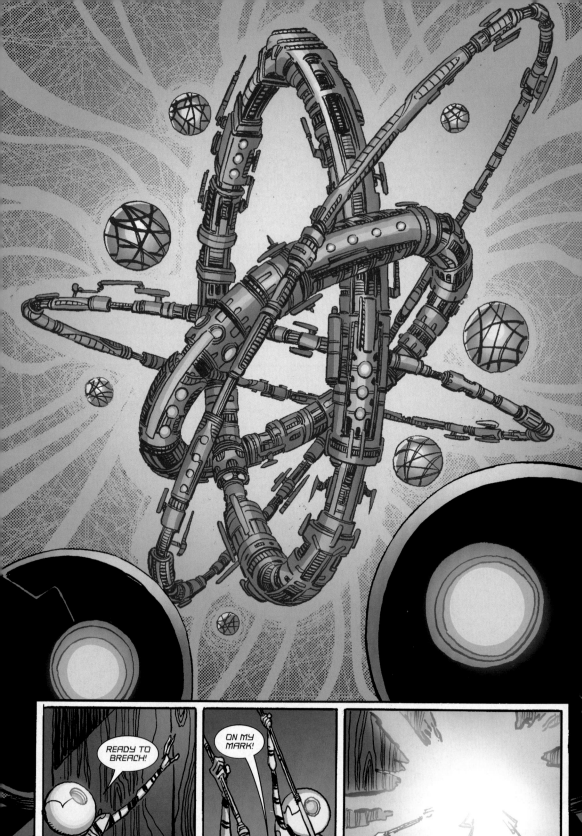

READY TO BREACH!

ON MY MARK!

EXECUTE.

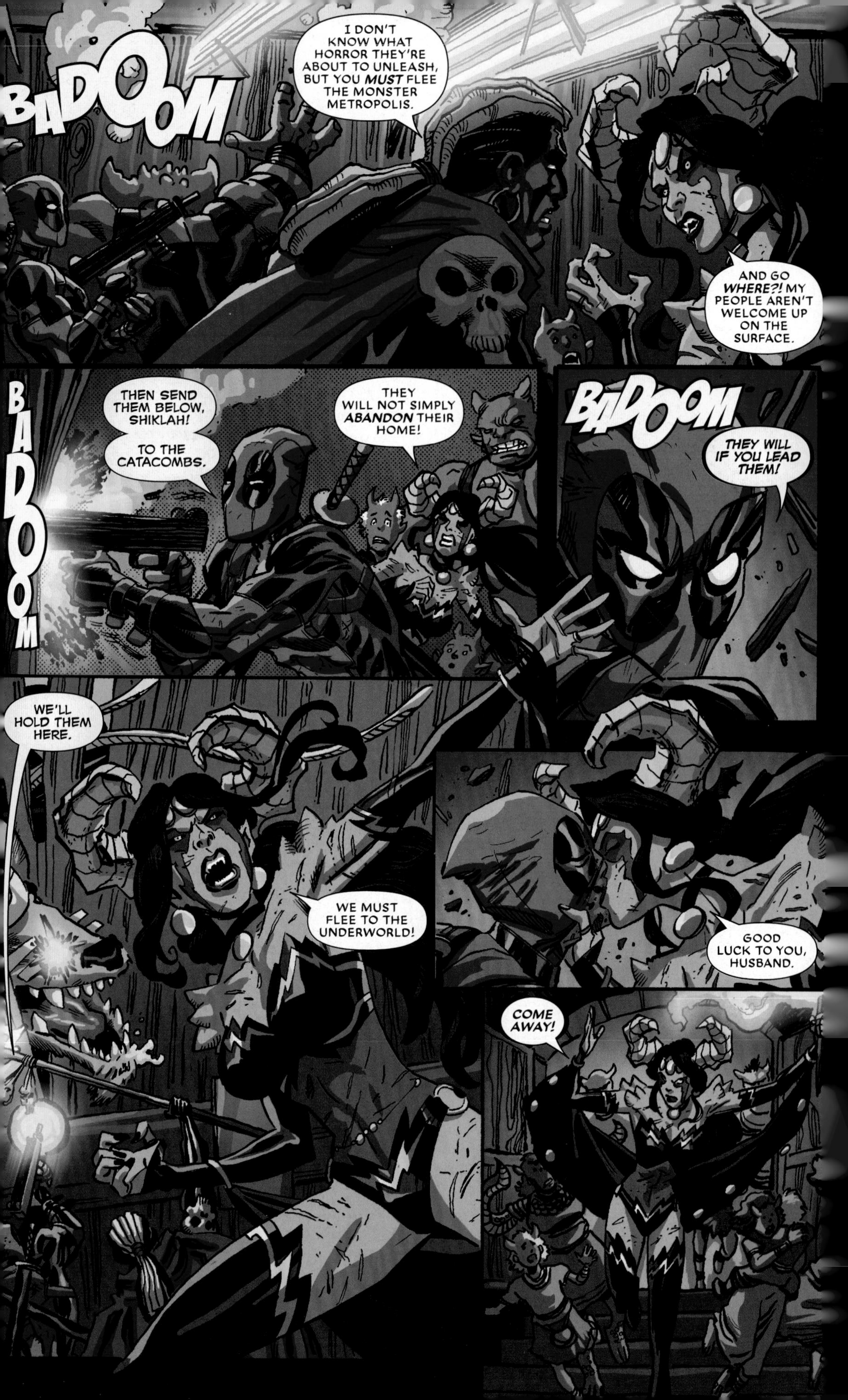
BADOOM
I DON'T KNOW WHAT HORROR THEY'RE ABOUT TO UNLEASH, BUT YOU *MUST* FLEE THE MONSTER METROPOLIS.
AND GO *WHERE?!* MY PEOPLE AREN'T WELCOME UP ON THE SURFACE.
BADOOM
THEN SEND THEM BELOW, SHIKLAH!
TO THE CATACOMBS.
THEY WILL NOT SIMPLY *ABANDON* THEIR HOME!
BADOOM
THEY WILL IF YOU LEAD THEM!
WE'LL HOLD THEM HERE.
WE MUST FLEE TO THE UNDERWORLD!
GOOD LUCK TO YOU, HUSBAND.
COME AWAY!

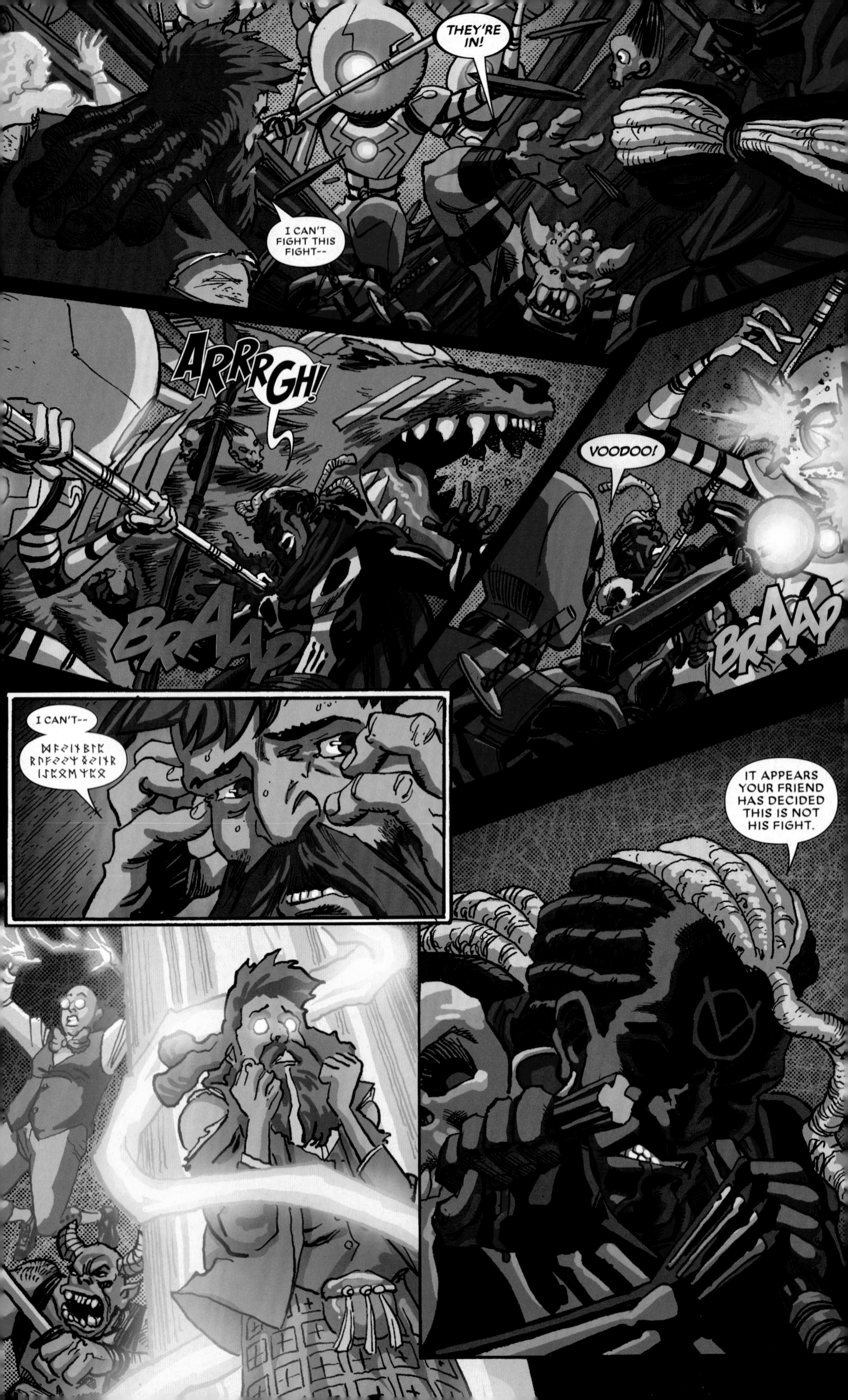
THEY'RE IN!
I CAN'T FIGHT THIS FIGHT--
ARRRGH!
BRAAAP
VOODOO!
BRAAAP
I CAN'T--
IT APPEARS YOUR FRIEND HAS DECIDED THIS IS NOT HIS FIGHT.

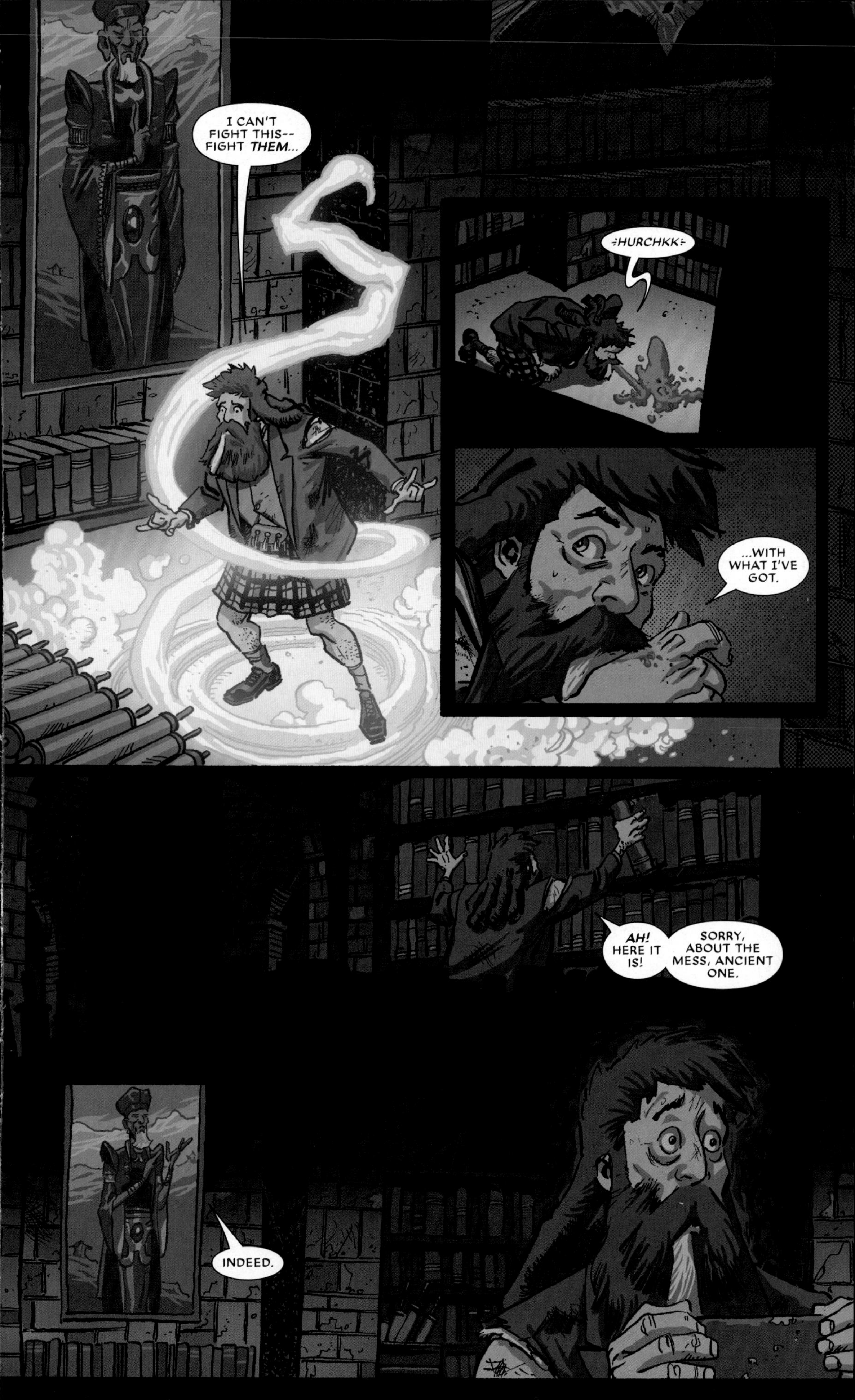
I CAN'T FIGHT THIS-- FIGHT *THEM*...
=HURCHKK=
...WITH WHAT I'VE GOT.
AH! HERE IT IS!
SORRY, ABOUT THE MESS, ANCIENT ONE.
INDEED.

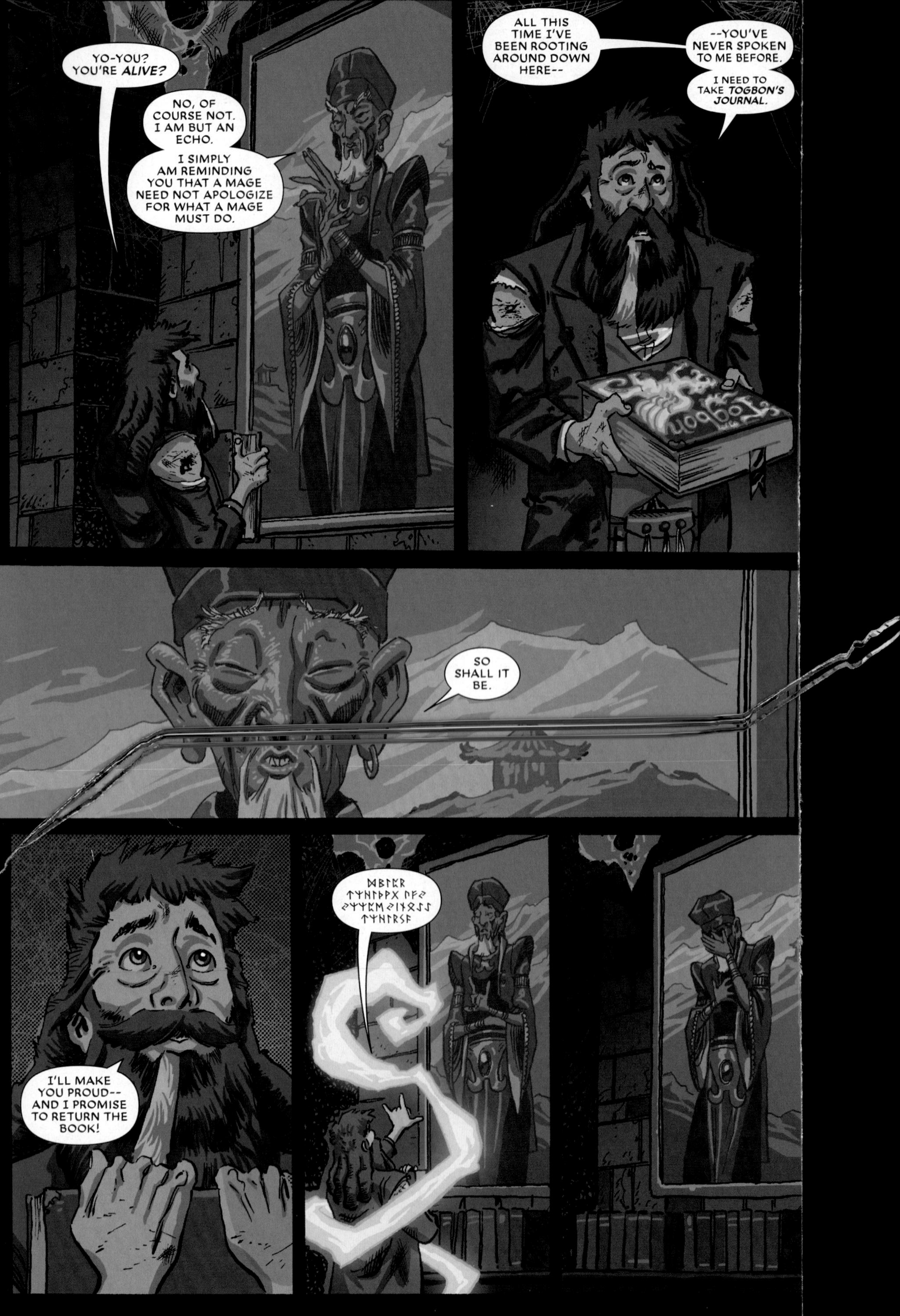
YO-YOU? YOU'RE ALIVE?
NO, OF COURSE NOT. I AM BUT AN ECHO.
I SIMPLY AM REMINDING YOU THAT A MAGE NEED NOT APOLOGIZE FOR WHAT A MAGE MUST DO.
ALL THIS TIME I'VE BEEN ROOTING AROUND DOWN HERE--
--YOU'VE NEVER SPOKEN TO ME BEFORE.
I NEED TO TAKE TOGBON'S JOURNAL.
SO SHALL IT BE.
I'LL MAKE YOU PROUD-- AND I PROMISE TO RETURN THE BOOK!

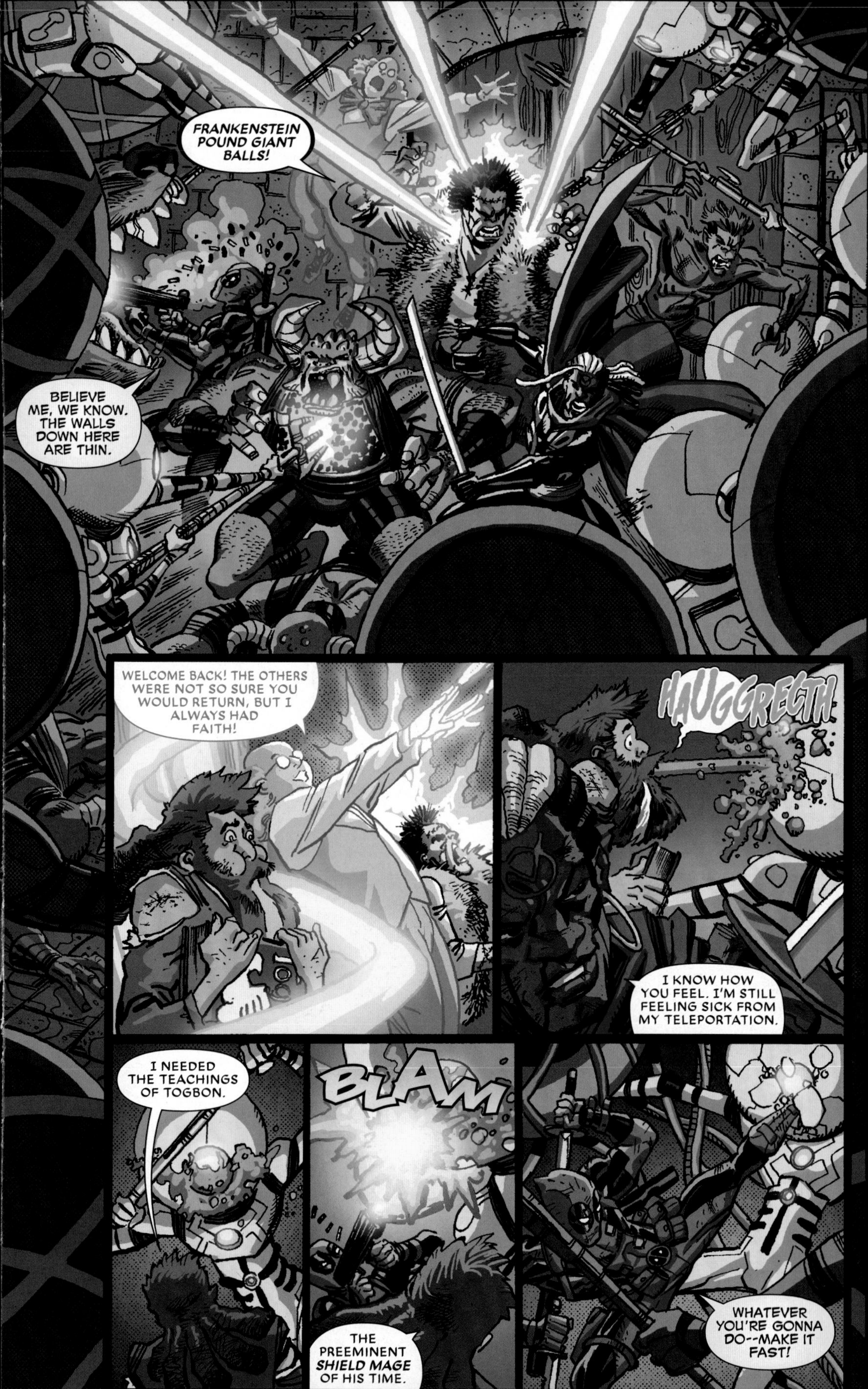
FRANKENSTEIN POUND GIANT BALLS!
BELIEVE ME, WE KNOW. THE WALLS DOWN HERE ARE THIN.
WELCOME BACK! THE OTHERS WERE NOT SO SURE YOU WOULD RETURN, BUT I ALWAYS HAD FAITH!
HAUGGRECTH
I KNOW HOW YOU FEEL. I'M STILL FEELING SICK FROM MY TELEPORTATION.
I NEEDED THE TEACHINGS OF TOGBON.
BLAM
THE PREEMINENT SHIELD MAGE OF HIS TIME.
WHATEVER YOU'RE GONNA DO--MAKE IT FAST!

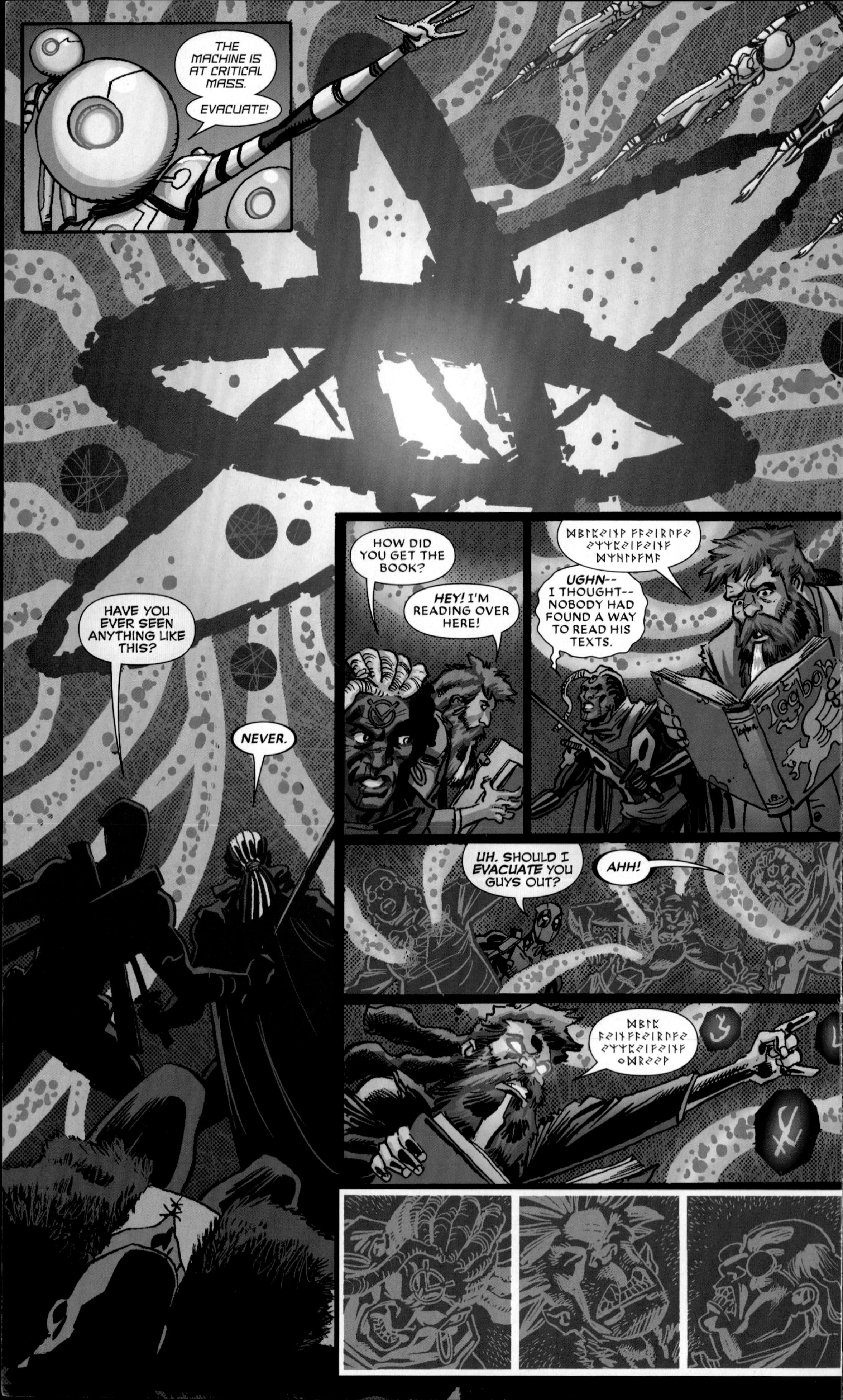
THE MACHINE IS AT CRITICAL MASS.
EVACUATE!
HAVE YOU EVER SEEN ANYTHING LIKE THIS?
NEVER.
HOW DID YOU GET THE BOOK?
HEY! I'M READING OVER HERE!
UGHN-- I THOUGHT-- NOBODY HAD FOUND A WAY TO READ HIS TEXTS.
UH. SHOULD I EVACUATE YOU GUYS OUT?
AHH!

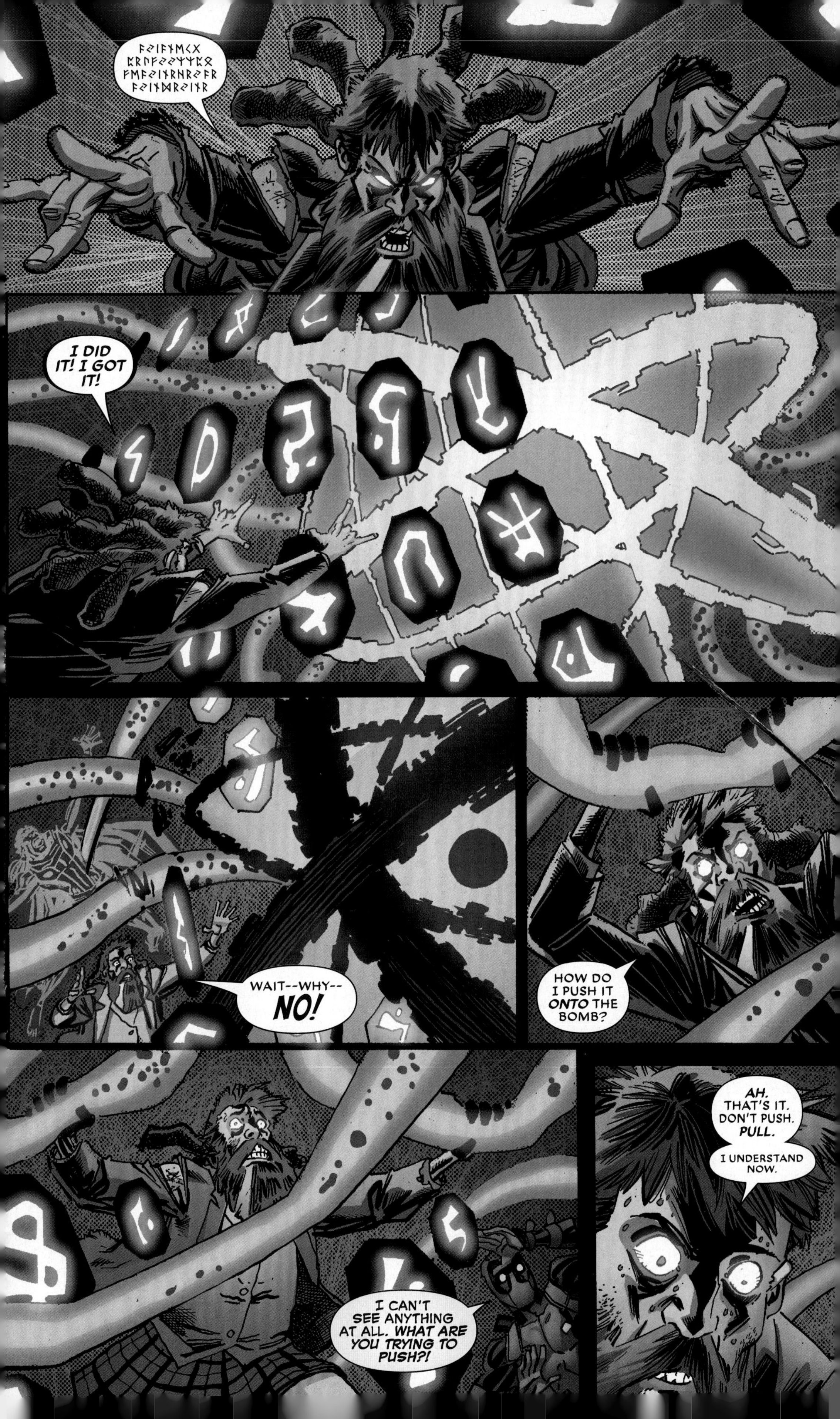
I DID IT! I GOT IT!
WAIT--WHY--
NO!
HOW DO I PUSH IT ONTO THE BOMB?
I CAN'T SEE ANYTHING AT ALL. WHAT ARE YOU TRYING TO PUSH?!
AH. THAT'S IT. DON'T PUSH. PULL.
I UNDERSTAND NOW.

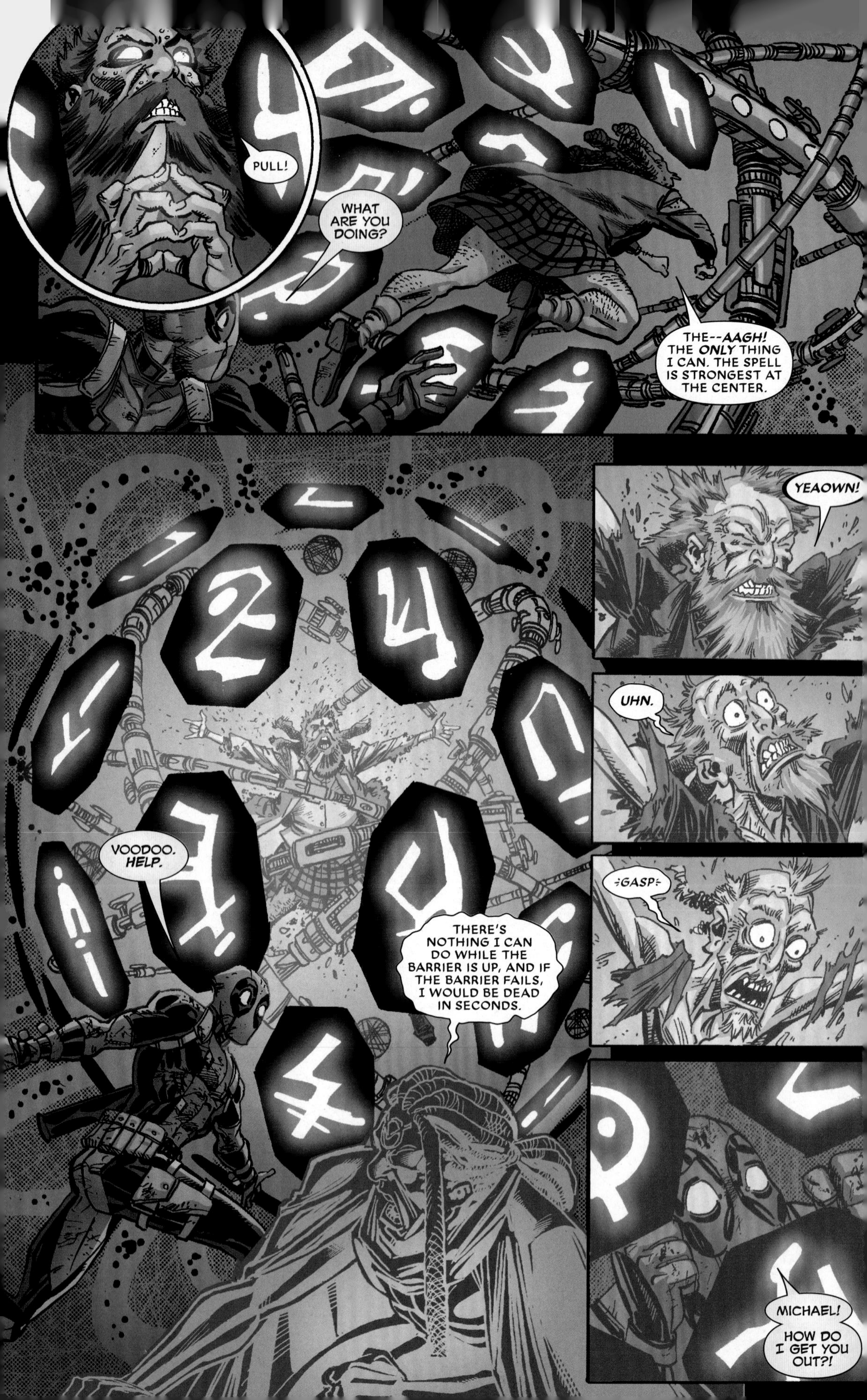
PULL!
WHAT ARE YOU DOING?
THE--AAGH! THE ONLY THING I CAN. THE SPELL IS STRONGEST AT THE CENTER.
YEAOWN!
UHN.
⸗GASP⸗
VOODOO. HELP.
THERE'S NOTHING I CAN DO WHILE THE BARRIER IS UP, AND IF THE BARRIER FAILS, I WOULD BE DEAD IN SECONDS.
MICHAEL!
HOW DO I GET YOU OUT?!

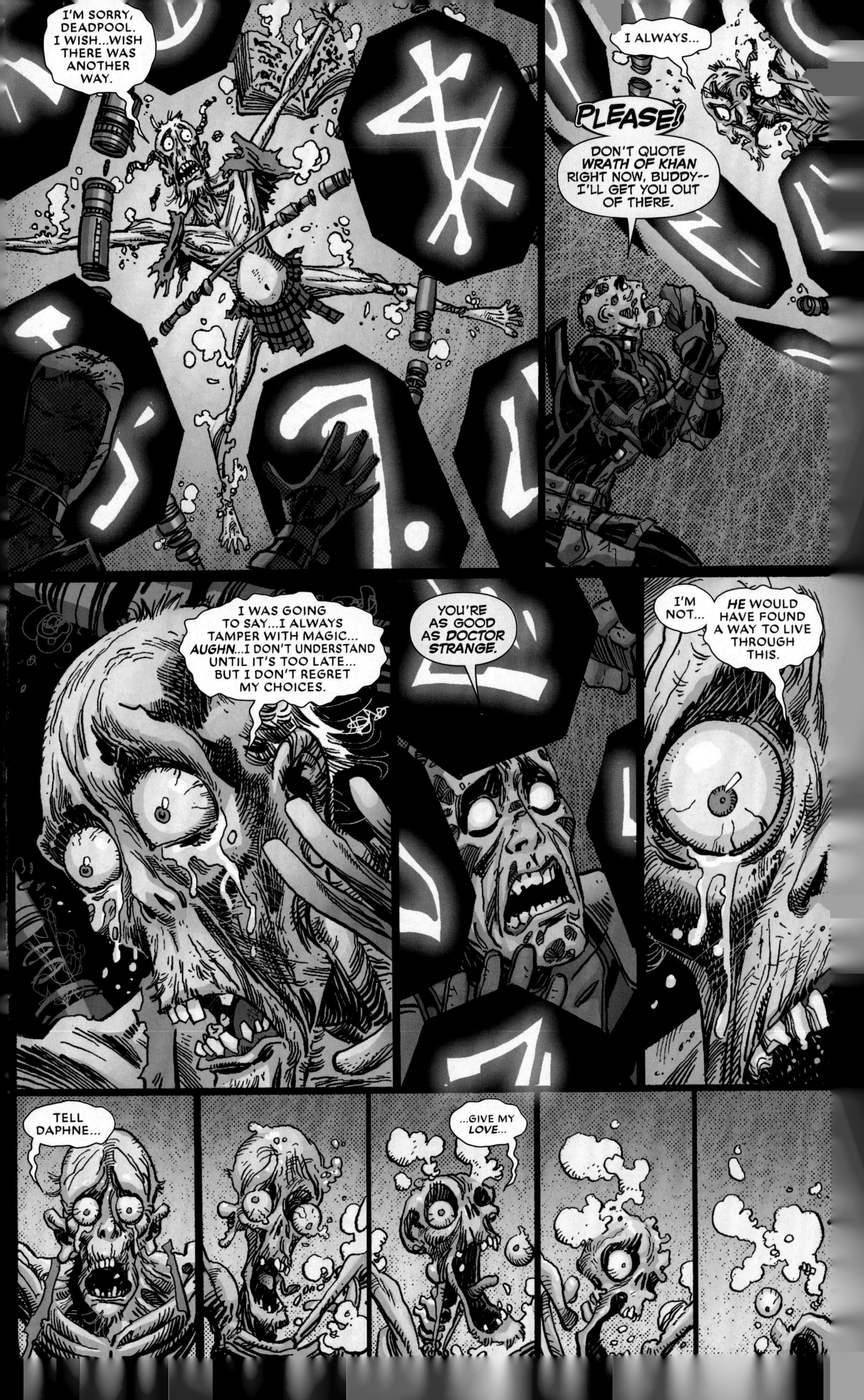
I'M SORRY, DEADPOOL. I WISH...WISH THERE WAS ANOTHER WAY.
I ALWAYS...
PLEASE!
DON'T QUOTE WRATH OF KHAN RIGHT NOW, BUDDY-- I'LL GET YOU OUT OF THERE.
I WAS GOING TO SAY...I ALWAYS TAMPER WITH MAGIC... AUGHN...I DON'T UNDERSTAND UNTIL IT'S TOO LATE... BUT I DON'T REGRET MY CHOICES.
YOU'RE AS GOOD AS DOCTOR STRANGE.
I'M NOT...
HE WOULD HAVE FOUND A WAY TO LIVE THROUGH THIS.
TELL DAPHNE...
...GIVE MY LOVE...

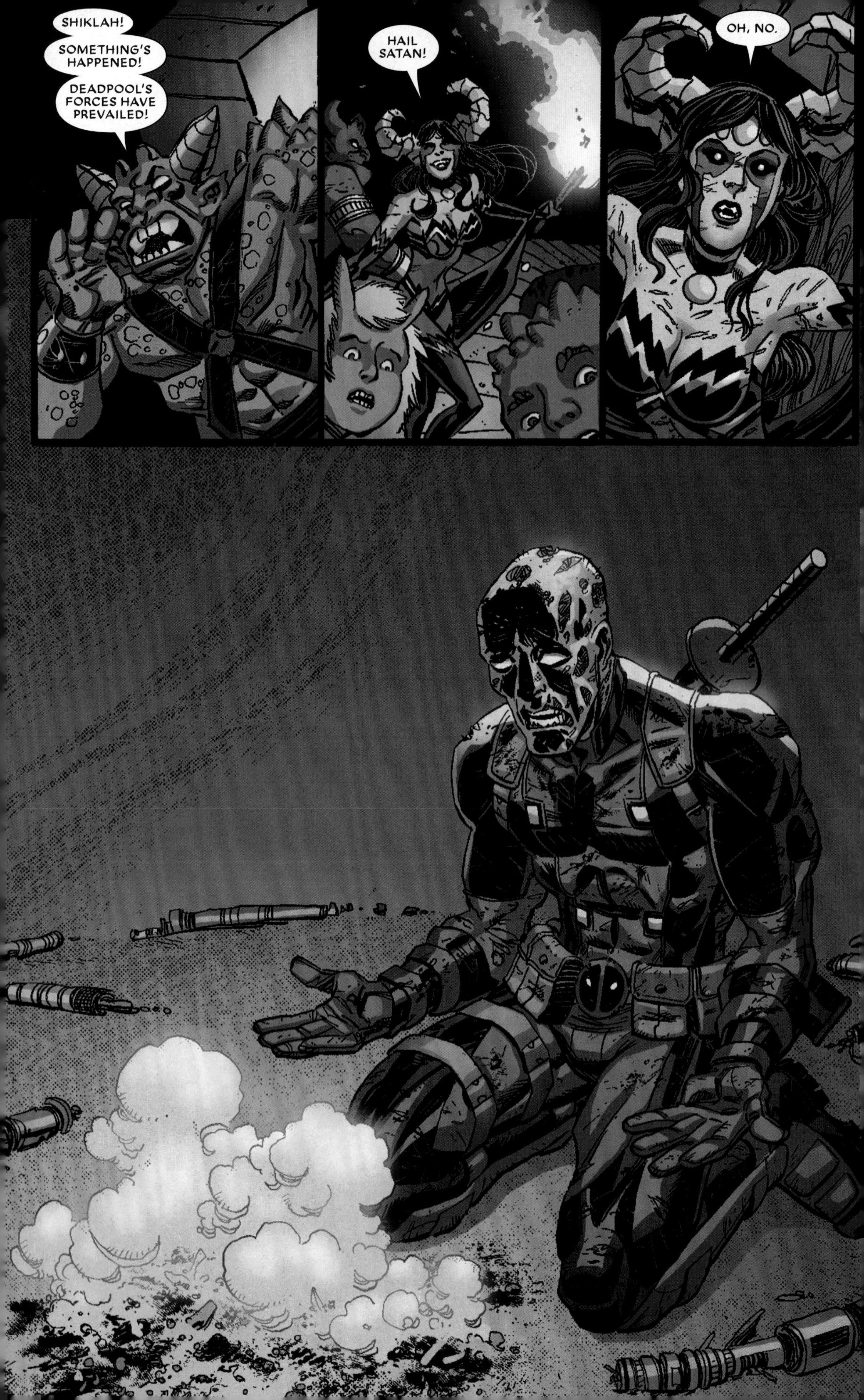
SHIKLAH!
SOMETHING'S HAPPENED!
DEADPOOL'S FORCES HAVE PREVAILED!
HAIL SATAN!
OH, NO.

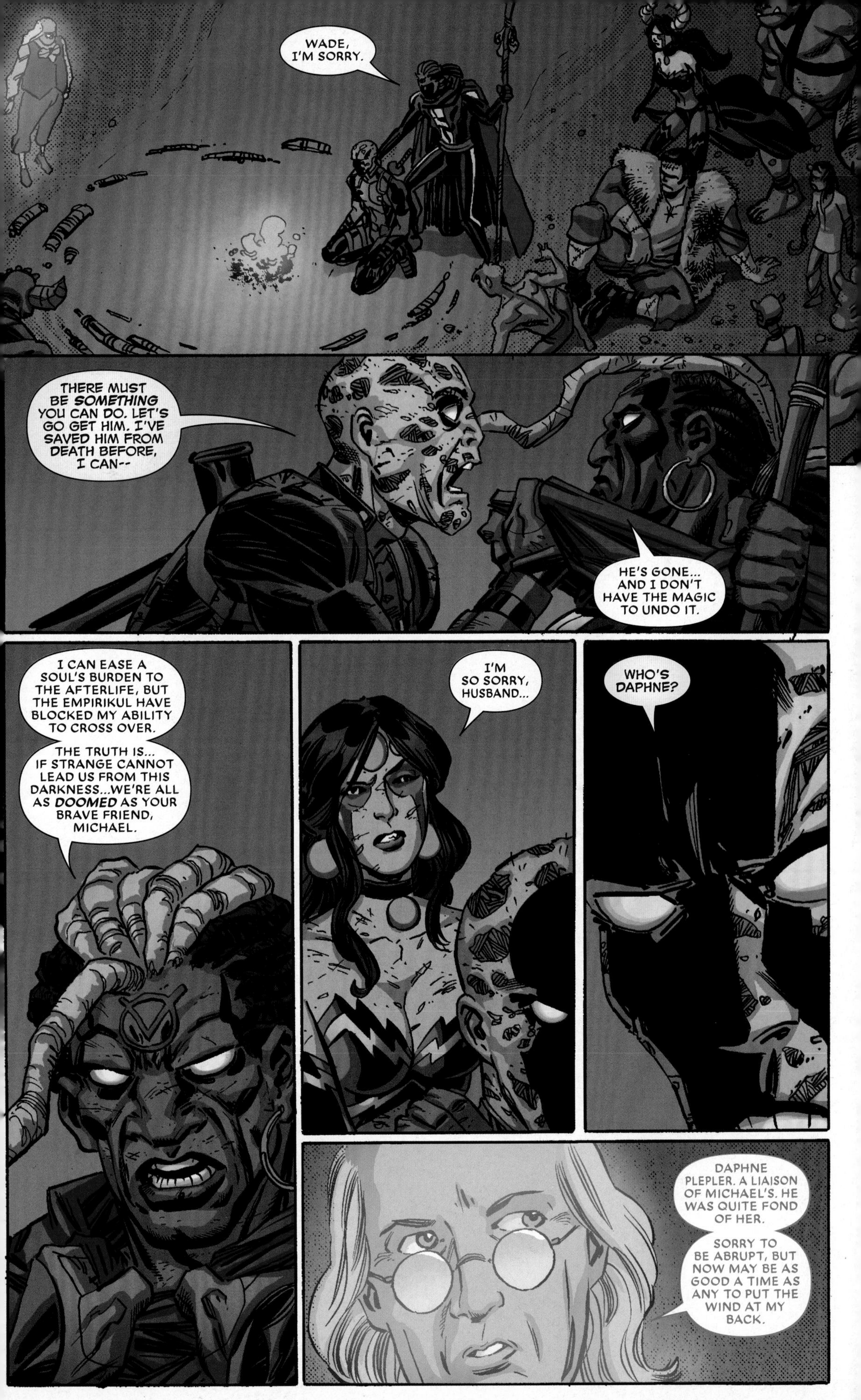

WADE, I'M SORRY.
THERE MUST BE *SOMETHING* YOU CAN DO. LET'S GO GET HIM. I'VE SAVED HIM FROM DEATH BEFORE, I CAN--
HE'S GONE... AND I DON'T HAVE THE MAGIC TO UNDO IT.
I CAN EASE A SOUL'S BURDEN TO THE AFTERLIFE, BUT THE EMPIRIKUL HAVE BLOCKED MY ABILITY TO CROSS OVER.
THE TRUTH IS... IF STRANGE CANNOT LEAD US FROM THIS DARKNESS...WE'RE ALL AS *DOOMED* AS YOUR BRAVE FRIEND, MICHAEL.
I'M SO SORRY, HUSBAND...
WHO'S DAPHNE?
DAPHNE PLEPLER. A LIAISON OF MICHAEL'S. HE WAS QUITE FOND OF HER.
SORRY TO BE ABRUPT, BUT NOW MAY BE AS GOOD A TIME AS ANY TO PUT THE WIND AT MY BACK.

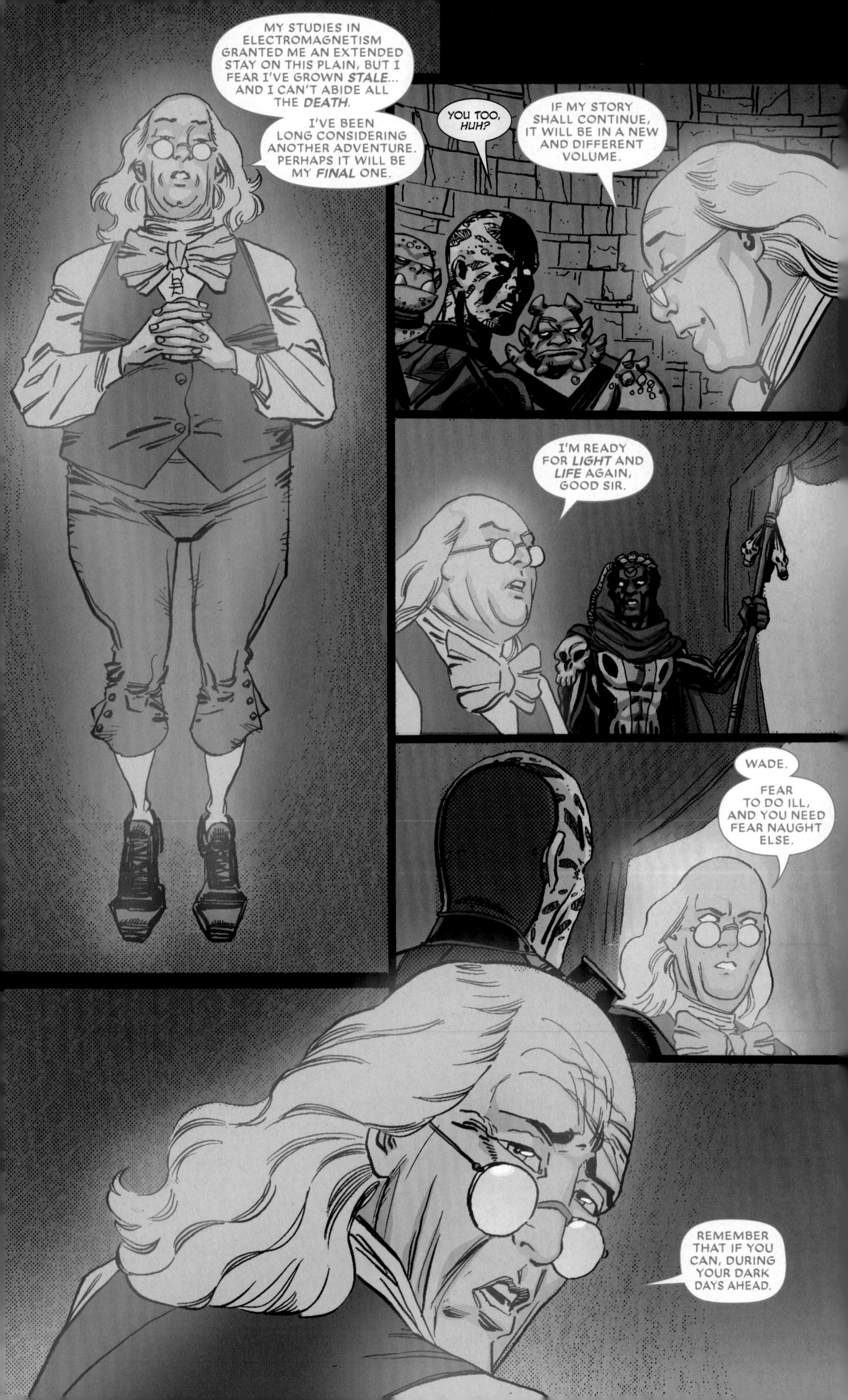

MY STUDIES IN ELECTROMAGNETISM GRANTED ME AN EXTENDED STAY ON THIS PLAIN, BUT I FEAR I'VE GROWN *STALE*... AND I CAN'T ABIDE ALL THE *DEATH*.
I'VE BEEN LONG CONSIDERING ANOTHER ADVENTURE. PERHAPS IT WILL BE MY *FINAL* ONE.
YOU TOO, *HUH?*
IF MY STORY SHALL CONTINUE, IT WILL BE IN A NEW AND DIFFERENT VOLUME.
I'M READY FOR *LIGHT* AND *LIFE* AGAIN, GOOD SIR.
WADE.
FEAR TO DO ILL, AND YOU NEED FEAR NAUGHT ELSE.
REMEMBER THAT IF YOU CAN, DURING YOUR DARK DAYS AHEAD.

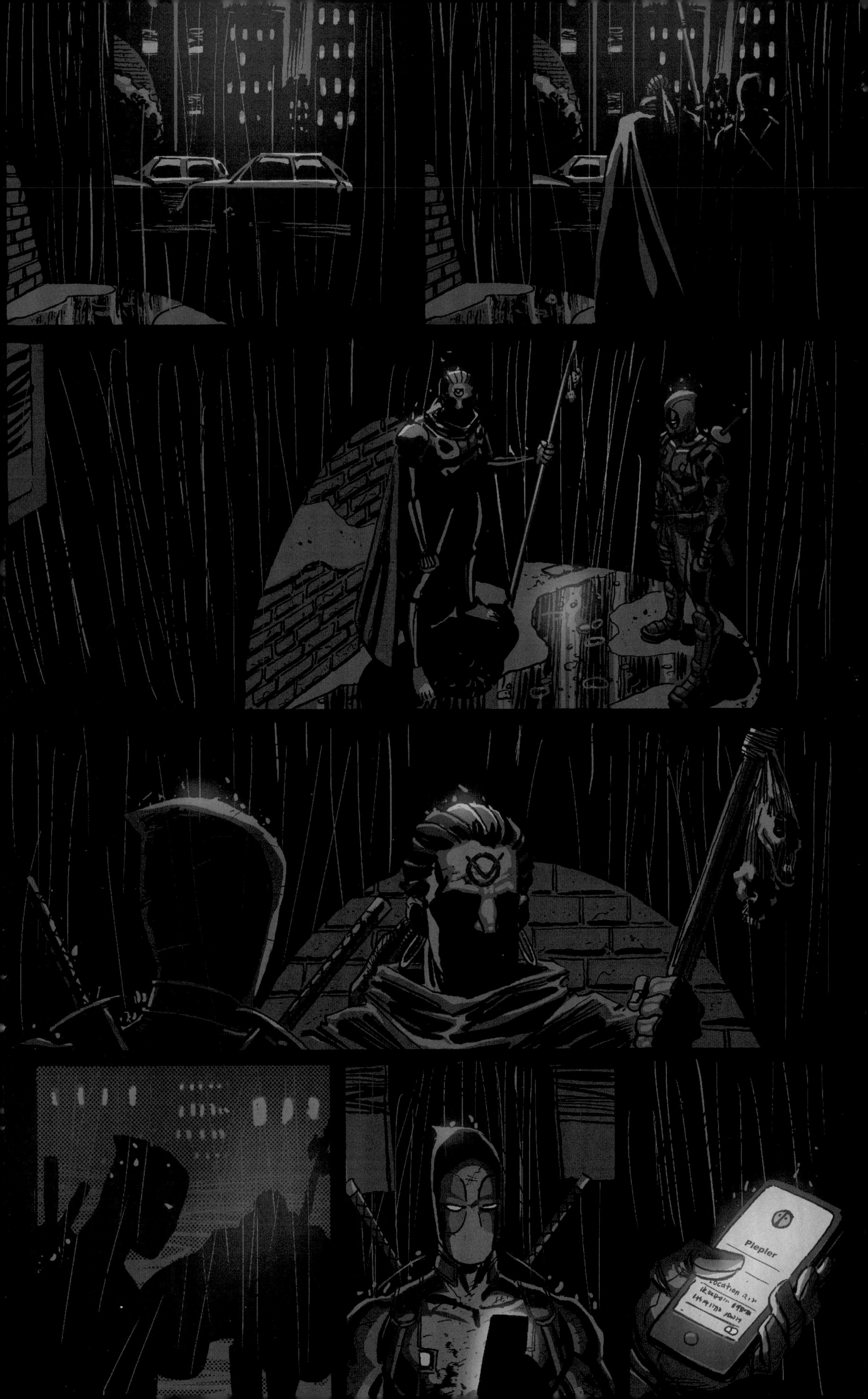
Plepler

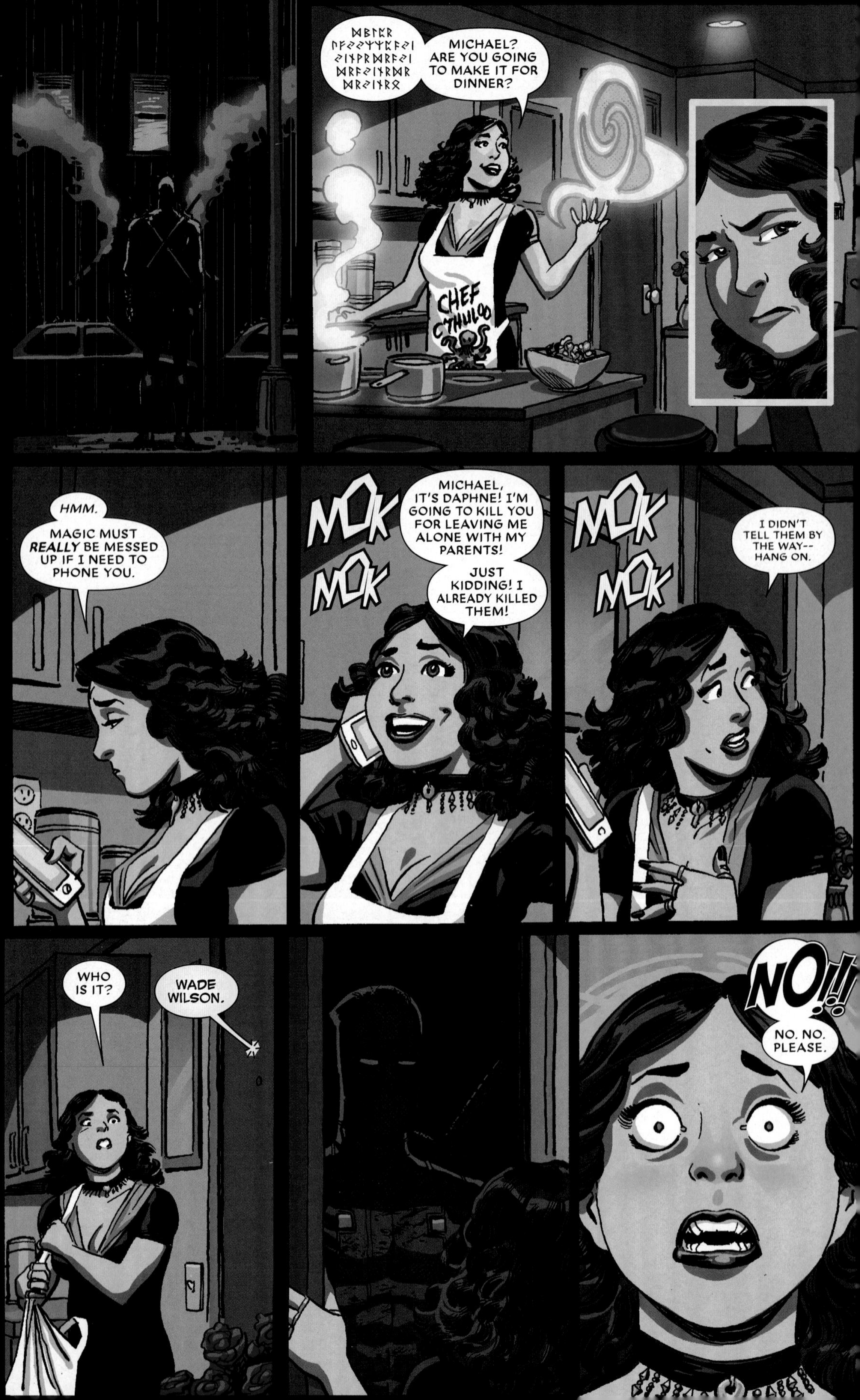
MICHAEL? ARE YOU GOING TO MAKE IT FOR DINNER?
HMM.
MAGIC MUST REALLY BE MESSED UP IF I NEED TO PHONE YOU.
MOK
MOK
MICHAEL, IT'S DAPHNE! I'M GOING TO KILL YOU FOR LEAVING ME ALONE WITH MY PARENTS!
JUST KIDDING! I ALREADY KILLED THEM!
MOK
MOK
I DIDN'T TELL THEM BY THE WAY-- HANG ON.
WHO IS IT?
WADE WILSON.
NO!!!
NO. NO. PLEASE.

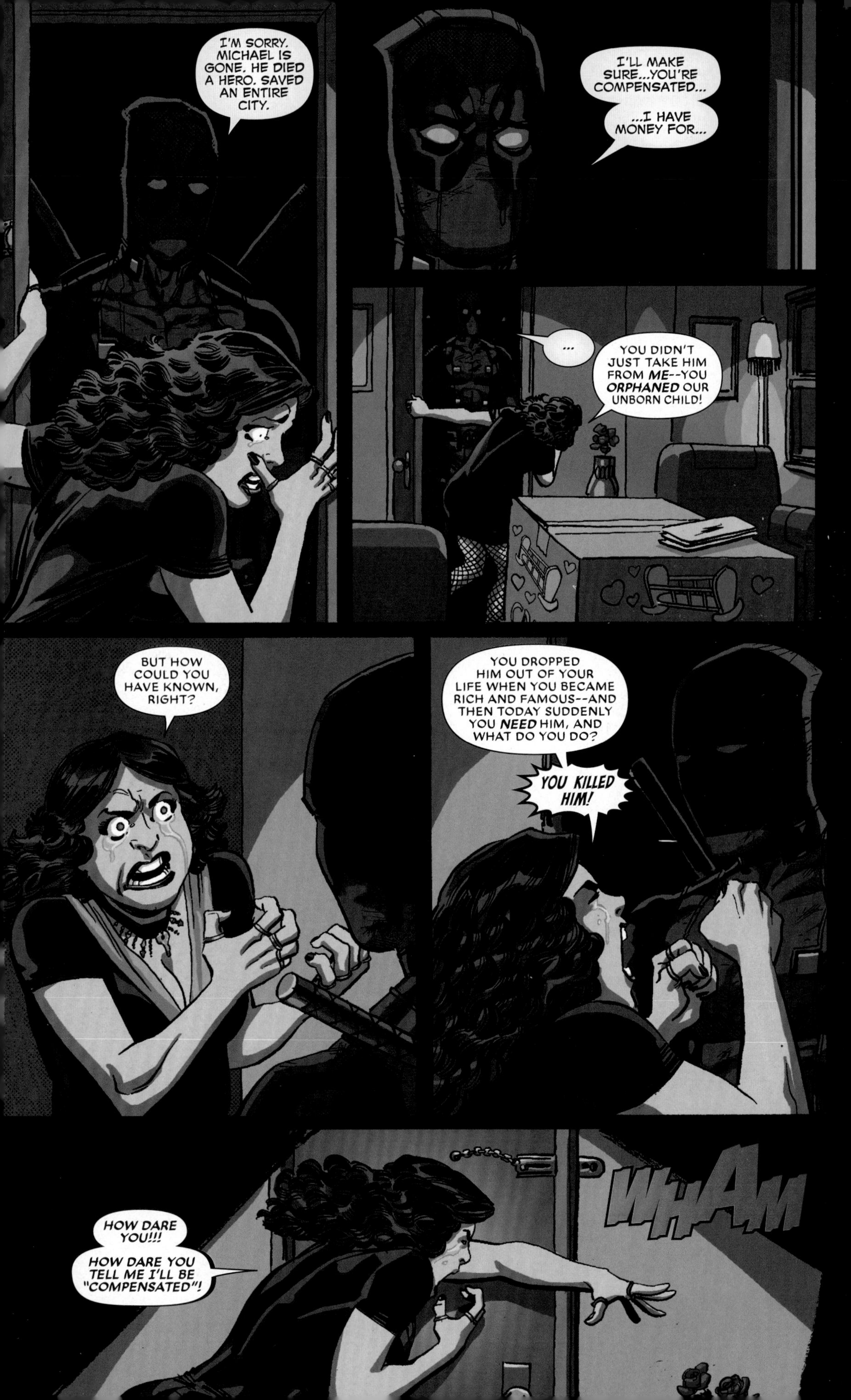
I'M SORRY. MICHAEL IS GONE. HE DIED A HERO. SAVED AN ENTIRE CITY.
I'LL MAKE SURE...YOU'RE COMPENSATED...
...I HAVE MONEY FOR...
...
YOU DIDN'T JUST TAKE HIM FROM ME--YOU ORPHANED OUR UNBORN CHILD!
BUT HOW COULD YOU HAVE KNOWN, RIGHT?
YOU DROPPED HIM OUT OF YOUR LIFE WHEN YOU BECAME RICH AND FAMOUS--AND THEN TODAY SUDDENLY YOU NEED HIM, AND WHAT DO YOU DO?
YOU KILLED HIM!
WHAM
HOW DARE YOU!!!
HOW DARE YOU TELL ME I'LL BE "COMPENSATED"!

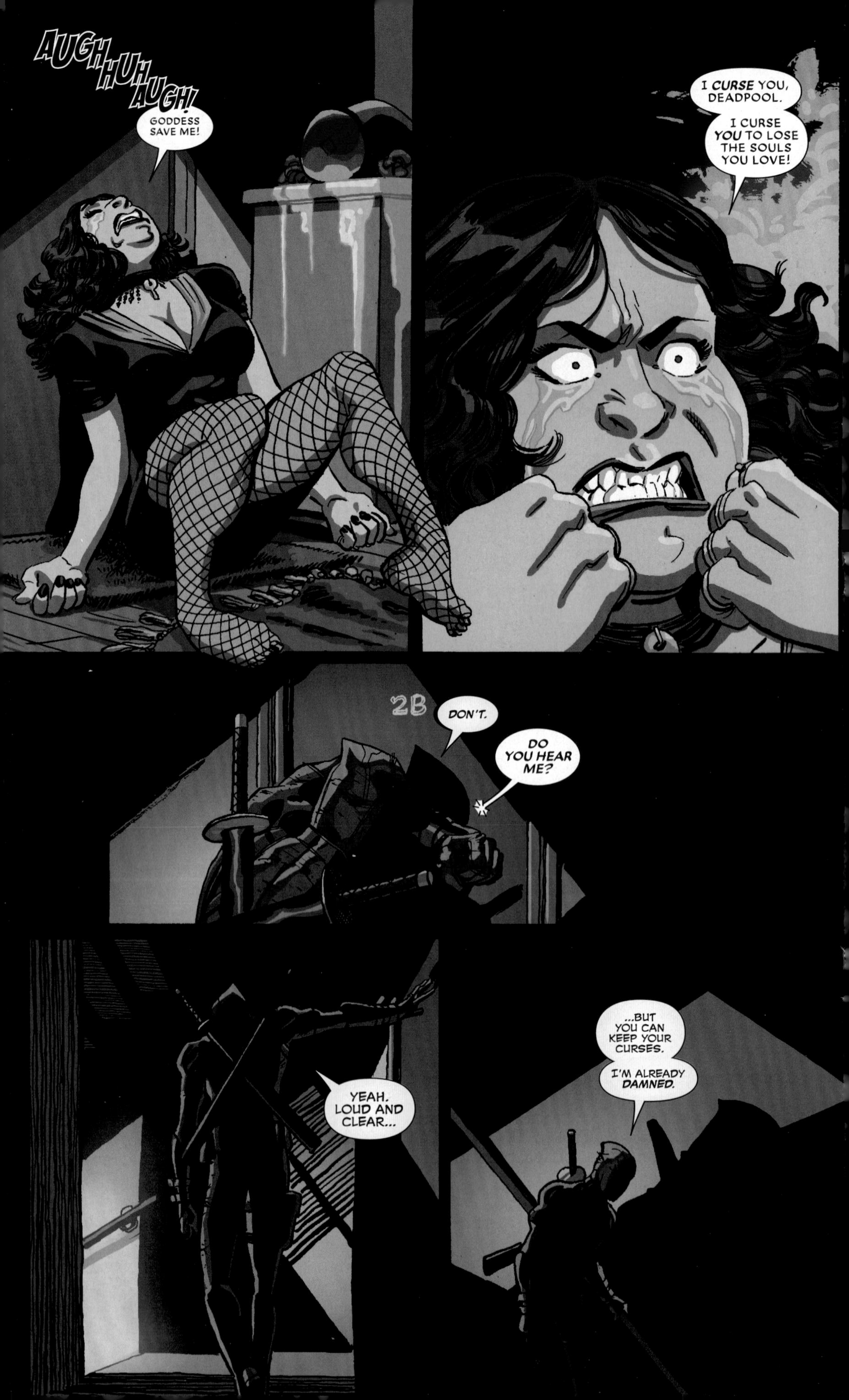
AUGH HUH AUGH!
GODDESS SAVE ME!
I CURSE YOU, DEADPOOL.
I CURSE YOU TO LOSE THE SOULS YOU LOVE!
2B
DON'T.
DO YOU HEAR ME?
YEAH. LOUD AND CLEAR...
...BUT YOU CAN KEEP YOUR CURSES.
I'M ALREADY DAMNED.

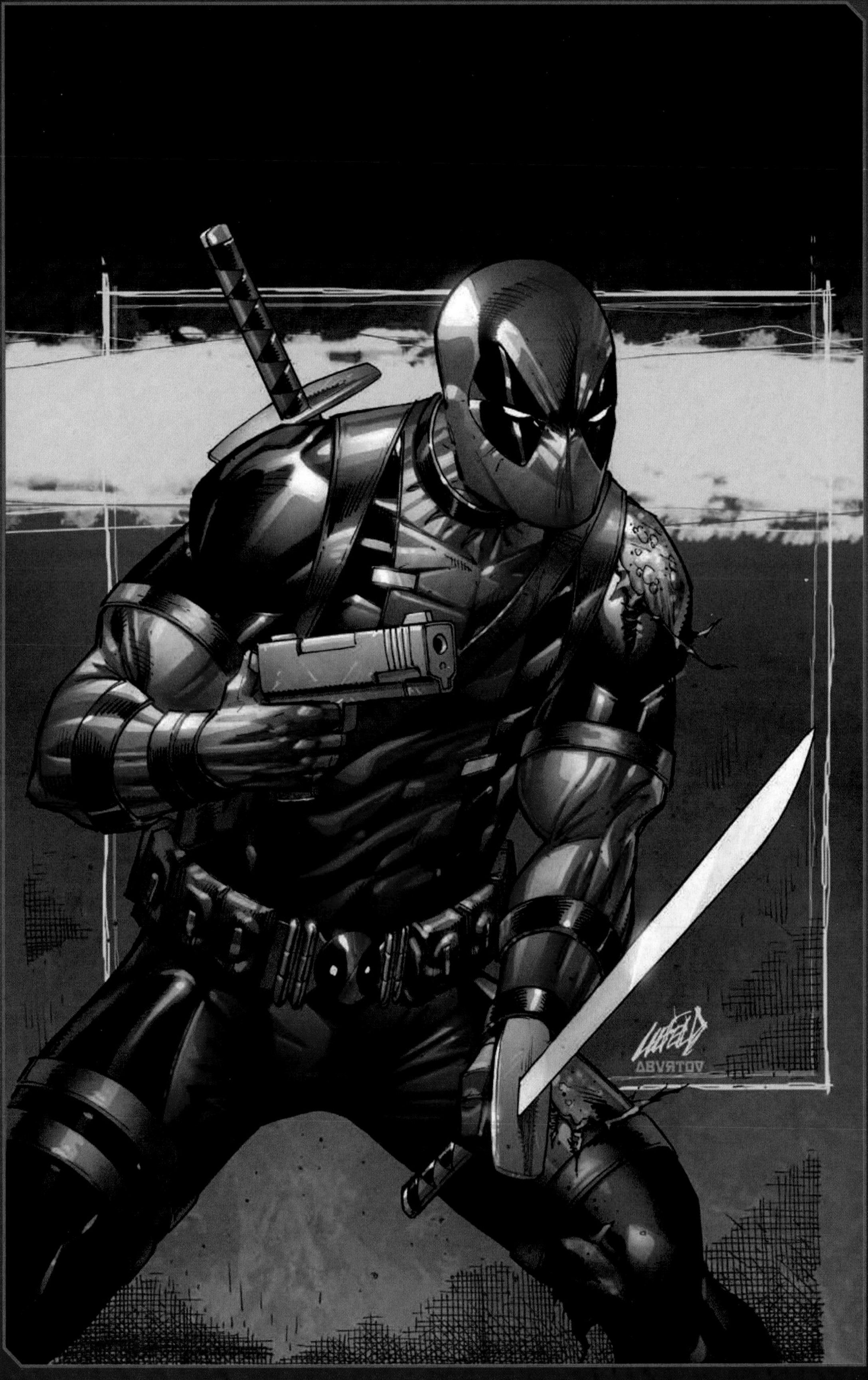

#13 variant by ROB LIEFELD & JESUS ABURTOV

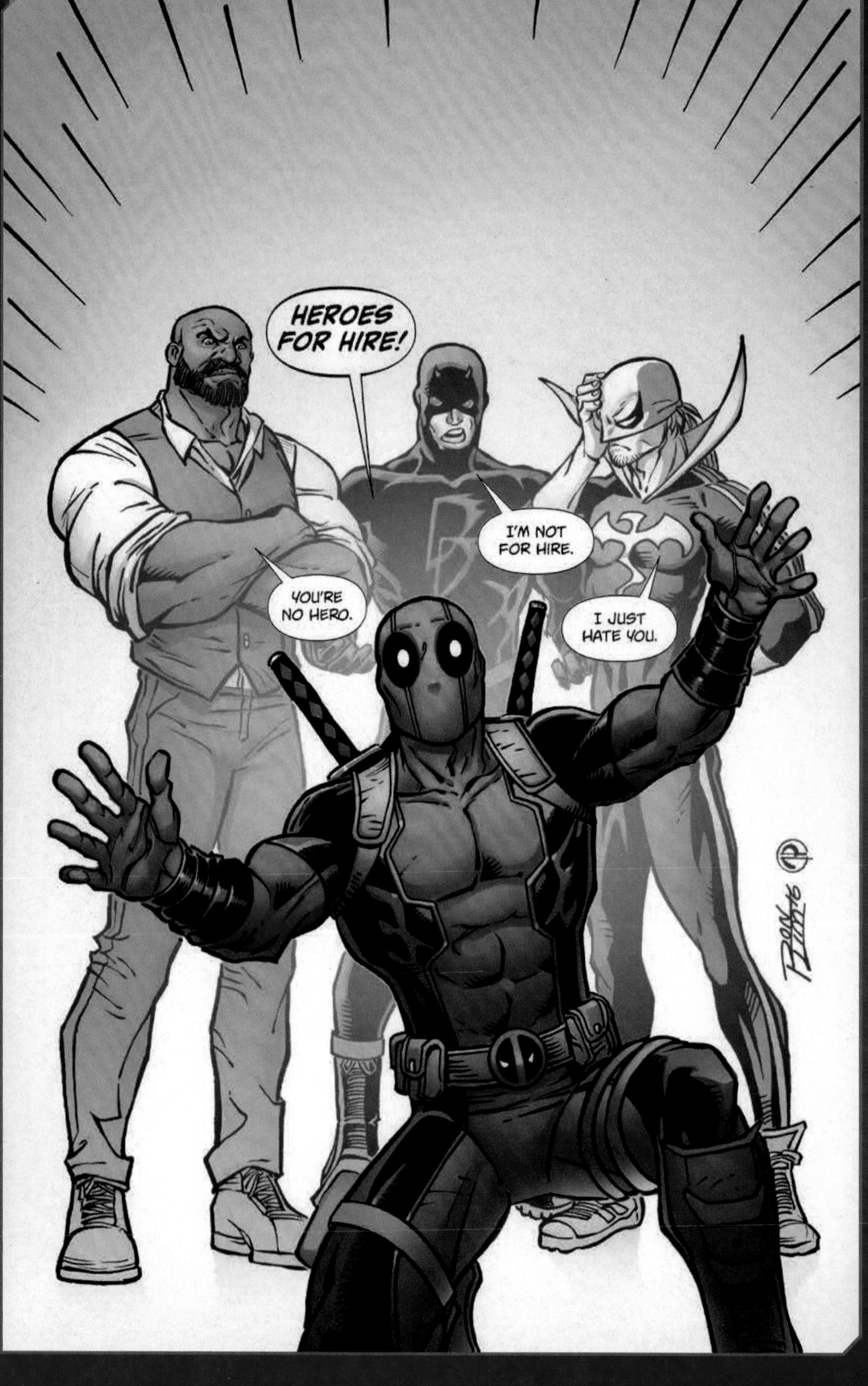
HEROES FOR HIRE!
I'M NOT FOR HIRE.
YOU'RE NO HERO.
I JUST HATE YOU.

#13 variant by RON LIM, TOM PALMER & FRANK D'ARMATA

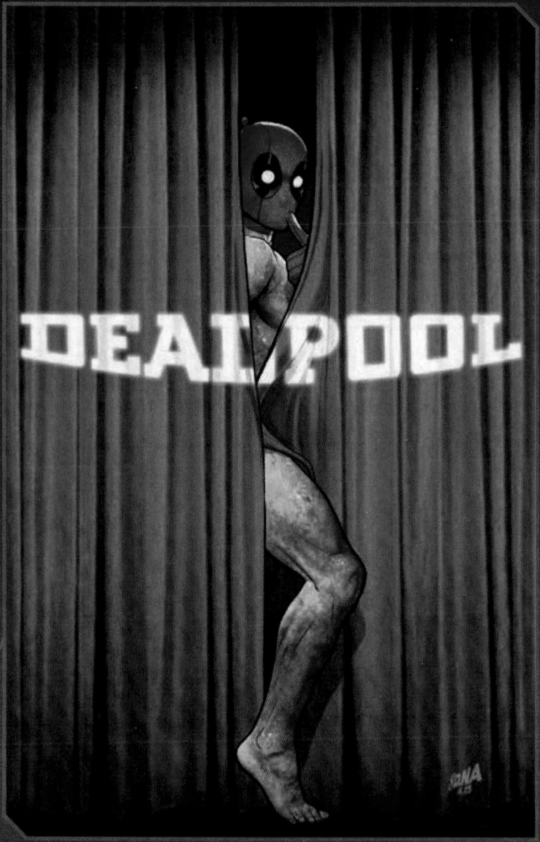
DEADPOOL

#13 variant by
DAVID NAKAYAMA

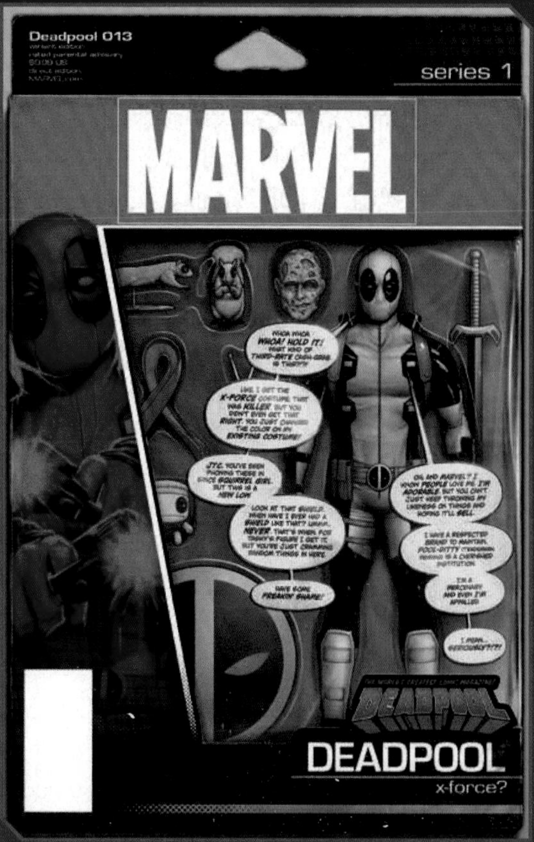
Deadpool 013
series 1
MARVEL
DEADPOOL
x-force?

#13 action figure variant by
JOHN TYLER CHRISTOHPER

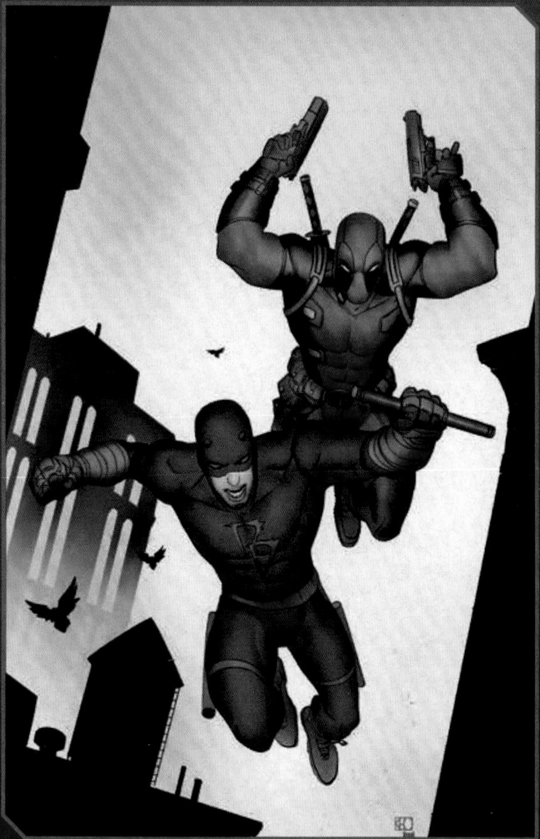

#13 variant by
KHOI PHAM & FRANK D'ARMATA

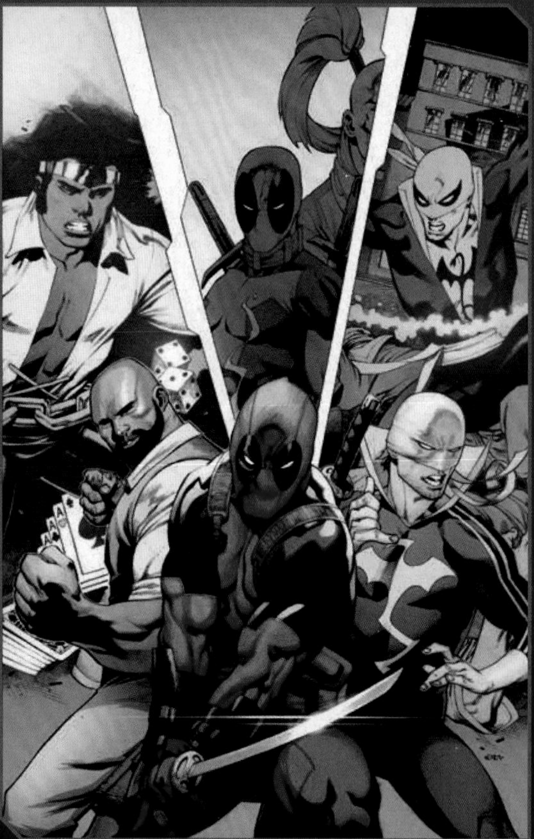

#13 variant by
CHRIS STEVENS & JASON KEITH

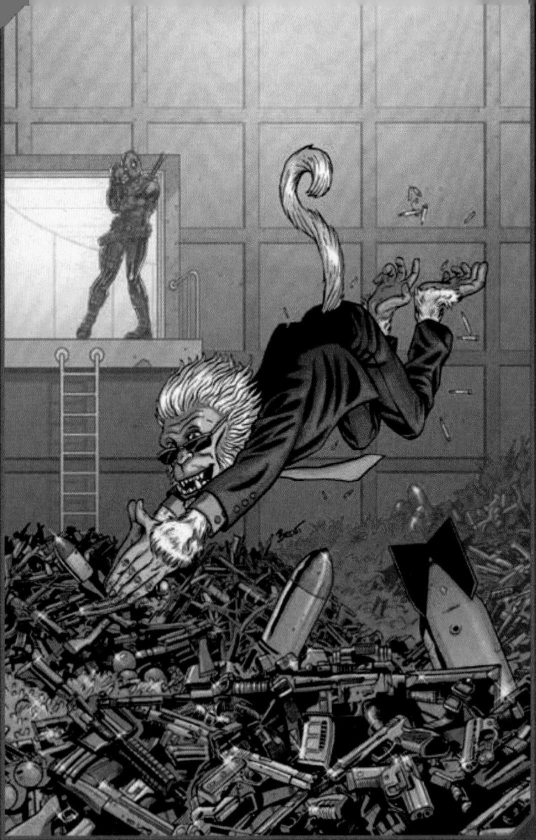

#13 variant by
BRENT SCHOONOVER & NICK FILARDI

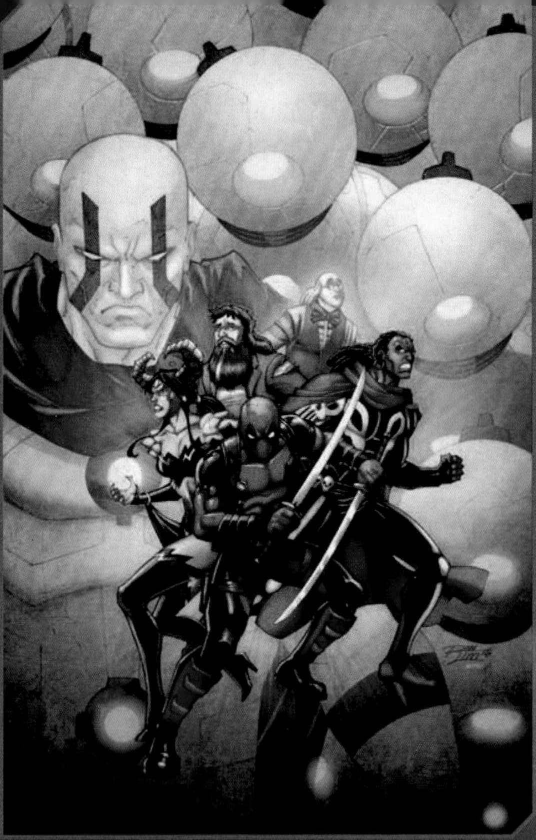

Last Days of Magic #1 variant by
RON LIM & CHRIS SOTOMAYOR

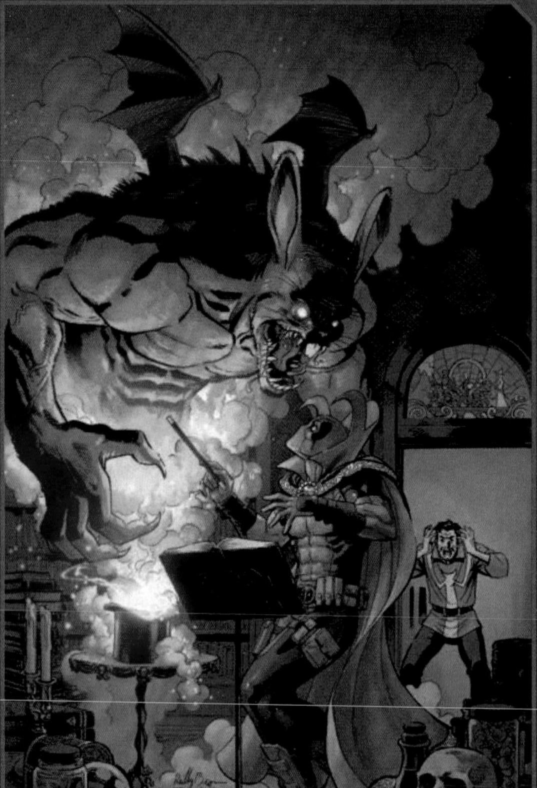

Last Days of Magic #1 variant by
REILLY BROWN